ETHICS AND THE ACQUISITION OF ORGANS

Transplantation is a medically successful and cost-effective way to treat people whose organs have failed—but not enough organs are available to meet demand. *Ethics and the Acquisition of Organs* is concerned with the major ethical problems raised by policies for acquiring organs. The main topics are the rights of the dead, the role of the family, opt in and opt out systems, the conscription of organs, living organ donation from adults and children, directed donation and priority for donors, and the sale of organs.

In this ground-breaking work, T. M. Wilkinson uses concepts from moral and political theory such as autonomy, rights, posthumous interests, justice, and well-being, in a context informed by the clinical, legal, and policy aspects of transplantation. The result is a rigorous philosophical exploration of real problems and options. He argues that the ethics of acquiring organs for transplantation is not only of great intellectual interest, but also of practical importance. As such, this book will be of profit not only to students and academics who work in applied ethics and bioethics, but also to the lawyers, policy-makers, clinicians, and lobby groups interested in transplantation.

ISSUES IN BIOMEDICAL ETHICS

General Editors
John Harris and Søren Holm

Consulting Editors
Raanan Gillon and Bonnie Steinbock

The late twentieth century witnessed dramatic technological developments in biomedical science and in the delivery of healthcare, and these developments have brought with them important social changes. All too often ethical analysis has lagged behind these changes. The purpose of this series is to provide lively, up-to-date, and authoritative studies for the increasingly large and diverse readership concerned with issues in biomedical ethics—not just healthcare trainees and professionals, but also philosophers, social scientists, lawyers, social workers, and legislators. The series will feature both single-author and multi-author books, short and accessible enough to be widely read, each of them focused on an issue of outstanding current importance and interest. Philosophers, doctors, and lawyers from a number of countries feature among the authors lined up for the series.

Ethics and the Acquisition of Organs

T. M. WILKINSON

CLARENDON · PRESS

OXFORD
UNIVERSITY PRESS

Great Clarendon Street, Oxford, OX2 6DP,
United Kingdom

Oxford University Press is a department of the University of Oxford.
It furthers the University's objective of excellence in research, scholarship,
and education by publishing worldwide. Oxford is a registered trade mark of
Oxford University Press in the UK and in certain other countries

First published 2011
First published in paperback 2015

Published in the United States of America by Oxford University Press
198 Madison Avenue, New York, NY 10016, United States of America

British Library Cataloguing in Publication Data
Data available

Library of Congress Cataloging in Publication Data
Data available

ISBN 978–0–19–960786–0 (Hbk.)
ISBN 978–0–19–870959–6 (Pbk.)

For my parents

Contents

Preface

It took me a while to write this book and many people and institutions have helped me. Claire Gallop, Steve Holland, Geoff Kemp, James Stacey Taylor, Suzie Wilkinson, and Stephen Winter read and commented on substantial chunks of the manuscript. I had valuable conversations with Paul Brown, Govert den Hartogh, Julian Lamont, John McCall, Andrew Moore, Stephen Munn, Julie Pedroni, David Price, Janet Radcliffe Richards, Kathy Smits, Stephen Streat, Steve Wilkinson, and Andrew Williams. I also want to thank the many diverse audiences for parts of the book from hospitals in Auckland, Manchester, and Houston to Philosophy departments as far apart as Otago and London.

I started and finished the book as a member of the Political Studies department at the University of Auckland, with six years in the middle working on ethics at Auckland's medical school. A politics department is where I feel most at home, but the book is very much better for the time I spent away, especially because of the help from clinical colleagues working in transplantation. The University of Auckland gave me three sabbaticals during the time it took me to write this book, which I much appreciate. I also appreciate the support of the Leverhulme Trust, which made me a Visiting Professor at the splendid Centre for Professional and Applied Ethics at Keele University. I want too to mention the Bioethics Council, a ministerial advisory committee I served on and then chaired. My period there coincided with the Council's work on xenotransplantation and the New Zealand government's revision of the Human Tissues Act, which gave me important insights into regulatory systems and policy formation.

Finally, I had intended to plagiarize P. G. Wodehouse's joke; I was going to thank my family without whose never-failing sympathy and encouragement, this book would have been finished in half the time. Really, I planned the joke before I started writing the book. In fact, Suzie has been a great help with the book, reading sections and discussing the topics with refreshing common sense, while Robert, Harry, and Julia have lately come to my talks, asked penetrating questions, and helped with the really boring parts of writing a book, namely the bibliography and index. So my thanks and love to them, and no jokes.

I have adapted, with the permission of the publishers, some of the material in this book from various articles and book chapters. These are:

'Parental Consent and the Use of Dead Children's Bodies' *Kennedy Institute of Ethics Journal* 11 (2001), 337–58.

'What's Not Wrong With Conditional Organ Donation?' *Journal of Medical Ethics* 29 (2003), 163–4.

'Individual and Family Consent to Organ and Tissue Donation: Is the Current Position Coherent?' *Journal of Medical Ethics* 31 (2005), 587–90.

'RacistOrgan Donors and Saving Lives' *Bioethics* 21 (2007), 63–74.

'Individual and Family Decisions About Organ Donation' *Journal of Applied Philosophy* 24 (2007), 26–40.

'Living Donor Organ Transplantation', in R. Ashcroft, A. Dawson, H. Draper, and J. McMillan (eds.), *Principles of Health Care Ethics* (2nd edn.) (Chichester: Wiley, 2007), 483–8.

'The Confiscation and Sale of Organs' *Res Publica* 13 (2007), 327–37.

'Consent and the Use of the Bodies of the Dead' *Journal of Medicine and Philosophy* (forthcoming).

1

Introduction

Organ transplantation replaces patients' failing or failed organs with new ones from other people. To take some of the major causes of organ failure that lead to transplantation, hearts fail because the heart muscle deteriorates, lungs fail because of emphysema, kidneys and pancreases fail because of diabetes, and livers fail because of irreversible scarring (cirrhosis). For people whose organs are failing or failed, the alternatives to transplantation are often grim. Dialysis, insulin, drugs, and surgery can keep people alive and while they are better for some patients than having an operation and then taking anti-rejection drugs, in many cases transplantation is unambiguously superior in the quantity and quality of life it offers. In some cases of acute organ failure, transplantation is the only way to keep patients alive for more than a few hours or days.[1]

Since the late 1970s, with improved drugs to prevent the recipients' bodies rejecting their new organs, organ transplantation has moved from the experimental to the routine.[2] Transplantation is now what we may think of as a medium-scale branch of medicine. It is nothing like as common as joint surgery, for instance, but nor is it rare. At the end of 2006, 173,339 people in the US were recorded as having a functioning transplant.[3] But as it has become routine, transplantation has been limited by the supply of organs. Not enough organs are available to meet demand. All sorts of policies and techniques have been adopted or proposed to try to increase the supply of organs or use those to hand more effectively, but transplantation remains unusual within expensive healthcare. Its public policy problem is not a shortage of money, but a shortage of the vital raw material.

Organs are, of course, within our bodies. Ordinarily, we think we have rights over our bodies. Our bodies, and our body parts, are not just resources to be allocated according to normal principles of public policy. That is why organ transplantation has not only the public policy problem of shortage, but the ethical problem of treating properly the people whose organs they are. Ethics and public policy are not separate. In the case of transplantation, the ethical and legal rules that determine whose organs may be taken and the consent that should be given undoubtedly limit the supply of organs, which is why the rules are controversial.

---

[1] For a vivid description of both life with organ failure and the benefits of transplantation, see Ronald Munson's excellent book, *Raising the Dead* (New York: Oxford University Press, 2002).

[2] See Nicholas Tilney, *Transplant: From Myth to Reality* (New Haven: Yale University Press, 2003), ch. 12.

[3] R. A. Wolfe et al., 'Trends in Organ Donation and Transplantation in the United States, 1998–2007' *American Journal of Transplantation* 9 (Part 2) (2009), p. 869.

Here are some examples of the controversies discussed in this book. Most countries have, in practice, a double veto for retrieving organs from the dead: people can veto the post-mortem retrieval of their organs and families can veto the retrieval of their dead relatives' organs. Should either or both of the vetoes be dropped to get more organs? In fact, and contrary to common belief, few countries require the consent of the deceased before retrieval, regarding family consent as sufficient. But should people's organs be taken if they have not agreed in advance? Because of scarcity, more and more living donors are being used. Are doctors thereby violating the ancient rule against harming their patients? Recent years have seen moves away from living donation by children and other incompetents and towards using adult donors who are unrelated to the recipients. Is either move justified? Organs from dead donors now go into a general pool for allocation. But should people be able instead to specify who should get their organs after they die? If they are live donors, should they be able to specify the recipients, as they may now for donation to family and friends? Organs are currently traded illegally, in black markets. Would allowing sale be an unethical way to get more organs? Would it even get more organs?

These questions are discussed in the academic fields of bioethics and applied ethics and by clinicians, lawyers, and policy-makers. Sometimes they even become politically prominent as when, for instance, the then British Prime Minister, Gordon Brown, decided that the UK should consider presumed consent.[4] The questions are important not only across disciplines but across countries too. Every place with a transplantation programme grapples with the ethical problems raised by scarcity.

As for the scope of the book, it focuses on the solid organs that are transplanted on the largest scale: kidneys, livers, hearts, lungs, and pancreases. That said, many of the issues discussed arise also for smaller-scale transplantation, such as transplanting small-bowels, for tissue transplants such as bone marrow, and for more experimental transplants, such as faces.[5]

Let me describe briefly the method this book uses to answer the ethical questions. The general approach is philosophical. Acquiring organs for transplantation raises tricky philosophical questions, for instance about why, if at all, we should regard the wishes of dead people as having moral force. Discussing these problems requires analysing and using staple concepts in moral and political theory, such as autonomy, rights, justice, and well-being. But any worthwhile discussion of transplantation must be informed by its relevant clinical, legal, and policy aspects. It is too easy otherwise to philosophize in the wrong direction, and anyone interested in the practical problems of acquiring organs needs to know what the theory has to do with their concerns.

---

[4] BBC News, 'Organ Donor System Overhaul Call', 13 Jan. 2008. A subsequent inquiry found against presumed consent. Its report and the topic of presumed consent generally are discussed in chapter 6.
[5] I largely ignore the topics of the criteria for death, donation after cardiac death, and the use of anencephalics. A great deal has been written about these topics, e.g. Robert Veatch, *Transplantation Ethics* (Washington, DC: Georgetown University Press, 2000) and Stuart Youngner et al. (eds.), *The Definition of Death* (Baltimore: Johns Hopkins University Press, 1999). Few seriously argue against using brain dead people as organ donors, whatever their views on whether brain death really is death.

In accordance with the interdisciplinary aspirations of the book, I start with a background briefing on transplantation in practice before describing the plan of the book. The aim is to describe the problem of shortage by explaining its nature, the reasons for it, and why it matters. It will become clear that the problem has no quick policy or technical fix.

THE SHORTAGE OF ORGANS

Because of appeals to donors and crisis stories in the media, everyone knows there are not enough organs for all those who need them. It is, however, surprisingly hard to say how big the shortage is. This is partly because the statistics are either difficult to get or soft and partly because the concept of 'shortage' is itself open to interpretation.

As a first approximation, let us say that the shortage is the gap between supply and demand. It is easy to find the statistics for actual supply and they are presumably reliable. For instance, 28,463 transplants were performed in the US in 2009.[6] While the data for supply are relatively easy to come by, the data for demand are another matter. The most common figure given is for people on a waiting list. In the US, for instance, 108,026 people were listed as waiting for organs (with some multiple organ listings). In the UK, 8,011 patients were listed as actively waiting for a transplant.[7] The figure is then commonly set against the number of transplants performed in a given year to give an implicit measure of shortage. But this is an unhelpful comparison. The number of transplants in a year gives a figure for annual supply but the number on a waiting list does not give a figure for annual demand. The waiting list consists of net increases in a given year plus the existing number of people already waiting. What is needed to set against annual supply is an estimate of fresh annual demand.[8]

A figure for fresh demand could be derived from net additions to a waiting list, that is, through comparing waiting lists across years. Some account would need to be taken of the number of people who died on the waiting list without receiving a transplant, some of whom should be counted as unsatisfied demand while others— those who died from causes unrelated to organ failure—should not. These figures are themselves likely to be soft, since whether someone has died from unrelated causes will sometimes be a matter of judgement.[9]

---

[6] For the US numbers, see the Organ Procurement and Transplantation Network's website, optn.transplant.hrsa.gov (last accessed August 2010); for the UK numbers, which are for 1/4/08–31/03/09 see www.uktransplant.org.uk (last accessed August 2010).

[7] The US number was taken from the website of the United Network for Organ Sharing, www.unos.org, and was current at 13 August 2010. The UK number was current at 24 August 2010 and was on www.uktransplant.org.uk.

[8] David L. Kaserman and A. H. Barnett, *The U.S. Organ Procurement System: A Prescription for Reform* (Washington, DC: AEI Press, 2002), pp. 16–18.

[9] As a matter of interest, medical students at my university, when studying anatomy, find that the death certificates of their subjects are wrong about the causes of death in roughly 40 per cent of cases. Private information.

Even assuming one can derive a demand figure from changes to the waiting list, one may question the use of waiting lists as indicators of demand. Suppose we take demand as meaning 'could benefit clinically', a definition we shall revisit. Organ listing should exclude people who could not clinically benefit, such as those too frail or ill to be able to withstand the operation or tolerate the regime of anti-rejection drugs. But waiting lists often do not include everybody who could clinically benefit. Practices vary from place to place and organ to organ, but waiting lists will often understate demand because people who have no realistic chance of getting the organ they need will not be placed on a list.[10] If the question is 'how many people could clinically benefit from an organ transplant?', the answer will be only a rough estimate.

In any case, clinical benefit may not be the right basis for demand. In economics, demand is not given by what would benefit someone but by whether the benefit is worth the cost. People may benefit from all sorts of things in the sense that, if free, they would rather have them than not. But how much of a service people want when it is free is not the right measure of demand. This is not to say that an organ transplant must be something a recipient would be willing to pay for, only that the cost of the resources involved must be taken into account. In many countries where transplants take place, recipients do not directly pay for the costs. Either the state pays or insurance firms do. At some point, third parties may reasonably refuse to pay. Suppose a liver transplant operation costs $250,000. To offer the operation to someone who would die without it but only acquire a 1 per cent chance of survival with it in effect values the saving of the life at $25 million. By contrast, the US Environmental Protection Agency has valued saving a life at $6.1 million.[11] One need not insist on a particular figure to accept the point that the expected clinical benefit may not be the right basis for demand.[12]

In theory, then, there could be a gap between the number of people who could clinically benefit from a transplant and the number of transplants that ought to be funded. However, transplants are cost-effective in practice. Patients with kidney failure are offered dialysis in rich countries and, compared with the continuing costs of dialysis, kidney transplants are cheaper, provide a better quality of life, and tend to add a few extra years of life as well. In the case of kidney transplantation, there may be no gap in practice between clinical benefit and cost-effectiveness. Compared with dialysis, it may be worth paying instead for kidneys to be transplanted into everyone who would benefit clinically. In the case of other organs, transplants

---

[10] Possibly people are sometimes listed or even transplanted even though they would predictably be better off not having the organ, as is alleged to occur in the US for reasons of financial gain. See Nicholas Tilney, *Transplant*, pp. 244–6.

[11] A figure cited in Cass Sunstein, *Worst-case Scenarios* (Cambridge, MA: Harvard University Press, 2007), pp. 200–1.

[12] Trisha Greenhalgh writes: 'From the patient's point of view, he or she generally wants to get better as quickly as possible. From the Treasury's point of view, the most cost-effective health intervention is one that returns all citizens promptly to taxpayer status and, when this status is no longer tenable, causes immediate sudden death.' *How to Read a Paper* (3rd edn.) (Oxford: Blackwell Publishing, 2006), p. 159. The problem of scarcity in health resources is finding an adequate third point of view.

do not dominate the alternative treatment in the way kidney transplants do for dialysis. But according to cost-effectiveness evaluations, transplants of livers, hearts, lungs, and pancreases provide a gain in quantity and quality of life big enough to make funding more of them worthwhile.[13] The financial limit is above that set by the actual supply of organs and, if more became available, it would be worth funding them. At some point, though, with a very large or unlimited supply of organs, it would not be worth funding a transplant despite the clinical benefit (although it is another matter whether people should be allowed to pay privately, as they may for unfunded pharmaceuticals in some state health systems).

To conclude this section, the demand for organs exceeds the supply, although the gap is hard to quantify. The shortage matters not only because organs are of clinical benefit to recipients but because they are of enough benefit to be cost-effective. But why are organs so scarce?

WHY ARE ORGANS SCARCE AND IS A SHORTAGE UNAVOIDABLE?

The gap between supply and demand could be closed either by reducing demand or increasing supply, or both. Demand, however, has been increasing because, among other reasons, transplants are increasingly worth having, especially as anti-rejection drugs improve, because the causes of organ failure, such as Type 2 Diabetes, have got worse, and because, as populations become older, more people's organs are failing. It is sometimes argued that the diseases causing organ failure are often preventable, for instance by not smoking, drinking less alcohol, and consuming fewer calories, and perhaps more could be done to prevent the causes of organ failure. However, one should neither overestimate the effectiveness of public health policies nor automatically see policies as desirable if they do work, since their success may come at too high a price in other values, such as the freedom to live one's life as one chooses. Suffice to say, the shortage is unlikely to be entirely avoided by reducing demand.

What about increasing supply? Many hope scientific developments in stem cell therapy, artificial organs, and the use of animal organs (xenotransplantation) will make existing organ transplantation redundant. But these hopes are not yet close to being realized.[14] Staying with existing transplantation, supply could be increased, although it is controversial whether it could be increased enough to meet demand. Let us examine some of the causes of a shortfall in supply, beginning with deceased donors.

The main problem with supply is that, although large numbers of people die each year, the overwhelming majority of them cannot have their organs transplanted.

---

[13] G. Machnicki et al., 'Economics of Transplantation: A Review of the Literature' *Transplantation Reviews* 20 (2006).

[14] Sir Roy Calne once said: 'Clinical xenotransplantation is just around the corner, but unfortunately it may be a very long corner.' Quoted in L. Bühler et al., 'Xenotransplantation: State of the Art Update—1999' *Frontiers in Bioscience* 4 (1999).

Dead donors are in the vast bulk of cases diagnosed brain dead in an intensive care unit. The organs of other dead people often cannot be transplanted because they will have deteriorated beyond being usable. Very few deaths are diagnosed as meeting brain death criteria.[15] Of those, some are excluded because their organs are not functional, or because they have medical contraindications such as HIV.[16]

Various factors affect the number meeting brain death criteria. Typical donors have suffered brain bleeds, for instance sub-arachnoid haemorrhage, or traffic accident, or other trauma. Countries with fewer road deaths or greater success in intensive care units in treating brain bleeds have fewer potential donors. The number of potential donors may also be affected by the number of intensive care beds and the practices within them, for instance whether to send to intensive care a patient who has no chance of survival.[17]

These factors are primarily to do with the number of potential donors. Other factors affect the ability to turn potential donors into actual donors. Some of these are organizational, for instance to do with whether an efficient procurement process is in place. Others are the ethical-legal factors this book explores, to do with, for instance, the kind of consent required and who has to give it. Sometimes the factors overlap; for instance, an efficient procurement system may go too far, ethically speaking, in trying to persuade families to donate. The individual chapters will present such data as there are about the relative importance of the ethical-legal factors in accounting for the organ shortage.

Would there be enough organs to meet demand if every deceased potential donor were an actual donor? We could compare the supply figures with the demand figures. The supply figures come from audits of potential donors.[18] The difficulty is in finding the comparable demand figures, for the reasons given earlier. Some writers argue there could be enough organs from deceased donors to meet demand.[19] Other writers claim that some organs could in principle be supplied in sufficient numbers but other organs could not.[20] Probably the gap between demand and the maximum supply of dead people's organs varies with time and place.

---

[15] Munson reports that 2 per cent of deaths are determined by brain death criteria in the US. See *Raising the Dead*, p. 183. I have seen lower estimates for other countries.

[16] What counts as a contraindication is itself a matter of choice. The general trend is towards taking organs that would have been rejected in the past as, for instance, too old or fatty. See Australian and New Zealand Intensive Care Society, *The ANZICS Statement on Death and Organ Donation* (3rd edn.) (Melbourne: ANZICS, 2008), p. 36.

[17] House of Lords European Union Committee, *Increasing the Supply of Donor Organs Within the European Union* (2008), pp. 114–17.

[18] One audit estimates that the US has between 10,500 and 13,800 potential donors each year. See E. Sheehy et al., 'Estimating the Number of Potential Organ Donors in the United States' *New England Journal of Medicine* 349 (2003), p. 673. A UK audit estimated that in 2008/9 there were 1,130 potential heartbeating donors (those who were diagnosed as brain stem dead). See UK Transplant *Potential Donor Audit: Summary Report for the 24 Month Period 1 April 2007–31 March 2009* available at <www.uktransplant.org.uk> (last accessed August 2010).

[19] Kaserman and Barnett, *The U.S. Organ Procurement System*, ch. 2.

[20] Sheehy et al. claim there would be enough kidneys and hearts from the dead to meet demand, but not livers. See 'Estimating the Number of Potential Organ Donors in the United States'.

Kidneys, parts of livers, and lobes of lungs can be supplied by living donors, and are available in increasing numbers. In 2009, the US had 6,387 living donors. In a comparable year, the UK had 927 living kidney donors, supplying a third of all kidney transplants.[21] The potential supply of kidneys, liver segments, and lung lobes from living people obviously exceeds demand. However, taking organs from living people is not like taking organs from dead people because the dead are beyond physical harm. So there will always be questions about how far demand for organs should be met by inflicting physical harm on the living. In any case, hearts and pancreases cannot be taken from living people without killing them.[22]

Whether there could be enough organs from the living and dead to meet demand is not as important a question as some might think. Radical critics of current procurement methods often stress the possibility of ending the shortage; defenders of the status quo the impossibility. But even if a shortage remains, retrieving more organs, with the consequent benefits to recipients, would be highly desirable.[23] The question is what policies would cause more organs to be retrieved and whether their price would be too high. As I said earlier, the public policy problem of transplantation is at root the shortage of its raw materials. The core ethical problem is that the organs are within people, who are not just raw material. To think sensibly about the numerous problems raised by attempts to increase supply, we need to work out what claims people have over their organs.

PLAN OF THE BOOK

The ethics of acquiring organs for transplantation is of great intellectual interest and of practical importance and yet, compared with other topics in bioethics, such as abortion and euthanasia, it is relatively underdone philosophically. This book fills the gap in a way that will be of profit not only to academics who work in applied ethics and bioethics, but also to the lawyers, policy-makers, clinicians, lobby groups, and even prime ministers interested in transplantation.

I have tried to meet the various needs of an interdisciplinary readership in the structure of the book and through signposting and cross-referencing. For example, chapters 2 to 4 lay out the philosophical foundations for the discussion in chapters 5 to 10 of problems specific to transplantation. Philosophers who work on rights or posthumous interests may not find much new in the foundations, but experience tells me that most other readers will. However, readers who are primarily interested in the practical problems of transplantation could go straight to the later chapters. They will see there enough cross-referencing to be able to find the relevant earlier parts of the book if they have questions about the foundations.

---

[21] See n. 6 for sources.

[22] Except in the most unusual circumstances. See chapter 8.

[23] 'The reduction of an evil from two instances to one is as important as its reduction from one to zero. One mark of an ideologue is to deny this.' Robert Nozick, *Anarchy, State, and Utopia* (Oxford: Basil Blackwell, 1974), p. 266.

Let me now describe briefly the content of the chapters. Chapter 2 discusses the rights we have over our own bodies. Although the ethical questions raised by organ transplantation are not entirely answerable in terms of rights, rights are central to deciding who ought to have the power to determine whether and what organs are taken from a living or dead person's body. I say a few things about what rights are before turning to rights over bodies. I distinguish a right of bodily integrity—essentially a right to veto invasions of one's body—from rights of personal sovereignty, particularly the right to permit invasions of one's body. I believe most people have both sorts of rights and I shall try to make the case for the rights by showing how they fit with our intuitions and by clearing away certain misunderstandings.

The next two chapters consider the claims people have over their bodies after they die. I argue that people do have rights over their bodies after they die, and these are rights of personal sovereignty. The obvious question arises of how anyone could infringe on a posthumous right. The deceased would not know about an infringement and would no longer exist to have a right infringed upon. Put in its usual philosophical terms, posthumous rights do not satisfy an 'experience requirement' and run into the 'problem of the subject'. Chapter 3 tries to show how nonetheless we could have posthumous interests. It gives some intuitive support to the possibility of posthumous harm before discussing the experience requirement and the problem of the subject. The chapter's way of explaining posthumous harm will be familiar to philosophers who work on the topic, but will be novel, accessible, and intellectually satisfying for people who do not. At the end, I show the relevance of the philosophical pyrotechnics to transplantation.

Assuming people can have posthumous interests, chapter 4 takes up the question of their moral force and, in particular, whether they should be protected by rights. I begin with the rights described in chapter 2, of bodily integrity and personal sovereignty, and show why we do not have a posthumous right of bodily integrity but do have posthumous rights of personal sovereignty. I explain what personal sovereignty rights imply for organ retrieval after death. I then assess and criticize alternative foundations for a claim to control what happens to our organs after death, to do with rights of religious freedom or protecting the sensibilities of the living. Finally, I reply to some objections to posthumous rights, which are to do with a certain view about autonomy over time, a view of rights as protecting choices rather than benefits, and a view that rights protect only against bad experiences, experiences the dead obviously would not have. The chapter then sets out how the interests of the dead can conflict with the claims of families and potential recipients, which foreshadows the themes of the next three chapters.

If individuals have rights over their bodies after death, what should be the role of their families? Families have a substantial role, in practice, in deciding what happens to a relative's organs, but it is a role that is often criticized. Chapter 5 assesses three main lines of argument about the family's role. The first says that families should decide in order to give best effect to the claims of the deceased. The arguments here are over whether the deceased transferred authority to the family or whether families know better than others what the deceased wanted. The second says that families have a legitimate claim in their own right to decide. The arguments here concern the family's distress, respecting family bonds, and religious and cultural diversity. The third says that families should decide because the alternative of overriding them would have excessive social costs, in particular by causing a net drop in the supply of organs. The chapter argues that we often do not know—but could do more to find out—whether families give best effect to the claims of the deceased; that the family do have a claim in their own right, but only the weak claim not to be distressed; and that the family should have a power of veto given the likely effect on the supply of organs if their refusal to donate were overridden.

It is often not known what people want to happen to their bodies after they die. Chapter 6 asks how a system for organ retrieval ought to respond. The chapter defends a policy under which organs may be taken where there is no good reason to think the deceased would have objected and where the family do not object. The philosophical argument, in the first part of the chapter, is mainly about why it is ethically permissible to take organs from people who did not consent. In the case of the dead, their rights do not require consent but instead only doing what is likely to be in their interests. The second part of the chapter connects the philosophical argument to the debates about presumed consent and opt-out systems for organ retrieval. These debates are riddled with error and confusion about existing practice. I shall explain how the policy defended in this chapter differs little from the practice of many countries. I shall also set out the currently fashionable idea that the choice to donate or not can be framed so as to encourage donation, an idea about which I shall be sceptical.

Chapter 7 is about the conscription of organs. It tests the earlier conclusions about rights over our bodies against the view that organs should be compulsorily reallocated to people whose organs have failed. Although conscription from the living should not be taken seriously, conscription from dead people should not be dismissed out of hand. I argue against it anyway. I describe and reject arguments for conscription based on justice, positive rights, and the needs of the sick. Conscription would wrongfully infringe on a right to control what happens to one's body after death. I argue, however, that young children are outside the scope of the rights-based argument. Whatever the other drawbacks of conscription, it cannot be rejected on the basis of children's posthumous rights because they do not have posthumous rights.

Up to this point, the book will primarily have focused on organ retrieval from the dead. Chapter 8 is about living donor organ transplantation. Living donation is, as we saw earlier, of major and growing importance in organ transplantation. Although living donation from adults is no longer especially controversial, the issues it raises are not only important but also raised by the much more controversial sale of organs. Living donation creates what appears to be a conflict between the duty for doctors to do no harm and the duty to respect the autonomous wish to donate. However, on closer inspection of harm and autonomy, the conflict is much less stark. Where a conflict does exist, I argue that people should be allowed to sacrifice autonomously their well-being to some degree. The chapter then considers whether

organs may be taken from children and other incompetents or marginally competent people. I argue that competent children should be allowed to donate, subject to
the same caveats as apply to adults, and I show how the correct view of harm
supports organ retrieval from the incompetent in certain cases.

The ethical problems of transplantation are about allocation as well as acquisition. Chapter 9 is about the ethical problems created when allocation and acquisition interact. On the acquisition side, transplantation has been dominated by the
ideas of gift and altruism. On the allocation side, it has been dominated by a
concern for an efficient and just distribution. I argue that the traditional view of gift
and altruism is confused about the concepts and the basis for highly inaccurate
descriptions of existing practice. I then turn to allocation. I consider cases of so-
called directed donation (e.g. 'you can give my organs only to someone who is
white') and schemes to give priority in receiving organs to people who are willing to
donate. Both directed donation and priority schemes can have practical drawbacks,
but the ethical objections to them are not strong. I criticize the prevailing view of
justice and efficiency, which rests on the fallacy of assuming that only strictly
impartial allocation rules are impartially defensible.

Chapter 10 is about the sale and purchase of organs. It lays out some of the options
both for permitting sales and preventing them. The chapter goes through some of the
evidence about how permitting sale might affect the supply of organs from both the
living and the dead. It then discusses a specific problem with the purchase of organs
from the dead before evaluating the effects on living sellers. I consider whether we have
a right to sell our organs and whether and how it would matter if selling makes sellers
worse off than not selling. I also consider the view that permitting sale would cause
exploitation and injustice. I next turn to the objection that sale undercuts altruism and
wrongly commodifies people, or parts of people. On the whole, I believe that
prohibiting sale infringes upon people's rights over their bodies and, in some circumstances—which may well be the actual ones—sale should be allowed. But I concede
there are certain circumstances when sale may be legally discouraged.

Although I disagree with much of the ethical reasoning common in the field of
transplantation, not all the practical conclusions of the book are particularly radical.
I argue that people should be able to veto the retrieval of their organs after they die,
which rules out conscription; that the family should keep its power to override the
deceased's agreement to donate; that it could be permissible to retrieve organs from
people who neither consented nor dissented; and that living adults should be
allowed to donate to strangers. These conclusions are in line with common practice.
I do argue for permitting the retrieval of organs from children in rare cases, for
permitting the sale of organs, and for letting people designate the recipients of their
organs, at least if the effect would be to make more organs available. These
conclusions are contrary to mainstream practice, although widely shared by many
who write on transplantation. It does not matter to me whether the practical
conclusions are radical. I have followed the arguments where they have gone.
I hope what follows is a better worked out and more coherent intellectual foundation than usual for deciding how organs should be acquired.

2

Transplantation and Rights over Our Bodies

Do people have a duty to donate their organs after they die? Some writers think so, and a few would have the state enforce the duty by conscripting organs. Should people be allowed to sell their organs? Many say they should not, fearing the risk to the sellers' health or the corrupting effect on social relations. How should scarce organs be allocated? Some say organs should be given to those who would benefit the most, while others argue for what they think are fairer allocations. These views can be loosely classified in these terms: moralism, which involves the enforcement of moral duties; paternalism, which involves stopping people from harming themselves; and distributive justice, which is about the goodness or rightness of allocations. Now consider the following examples.

(1) Suppose a man refuses to donate a kidney to his son, despite having promised he would. With certain further details, we would be justified in holding this man's refusal to be morally wrong. Suppose, moreover, that society finds his behaviour repugnant. Nonetheless, few would say this man should be forced to submit to removal of his kidney for transplant into his son. Some interest or claim of this man outweighs his son's need and the man's earlier promise.[1] It also outweighs repugnance. For all that society might find his refusal repugnant, it may not act on that feeling by taking the man's kidney.

(2) Suppose a competent woman refuses the removal of a cancerous kidney even though removal is necessary to save her life. It is widely accepted that her kidney may not be removed. People have a duty not to take her kidney when she refuses even when it is in her interests to have the kidney removed.

(3) Consider some reasons for kidney conscription, that is, compulsorily taking the second kidney from living people with two. On the face of it, conscription would be recommended by utilitarianism, because the loss to the person of one kidney would likely be outweighed by the gain to the recipient who has no functioning kidney; by egalitarianism, because conscription would reduce the inequality between those with two kidneys and those with none; and priority to

---

[1] See the discussion of the relevantly similar 1978 American case of *McFall v. Shimp* in Michele Goodwin, *Black Markets: The Supply and Demand of Organs* (Cambridge: Cambridge University Press, 2006), pp. 63–6. McFall needed bone marrow to live and tried to get the court to force his cousin and friend Shimp to provide it. Judge Flaherty, trying the case, described Shimp's refusal as 'morally indefensible'. But he found for Shimp nonetheless, saying 'Forcible extraction of living body tissue causes revulsion in the judicial mind.' See the quotation in Cécile Fabre, *Whose Body Is It Anyway? Justice and the Integrity of the Person* (Oxford: Clarendon Press, 2006), p. 109.

the worst off, since those with no kidneys are worse off than those with two, and worse off than those with two would be after one is taken off them. Despite the apparent convergence on conscription of these widely held views of justice, conscription is not taken seriously as a matter of policy. Indeed, virtually no one suggests even conscripting blood, let alone kidneys. Our body parts may not be conscripted even when conscription would do more good than harm and have apparently fairer outcomes.

If we compare the three examples with moralism, paternalism, and distributive justice, we see that people's claims over their bodies limit what may be done in the way of enforcing moral duties, stopping people harming themselves, or aiming for a just allocation. Whatever these claims are, they must be weighty ones. The concept that best expresses these claims is the concept of rights.

Ethical thinking about transplantation is dominated not by rights, but by the ideas of donation and consent. However, donation presupposes that the organ is the person's to give, not no one's or someone else's or a resource for social use; and the emphasis on consent implies that people have rights to give or withhold consent. Indeed, thinking through the rights people have and how they fit with the interests of other people turns out to answer many of the ethical questions raised by the procurement of organs. For instance, deciding whether the state may stop people selling their organs or may allow families to veto their relatives' wishes to donate depends substantially on how we understand the rights we have over our bodies.

The purpose of this chapter is to give an account of the rights that are relevant to transplantation. Rights are the subject of an enormous and sophisticated literature in political and legal philosophy and I shall be drawing on some of its ideas in the later chapters on topics specific to transplantation. It is convenient, however, to set out these ideas in advance, and that is what this chapter does. I do not think the chapter breaks new ground in thinking about rights, but I do think the ideas will be new and illuminating for readers without a background in political and legal philosophy. I have selected the ideas most relevant to transplantation and developed them only as far as I think is needed. Nonetheless, those who are primarily interested in the specific topics discussed later could start there and refer back to this chapter as they need to.

The chapter first explains the idea of moral rights. It then argues that we have rights of bodily integrity and rights to individual autonomy, which I shall characterize as 'personal sovereignty'. The chapter spends some time developing a model of personal sovereignty in the light of apparently conflicting practices and of the doctrine of informed consent in medicine. It concludes by replying to some criticisms of a rights approach. In addition to giving its own account of rights, to be used later in the book, the chapter also introduces concepts, such as negative and positive rights, autonomy, informed consent, and ownership, that figure prominently in discussions of transplantation.

MORAL RIGHTS

The term 'rights' can be used in various ways.[2] This book mostly takes rights in the sense of moral claims—moral constraints on the behaviour of others—with considerable weight. We may distinguish moral from legal rights. Moral claim rights are normative and they offer critical standards to assess social practices, including the law. However, although I am focusing on moral rights, moral and legal rights often overlap in content and they conceptually have much in common. For example, murder infringes on both a legal and a moral right. And moral claim rights, like legal claim rights, entail duties.

To get a sense of the force of a right, take a familiar example in modern moral philosophy. Suppose the only way in which one can save five patients is by giving each a transplant, and suppose the only source for the transplants is a healthy friendless man who appears for a check-up. Each of the five would live happily for many years following a transplant and usually it is worse when five lives are lost than when one life is lost. Nonetheless, virtually everyone thinks that it would not be permissible to kill the healthy man in order to save the lives of five patients. The man has a right not to be killed, and this right outweighs the greater gain of saving a net four lives.[3] This is an example of what it means to say that a right has considerable moral force. Put another way, rights are peremptory, and this includes being able to override the greater good.[4]

Some rights may be absolute, that is, rights where every infringement is a violation, meaning an all-things-considered wrongful act.[5] But consider another case: a baby is crawling towards a cliff edge and the only way to save her in time is to push a man out of the way (but not over the cliff). Suppose that the man would not have consented even though he would suffer no harm beyond that of being pushed. Ordinarily, people have rights not to be pushed over but, in this case, it is permissible to push. There are two ways to interpret this conclusion. One is to say that at least some rights can be overridden for at least some benefits. On this interpretation, the rights are not absolute because they may be infringed upon without being violated. The other is to say that rights might be so specified so that they never need overriding. For instance, in this case, the right not to be pushed

---

[2] Virtually any book on rights in political or legal theory gives a full account. L. W. Sumner, *The Moral Foundation of Rights* (Oxford: Clarendon Press, 1987), ch. 2 is particularly clear.

[3] Judith Jarvis Thomson, *The Realm of Rights* (Cambridge, MA: Harvard University Press, 1990), p. 135.

[4] That rights are peremptory is a commonplace among rights theorists. See e.g. Jeremy Waldron (ed.), *Theories of Rights* (Oxford: Clarendon Press, 1984), p. 14; Sumner, *The Moral Foundation of Rights*, pp. 8, 12. To say that rights are peremptory is to make a conceptual point about rights which one can accept even if one thinks that there are no rights. Joseph Raz argues that the duties imposed by rights are peremptory in ruling out certain countervailing reasons rather than that the interests protected by rights are weightier. See Joseph Raz, *The Morality of Freedom* (Oxford: Clarendon Press, 1986), pp. 195.

[5] Judith Jarvis Thomson, *Rights, Restitution, and Risk* (Cambridge, MA: Harvard University Press, 1986), pp. 51–2.

could be specified more fully as the right not to be pushed over for no good reason and, because saving a baby is a good reason, the man does not have a right to be infringed upon.[6] Sometimes it is correct to think that the apparent problem of conflict between rights and the good can be avoided by restating the rights. One example is given in chapter 6, where I argue that people whose wishes are not known do not have rights infringed upon when others attempt to follow their wishes as closely as possible. However, some writers argue that rights may never be overridden and, in those cases where we are tempted to think otherwise, what is required is a more careful statement of the right. Unlike these writers, I doubt all overridings can be explained away by restatement.

I do not say that the peremptoriness of rights captures common usage. Rights are often taken in a hyperinflationary aspirational sense, standing for any good thing the speaker wishes to be done. But rights should not have their value inflated away. The complaint is not the relatively trivial one that the aspirational are misusing the words; it is the more important complaint that rights, as understood here, have considerable moral weight, and they are held much more sparingly than when taken in the hyperinflationary aspirational sense.[7] If we want the concept of rights to mark out special moral weight, we have to be careful how we use it. Otherwise we run the risk of declaring everything to be top priority, which is another way of saying nothing has priority.

There is another reason to be careful in ascribing rights. Because claim rights entail duties, they constrain the freedom of people besides the rightholder. Each time we say someone has a right, we say that others must pay the cost of having their freedom restricted. The cost of rights helps explain why people sometimes have interests that are morally considerable but are not protected by a right. Despite being morally considerable, others should not be put under a duty that corresponds to the interest. Examples have to be argued for, since any is likely to be controversial, but here is one from later in the book: people who need an organ to be transplanted into them have a morally important interest but typically no right to the organ. They have no right because no one is under a duty to supply the organ.

Even if I have a right to do something, it is an open question whether I ought to do it.[8] The man in the earlier example acted immorally in refusing to donate to his son. His right gave him the freedom to choose whether to donate or not, and he exercised his freedom wrongly. Consider also the right of free speech: I may still act selfishly, thoughtlessly, spitefully or in some other morally discreditable way in saying something I have a right to say. Having a right to give or withhold your

---

[6] Thomson argues that there are limits to the specification strategy. See Thomson, *The Realm of Rights*, chs. 3 and 4. John Oberdiek defends specification and criticizes the idea that rights are overridden in 'Specifying Rights Out of Necessity', *Oxford Journal of Legal Studies* 28 (2008).

[7] For these contrasting senses, see Lawrence Gostin (ed.), *Public Health Law and Ethics: A Reader* (Berkeley and Los Angeles: University of California Press, 2002), pp. 15–19. Joel Feinberg, *Social Philosophy* (New Jersey: Englewood Cliffs, 1973), chs. 4–6 remains an excellent guide to different types of rights claim.

[8] See Jeremy Waldron, 'A Right to Do Wrong', in his *Liberal Rights* (Cambridge: Cambridge University Press, 1993).

organ does not tell you whether to give or withhold it. Because the exercise of a right is a matter for moral guidance and appraisal, rights are not the total of ethics.

I want to say something here about how rights can protect even relatively trivial exercises of them. It is often said, in discussion of transplantation ethics, that people refuse to donate for poor reasons, for instance because they are squeamish about contemplating their bodies being cut up after death, or because of false beliefs, for instance that agreeing to donate will cause their deaths to be hastened or their bodies to be used in anatomy schools. Perhaps some refusals should be protected, for instance those based on a deep religious commitment, but why, it is asked, should their misguided refusal to donate have a right's protection? Yet there is nothing unusual in trivial exercises of a right. What people do may be for trivial reasons and yet be protected. For instance, New Zealand has political rights which allowed the Bill and Ben Party to form and be included on the 2008 general election ballot paper, and people could vote for it even though it was a joke. It is an interesting question why rights can protect trivial exercises of them. One answer might be that it would be unwise to try to tailor rights to protect only important exercises because then, as in the political case, some authority would have to decide what was and what was not important, a power clearly open to abuse. Another answer might be that rights let people know who is entitled to do what, with benefits in certainty and coordination that would be lost with ad hoc exceptions.[9] Still, whatever the explanation, it is clear that rights can protect trivial exercises. Whether they do in the case of organ retrieval remains to be seen.

Now we have in hand some of the ideas that underlie rights, we can turn to the rights most relevant in discussions of transplantation. These are rights over our bodies. The next few sections describe and, so far as possible, justify rights of bodily integrity and personal sovereignty. The final sections review political philosophy so as to explain how this chapter's view of rights compares with other views and to defend the rights against certain general criticisms.

BODILY INTEGRITY

It is widely accepted that competent people have a right of bodily integrity. Think back to the three examples at the start of this chapter. The man who refused to donate to his son had a right not to have his kidney transplanted even though his refusal was immoral. The woman with cancer was entitled to veto a nephrectomy even though she needed it. We all have a right against our organs being taken, despite an apparent consensus among popular theories of justice in favour of conscription. The examples show the weight of a person's refusal of intrusions into her body. If someone says 'no nephrectomy', then no nephrectomy. As I said, the most natural, and indeed common, way to describe the very significant weight attached to this refusal is to say that the person has a right.

[9] T. M. Scanlon, 'Rights, Goals, and Fairness', in his *The Difficulty of Tolerance* (Cambridge: Cambridge University Press, 2003).

Perhaps the most famous statement of the right to bodily integrity is by Justice Cardozo in the case of *Schloendorff* v. *The Society of New York Hospital* (1914). Cardozo wrote, 'Every human being of adult years and sound mind has a right to determine what shall be done with his own body; and a surgeon who performs an operation without his patient's consent, commits an assault, for which he is liable in damages.'[10] There are important and interesting questions about the content of the right to bodily integrity. The right is usually taken to forbid even relatively trivial touching without consent,[11] but it does not forbid accidental jostling on a bus. Does the right forbid spraying the passenger cabins of aircraft with insecticide while the passengers are in their seats, as used to happen on arrival in New Zealand? Would it forbid spraying people with a vaccine, if that were possible? The right entitles people to refuse medical treatment; does it also give them the right to be disconnected from lifesaving machinery? Although these are interesting questions, we can ignore them here. Whatever a right to bodily integrity protects, it certainly protects against the non-consensual removal of one's organs.

If we look over the examples, and influential interpretations of the right to bodily integrity, it is clear that it is negative, that is, it is a claim against invasion of the body.[12] The right to bodily integrity is not a right to command that anything happen to one's body. It need not even be the right to permit intrusions into one's body, since the right to bodily integrity might not be one that can be waived through consent. Consider the Jesus Christians, a sect some of whose members want to become living kidney donors for religious reasons. Their right to bodily integrity is no reason to accept their offers, whatever other reasons there may be. If their organs are not taken, they do not thereby suffer an unconsented invasion of their bodies.

The right to bodily integrity is thus a limited and negative one. It is also almost entirely uncontroversial and often considered of great weight. To quote another influential statement, 'under a free government at least, the free citizen's first and greatest right, which underlies all the others—the right to the inviolability of his person, in other words, his right to himself—is the subject of universal acquiescence'.[13] Indeed, some critics of medico-legal decision-making complain about the insufficiency and obviousness of these rights. Jay Katz, having quoted the courts in *Schloendorff* and *Pratt*, notes that they do not go beyond the obvious points about the wrongness of the surgeons' actions and, for all their language of sovereignty, do not give doctors duties actually to inform patients or ensure they understand their options.[14] But in not going beyond the obvious, they do state the obvious.

---

[10] Quoted in Jay Katz, *The Silent World of Doctor and Patient* (Baltimore and London: Johns Hopkins University Press, 2002), p. 51. Mrs Schloendorff, while unconscious, had a fibroid tumour removed contrary to her repeatedly expressed wishes.

[11] Thomson, *The Realm of Rights*, p. 205.

[12] I set aside the point that one's right to bodily integrity might be the basis for a positive right that others protect it, for instance through a police force.

[13] *Pratt v. Davis* (1905), quoted in Katz, *The Silent World of Doctor and Patient*, p. 51. 'The inviolability of the person' clearly includes the body. Dr Pratt removed Mrs Davis's uterus and ovaries after deceiving her into believing he would only repair some superficial rectal and cervical tears.

[14] Katz, *The Silent World of Doctor and Patient*, pp. 50f. Onora O'Neill makes a similar point about the limited value of a right to refuse treatment, although she says 'Undoubtedly such rights are of great

Why is the right to bodily integrity both uncontroversial and taken to be of such importance? I suspect we simply have solid intuitions about bodily integrity, and those who want to disagree have some hard explaining to do. The intuitions are basic and any moral theory would have to explain them and not conflict with them. Certainly if we think back to the example of killing the healthy man to save five lives, it is hard to see a moral theory that was more plausible than the intuitive conclusion that it is wrong.[15]

I do not say here that the right to bodily integrity is basic in the sense that it cannot be derived or explained in some deeper theory, only that the intuitions about bodily integrity are not justified by the theory but rather do the justifying of the theory. Let me explain. Judith Jarvis Thomson says the right to bodily integrity is justified by the recognition that people are individuals and not mere cells in an organism.[16] She also says that rights over our own bodies underlie our other rights, that we could not have, say, property rights or rights not to be harmed, without also having rights over our bodies. Consider Warren Quinn's explanation of the precedence of negative rights over positive rights. He writes,

> A person is constituted by his body and mind . . . For that very reason, it is fitting that he have primary say over what may be done to them—not because such an arrangement best promotes overall human welfare, but because any arrangement that denied him that say would be a grave indignity. In giving him this authority, this morality recognizes his existence as an individual with ends of his own—an independent *being*.[17]

Some writers try, then, to locate a right to bodily integrity within theories of rights and value. Nonetheless, the role that bodily integrity plays is not that of derived conclusion. While bodily integrity may logically follow from the deeper theories, normatively the justification goes the other way. The theories themselves are justified because of intuitions about bodily integrity.[18] For instance, Quinn is basing his views about negative rights on the intuitions he assumes we share about the especial horrors of assaults on our minds and, to a lesser but still very important extent, our bodies.

Bear in mind that bodily integrity is both uncontroversial and weighty when we later come to controversy within political commentary and bioethics about rights, about whether they are given too much significance, and whether they are inconsistent with community or with people's responsibilities. In the initial three examples, even critics of rights agree that people's kidneys may not be taken, which suggests that people have at least some rights and they trump many other considerations.

---

value.' See Onora O' Neill *Autonomy and Trust in Bioethics* (Cambridge: Cambridge University Press, 2002), p. 26.

[15] Thomson, *Realm of Rights*, p. 135. As Bernard Williams wrote about infanticide ' . . . "You can't kill that, it's a child" is more convincing as a reason than any reason which might be advanced for its being a reason . . .' *Moral Luck* (Cambridge: Cambridge University Press, 1981), p. 81.

[16] Thomson, *Realm of Rights* ch. 8.

[17] Warren Quinn, *Morality and Action* (Cambridge: Cambridge University Press, 1993), p. 170 (emphasis in original). See also pp. 170–2.

[18] Compare Raz, *The Morality of Freedom*, pp. 168–70, on core and derivative rights.

PERSONAL SOVEREIGNTY

Although considerations of bodily integrity justify weighty rights over our body, those rights are limited in scope. We surely have rights over our bodies in addition to those protecting us from invasion. In the initial example, the father who refused to donate a kidney to his son could not be made to. But suppose he had wanted to donate a kidney. Both refusal and offer are choices about one's body, but only the father's refusal is protected by a right of bodily integrity. If the father were not allowed to donate his kidney, his body would remain intact and its integrity uninvaded. Yet we may well think the decision to donate should be up to him. It is his body.

The most common way to express the idea that people should decide what to do with their own bodies is in terms of autonomy. Since autonomy means 'self-rule', it is a proper term to use. However, autonomy is variously used to describe a view of free will, independence in decision-making, and the authentic realization of values, none of which I want to be committed to. So I shall follow Joel Feinberg in using 'personal sovereignty' rather than autonomy to describe the model of claims over one's body that I favour, personal sovereignty being only one limited interpretation of autonomy. Much of the task of defending personal sovereignty consists in sharpening up its description and the analysis of opposing claims. This section only begins the task; the rest of the book does much more.

Consider this analogy to the wish to donate:

> if a man or woman voluntarily chooses to have a surgical operation that will render him or her infertile and a physician is perfectly willing to perform it, then the person's 'bodily autonomy' is infringed if the state forbids it on some such grounds as wickedness or imprudence. If no other interests are directly involved, the decision is the person's own and 'nobody else's business,' as we say, or 'a matter between the person and his/her doctor only.'[19]

By analogy, the decision to donate gives the state a duty not to interfere in the consensual links between willing donor and willing doctor. People may make imprudent decisions or 'wicked' decisions (where the wickedness is of a sort that does not harm others), but what they decide to do should not be prohibited by the state. However, note the quotation's qualifications: the assertion of individual freedom to act assumes that the decisions are voluntary and the acts would not directly affect the interests of others.

Donating organs or seeking sterilization are just two examples where we may think people have rights over their bodies that go beyond the right to veto invasions of bodily integrity. At first glance, consensual sex, consensual cohabitation, freedom of movement, or the freedom to eat unhealthily are other examples of decisions beyond bodily integrity that it is widely accepted the parties involved should be free to make. Perhaps the most important way in which the rights go beyond bodily integrity is in protecting the ability to forge links with consenting others. As I said

---

[19] Joel Feinberg, *Harm to Self* (New York: Oxford University Press, 1986), p. 53.

earlier, I shall classify these rights over the body under the heading of 'personal sovereignty'.

Feinberg takes personal sovereignty to be '*de jure* self-government interpreted on the analogy to a political state, as sovereign authority to govern oneself that is absolute within one's own moral boundaries'.[20] His idea of personal sovereignty is that we have a sphere within which we may decide what happens—we are sovereign—and this sphere consists of what is personal to us —hence 'personal sovereignty'. As for what is within the sphere, he writes,

> the kernel of the idea of autonomy is the right to make choices and decisions—what to put into my body, what contacts with my body to permit, where and how to move my body through public space, how to use my chattels and physical property, what personal information to disclose to others, what information to conceal, and more.[21]

Whatever exactly is within this sphere, it should include decisions about our bodies. Our bodies—unlike property in the external world—are as personal to us as anything can be.

Feinberg's view that people should be sovereign within their spheres is limited to decisions made by people who are capable of autonomy, and whose decisions satisfy some requirement of voluntariness, which rules out choices that are coerced, manipulated, made in the absence of adequate information, while drunk, and so on. Obviously, all of these conditions require a good deal of elaboration, which Feinberg supplies, but let us take it that the conditions are undemanding enough to allow for at least most adults' decisions to satisfy them.

As with bodily integrity, the thesis that we ought to be personally sovereign rests on intuitions that cannot be demonstrated. Perhaps the most persuasive summary way of putting it is that people ought to be able to run their own lives and, if we ask what counts as within one's own life, decisions about one's body certainly do. In related and more philosophical terms, David Archard writes, 'The giving and withholding of consent fixes what is permissible and impermissible in our relations to others, and has this power as an expression of our fundamental moral status as independent, self-governing agents entitled to determine what may and may not be done to us.'[22] The quotation nicely brings out the core intuition that each of us should be able to run our own lives, which both limits what we may do to others and what they may do to us. Out of the core intuition, one needs to construct a model which describes and explains how the decisions are supposed to fit with the interests of others or with decisions that are bad for the person deciding. The models can become rather elaborate. As we go through a model's needed qualifications, explanations, and sub-arguments, and try to fit it with other theories, we must not lose sight of the summary statement that people should be able to run their own lives.

---

[20] Joel Feinberg, *Harmless Wrongdoing* (New York: Oxford University Press, 1990), p. xvii.
[21] Feinberg, *Harm to Self*, p. 54.
[22] The quotation is from David Archard's untitled review of Joan McGregor et al., *Journal of Applied Philosophy* 24 (2007), pp. 209–10.

It is all very well to say people should be able to run their own lives, but what if they would make decisions that are bad for them or others? To take a concrete, if daft, example from Amartya Sen: we might think people should be free to wear miniskirts, but would we still think that if doing so caused cancer in the eye of the beholder?[23] What if miniskirts caused cancer in those who wore them?

When it comes to harms that we cause ourselves, Feinberg's all-things-considered view is that people should be able to make these choices for themselves even if they turn out to be catastrophic. This conclusion is not as hardline (or implausible) as it might seem. Feinberg, recall, is restricting his claims about the personal sphere to decisions that are voluntary, and this does not include decisions made by young children, or the grossly misinformed, or the coerced, or the drunk. No doubt many or most of the decisions a person would make that are truly disastrous to herself would not receive the protection of personal sovereignty that Feinberg has in mind. Nonetheless, some believe that Feinberg goes too far in letting people harm themselves. In chapter 8, I consider ways in which personal sovereignty might be weakened to permit some paternalism. They turn out to make little difference when it comes to organ transplantation.

What, then, of decisions that are disastrous or even just bad for other people? There are two relevant points to make here. First, not every bad effect on a person counts as a harm. Fleeting distaste does not, for instance. A harm must be a setback to an interest.[24] A 'harm to others' principle would not sanction interferences with free action on the strength of other people's mere dislikes. Second, a harm to others principle does not say just any harm caused by someone's action is enough to justify preventing it. To take a well-known example, if I beat you in a competitive examination, I might well have harmed you, but my beating you should not be prevented.[25] The harm caused to others is a reason to be weighed in favour of prevention, but it is a reason that might be outweighed by, for instance, the importance of free action or the social benefits of competition. Thus it is quite possible that, even if an action did cause harm to others, the interest in it would justify allowing someone to carry on. If others would suffer harm from our decisions about our bodies, there is a reason against our being allowed to make the decisions. But the reason to let us decide about our bodies will usually be stronger.

The idea that people should run their own lives is often expressed in terms of a private sphere with absolute powers of decision. It is an old criticism of liberalism that no decisions are purely self-regarding and what people choose to do does not affect only them.[26] The interest in controlling our bodies can be set against other

---

[23] A. Sen, *Collective Choice and Social Welfare* (San Francisco: Holden-Day Inc., 1970), p. 60.

[24] Feinberg, *Harm to Others*, pp. 45–6. Much of Feinberg's four volumes on the limits to the criminal law are about how to arbitrate between personal claims and the avoidance of harm to others. They are intended to provide a much-needed elaboration of John Stuart Mill's principle of liberty.

[25] Feinberg, *Harm to Others*, p. 219; J. S. Mill *On Liberty* (Harmondsworth: Penguin English Library, 1982), ch. 5, part 3.

[26] Patrick Devlin, *The Enforcement of Morals* (London: Oxford University Press, 1965). Feinberg's solution to this problem is to fall back on qualifications to self-regarding. What counts is not that a decision is purely self-regarding, which would be at least rare, but that it is 'chiefly' or 'primarily' self-regarding. See *Harm to Self*, p. 56.

people's claims in two different ways. One is to keep the sphere of decision, within which our authority to govern is absolute, but have its borders fluctuate according to the interests of others. The authority to govern would be protected by a right that is specified so it does not conflict with the weightier interests of others. The other is to have the interest in bodily control protected by a right that is not absolute. The right could be overridden by the interests of others or, in other words, the interests of others could, in certain circumstances, make infringing on a right justifiable. It does not greatly matter for our purposes whether we adopt the specification strategy or the overriding strategy, or both. The important point is that people have a claim to determine what happens to their own bodies that is weighty enough to be normally decisive and which should be protected by a right.

As I said, the rights of personal sovereignty go beyond the limited rights of bodily integrity in allowing people to forge links with others. That is why, in Feinberg's example of voluntary sterilization, people should be allowed to have the operation. But the rights are negative, rights to be free from interference. For anything said here, personal sovereignty does not give a doctor a duty to perform the sterilization. To take another example, the state has a duty not to ban interracial cohabitation because people have a right to cohabit with whomever they wish who is willing and able to consent to cohabiting with them. The right to cohabit with someone from another race is not the right to have a partner of another race supplied. Many writers believe that personal autonomy requires more than the absence of interference and needs positive rights too, that is, rights to be supplied with the resources they need to run their lives. Other writers have doubts about positive rights. I do not take a stand on this here; I merely want to note that doubts about positive rights are not relevant to the negative rights of personal sovereignty.

Although the rights of personal sovereignty are negative, the implications of personal sovereignty may not be. We may have reasons to help people run their own lives even though our reasons are not duties correlative to their rights. Suppose you want to borrow some money from me to pay to study for a law degree. You have no right to the money. If I withhold the loan because I think you would be better off doing something other than a law degree, I fail to honour your personal sovereignty although I infringe on no right of yours. If, by contrast, I do not give you the money because I want it to help someone else, I do not fail in any way to honour your personal sovereignty. I make these points again in a section of chapter 8 on doctors' entitlements to refuse to transplant organs.

CONFLICTS WITH PERSONAL SOVEREIGNTY

Whereas bodily integrity is both largely uncontroversial and a solid element in our moral thinking, personal sovereignty is more controversial. The personal sovereignty model says that people should be able to make choices over what happens to and how they use their own bodies. On the face of it, this model is inconsistent with common practices in many countries. Medicines are regulated: substances cannot be called medicines unless they have been approved through some regulatory regime, and even then access to them is often under the control of doctors. Many countries make people wear helmets when riding motorcycles or seatbelts when in cars. Substantial bodily harm is an exception to *volenti non fit inuria* (to one who consents, no harm is done): a person causing such harm commits an offence no matter how voluntary the consent of the victim (or 'victim'). There are limits to what one can contract to. For instance, someone in breach of a labour contract typically may not be forced to do what was promised, even if the contract included a waiver of the right against specific performance. And, to take an example of direct interest, many countries criminalize the sale or attempted sale of organs. All of these look like examples where the model of personal sovereignty is not followed.

When the examples involve transplantation, as the sale of organs does, they will be considered in detail later on. It is worth foreshadowing briefly here some of the responses to the apparent conflict between personal sovereignty and legal and social rules. One response is to say that if personal sovereignty really does conflict with a rule, so much the worse for the rule. The conflicting exceptions do not stand up to critical scrutiny precisely because they conflict with personal sovereignty. Another response is to say that, in the event of a conflict, personal sovereignty must yield or be abandoned. Perhaps, if we reflectively endorse the rule, the sphere in which personal choice is sovereign should have its boundaries drawn differently, or perhaps we should look for some different account of the rights we have over our own bodies. A third response is to deny that the apparent exceptions to personal sovereignty really are exceptions. Consider, for instance, the regulation of medicines, which limits what we can put into our bodies. This limit need not restrict personal sovereignty. Many people welcome regulation so that they themselves do not have to sort the good medicines from the bad and useless, at considerable cost in time and risk of error. Put like that, regulation can be thought of as a sovereign delegation of decision-making, in which case it gives effect to personal sovereignty rather than conflicting with it. The personal sovereignty model is sophisticated enough not to require that people make their own choices. People often have choices about their choices.

This section was the merest sketch. More will be said in the relevant chapters about conflicts with personal sovereignty.

PERSONAL SOVEREIGNTY AND INFORMED CONSENT

Informed consent is at the heart of modern medical ethics. In sum, informed consent is public consent given voluntarily with an adequate understanding of the relevant facts. The requirement of public consent makes consent formal and visible, and not identical with an approving state of mind. The requirement of voluntariness rules out coercion, force, and manipulation. It also rules out choices made by those without the capacity for voluntary choice, such as the heavily drunk or young children. The requirement of adequate understanding is often taken to impose a duty on whoever is seeking consent to ensure that the information is put in such a way that it is accurate and understandable and, more demandingly, actually understood. The requirement of relevant facts sets a disclosure requirement for those seeking consent and a limit to the facts that need be disclosed.[27]

We must be careful not to fetishize informed consent. Consent is not a freestanding principle with independent moral force.[28] Consent is second order, arising out of some entitlement such as a right over our own bodies. That is why you, a stranger, cannot consent to an operation on me; you do not have a right over my body.

The connection between informed consent and personal sovereignty is largely a conceptual one. The personal sovereignty model is a way of capturing the idea that people should rule themselves. The way to have people ruling themselves is to let them make decisions about themselves in an informed way. There are other reasons for informed consent besides the direct conceptual connection between personal sovereignty and informed consent. One is the connection between the wishes of patients and their well-being. It is often argued that people are the best judges of their own interests, and so having people make choices for themselves will typically be better for them than having the decisions made by someone else. (Hedging and caveats are needed to make the best-judge view plausible.) Another reason for informed consent is its prophylactic role in preventing abuse and mistake. A patient could be treated without giving informed consent although he or she wanted the treatment and would have consented anyway. But a rule against treatment without consent protects against treatment that a patient did not want and would not have consented to. After all, if it is possible to get consent, why would someone not try, unless for bad motives?

Although they are conceptually connected, requiring informed consent is not always a sufficient or ideal way to respect personal sovereignty. First, consent is not enough because it implies a choice from among a limited menu of alternatives. Choice from a limited menu fails to capture the idea that people can forge their own links with consenting others.

Second, the connection between informed consent and personal sovereignty needs qualifying to take account of the earlier point about delegation. People do not simply have choices and preferences on one level; they have choices and preferences about their choices. People often want to delegate decision-making to save themselves effort or to increase the chances that the decisions will better, as judged by their own lights. Delegation is a familiar phenomenon and an expression of personal sovereignty. Suppose people wish to delegate their medical decisions, as they often do when, for instance, they ask doctors 'What would you do?' Some practitioners act as if they believe patients should be forced to give informed consent as a condition of treatment and should not be allowed to avoid considering the costs and benefits. Whatever the merits of this view, it is not one justified by respect for personal sovereignty or, at least, not directly.

---

[27] T. M. Wilkinson, 'Research, Informed Consent, and the Limits of Disclosure' *Bioethics* 15 (2001).
[28] Neil Manson and Onora O'Neill, *Rethinking Informed Consent in Bioethics* (Cambridge: Cambridge University Press, 2007), pp. 72–7.

Third, the prophylactic reason for consent sets a default rule: in the absence of consent, the patient may not be treated. This rule makes less sense when it is not possible to get consent from the patient, for instance when the patient is unconscious (or dead). Everyone recognizes that treatment should not be denied to the unconscious on the grounds that they have not consented, so no one endorses the 'no treatment' default rule in that case. But it is quite common to argue that certain things may not be done to the dead, even when there are grounds for believing they would have wanted them to be done, when they had not consented in advance. This conclusion, I shall argue in chapter 6, is one example where fixating on consent fails to serve its underlying values.

SELF-OWNERSHIP AND PROPERTY RIGHTS

Personal sovereignty is not the only model of rights over our bodies. Another philosophically prominent model is self-ownership. According to this model, we own ourselves, meaning we have property rights in ourselves. I spend little time on self-ownership because I doubt it is an alternative to personal sovereignty that is both genuine and plausible. As I shall explain, self-ownership is either a redescription of personal sovereignty, so plausible but not a genuine alternative; or it is genuinely different, but in ways which make it implausible.

Put as simply as 'we own ourselves', self-ownership could be a way of saying the same thing as personal sovereignty but in different language. Self-ownership would obviously then not be an alternative to personal sovereignty at all.[29] Strikingly, the common arguments for the thesis of self-ownership rely on the same intuitions as those that motivated the model of personal sovereignty.[30] That is, people are self-owners because they ought to be in control of themselves and not under the control of others. How, then, could self-ownership differ from personal sovereignty?

The version of self-ownership that has attracted the most philosophical attention is found within libertarian political philosophy. The libertarian version contains distinctive elements. Libertarians use self-ownership to argue for a right against taxation of the income from one's labour or for rights to alienate oneself, for instance through voluntary slavery.[31] The personal sovereignty model I have described need not have these radical implications for taxation and contract,

---

[29] Thomson's discussion of first property is much like this. See *The Realm of Rights*, ch. 8. See too David Archard, 'Informed Consent: Autonomy and Self-ownership' *Journal of Applied Philosophy* 25 (2008).

[30] Although I should mention Hillel Steiner's arguments, which purport to be non-moral and conceptual. For him, competent adults start off with equal rights (which they can waive and alienate) because the alternatives are either that people have no rights, which would cause insoluble moral deadlock, or that some have rights over others, a position for which no non-arbitrary reason can be given. See *An Essay on Rights* (Oxford: Basil Blackwell, 1994).

[31] Robert Nozick, *Anarchy, State, and Utopia* (Oxford: Basil Blackwell, 1974) is the best-known work of libertarian political philosophy, and he makes these claims about self-ownership. G. A. Cohen is the most important philosophical critic. See his *Self-Ownership, Freedom, and Equality* (Cambridge: Cambridge University Press, 1995).

which is a benefit of the personal sovereignty model, since the implications are highly controversial (and implausible).

The self-ownership model takes its rights to be property rights.[32] Some writers on transplantation, who are not libertarian, also argue that people do or should have property rights in their own body parts. For them, the virtue of property rights lies in their greater certainty. For example, rules about intestacy could be applied to organs when the deceased had not made their wishes known.[33] But many dislike the idea of property rights in bodies and others think it is a conceptual misdescription. These are large disputes, to be avoided if possible in thinking about transplantation. Insofar as the aim is greater certainty, we need not settle the question of property rights. Certainty requires setting out who is allowed to decide what. Arguing about whether having the right to decide is a property right is secondary.

Both personal sovereignty and self-ownership, in its libertarian version, would rule out conscription of organs from the living, or the dead, if rights extend beyond people's deaths. As for living donor transplantation, and controversies over what organs may be donated, both views would at first glance say that one's organs are one's own to dispose of as one wishes, which is compatible both with condemning morally certain ways of exercising those rights and with being sensitive to the ways in which people's voluntariness might be compromised. At this stage, then, it is hard to see how self-ownership or personal sovereignty would differ in what they had to say about organ retrieval. Both would require developing if they are to be properly compared and contrasted. However, to avoid being sidetracked, I shall concentrate on developing the personal sovereignty model. That has the polemical advantages of not being tied to concepts of property and ownership, and not being associated with libertarianism, all of which tend to put off those who are not libertarians.

CRITICISMS OF RIGHTS

In political philosophy, rights have been criticized for their metaphysical extravagance, requiring non-existent entities; for being pernicious in encouraging anarchy; for encouraging or at least being based on selfishness; and for representing and causing 'atomism' rather than community.[34] A proper discussion of these classical criticisms would be too far off the point of a book on transplantation, and there are in any case plenty of proper discussions—indeed, refutations—available.[35]

---

[32] Steiner, *An Essay on Rights*, claims that to do the job of rights, rights must be property rights.

[33] David Price, *Human Tissue in Transplantation and Research: A Model Legal and Ethical Donation Framework* (Cambridge: Cambridge University Press, 2009), ch. 8.

[34] See Jeremy Waldron (ed.), *Nonsense Upon Stilts* (London: Methuen and Co., 1987) for excerpts from Bentham, Burke, and Marx that make these criticisms as well as for a long essay by Waldron defending rights.

[35] Among these, see Stephen Holmes, *The Anatomy of Antiliberalism* (Cambridge, MA: Harvard University Press, 1993).

I want to respond to the criticisms of rights talk that seem to come up in discussion of transplantation, criticisms which have affinities with the classical objections. There seem to be three main ones: that rights are typically unfounded; that to talk of rights involves a needless circuit; and that rights are excessively individualistic.

The worry that rights are unfounded is sparked by the countless writings in bioethics that seem to pluck rights from thin air.[36] An assertion of a right has to be justified, and still more does it have to be justified when the right would impose duties. In the sense that a right must be justified, rights must be the conclusions of an argument. However, rights to bodily integrity and personal sovereignty are not plucked from thin air. I have tried to justify the rights by pointing to the ways in which they are supported by fundamental intuitions.

The worry that rights involve a needless circuit can be explained like this: given that rights talk can be translated into talk about duties, and given that rights have to be justified in terms of the importance of the interests or choices they protect, anything said about rights can be said in other ways, and said better. So citing rights is at least pointless and perhaps unhelpful. The reply is, in a sense, the whole book, which shows that citing rights has a point and does help. I think that, given the importance of organs in saving lives and improving their quality, ordinary thinking about the ethical and legal consent regime presupposes some idea that is equivalent to or very close to rights. Moreover, the sophisticated legal and philosophical discussion of rights includes ideas about overriding rights and specifying them carefully that can be fruitfully applied to the topics of the book. To be sure, what is put in terms of rights could be put in some other way. But it would be more convoluted, perhaps misleading, and would mischaracterize what people care about.

There can be, furthermore, an advantage in framing a discussion in terms of rights. People often agree on what should be done without agreeing on the underlying reasons. Cass Sunstein argues that policy should search for '*incompletely theorized agreements* on what to do—agreements on the right practice amidst disagreements or confusions about the specific theory that best justifies that practice'.[37] Rights can be the basis for just such agreements because people often accept that certain interests should be protected even as they disagree about why. An example is the right to non-interference with our bodies, which may be defended on the differing grounds of autonomy, well-being, or self-ownership.

The final criticism I want to consider is that rights are objectionably individualist. The root idea is that rights protect individuals' interests at the expense of a wider grouping, whether family, community, nation, or world, and rights give too much weight to the individuals' interests or else wrongly presuppose that their interests are separate to, even antagonistic to, the interests of the wider group. The criticism

---

[36] Norman Daniels, *Just Health* (Cambridge: Cambridge University Press, 2008), pp. 14–15.
[37] Cass Sunstein, *Worst-case Scenarios* (Cambridge, MA: Harvard University Press, 2007), p. 121 (emphasis in original).

arises partly because of the historical connection between rights and the moral individualism of the liberal tradition.

Rights are certainly individualistic in the sense that, as Carl Wellman writes, 'Every right is possessed by some individual right-holder'. But ' . . . these possessors need not be individual persons'.[38] Rights may be held by groups too, as they obviously are when held by corporations and other artificial persons. Wellman continues: 'it is essential that each right and each right-holder be individual in the adjectival sense defined as "Existing as a separate indivisible entity . . . Single as distinct from others of the same kind"'.[39] Wellman's view is common across many conceptual accounts of rights. The concept of rights does not presuppose anything about the separate interests of individual humans. The individualism of the concept of rights is only contingently connected to the moral individualism of the liberal tradition.

Nonetheless, this book does defend an account of rights recognizably within the liberal tradition, so the charge of excessive individualism will have to be confronted more directly. The view that we each have rights to make our decisions and act on them is an individualistic view. It says that individuals should not have things done to them or be prevented from acting or be forced to act in certain ways if they do not want to, whether by the state, their community, or their family. But this is a view about what people's rights are. It is not a view about how people would or ought to exercise their rights. If people wish to make their decisions for themselves without consulting their families, then the personal sovereignty model permits this. But it also permits people to consult as widely as they wish and defer to the decisions of their families, community leaders, religious leaders, or whomever. So the personal sovereignty model does not see people as selfish or solitary (or altruistic or community-minded). It does not look to the reasons people have for exercising their rights at all.[40]

That some rights exist should not be controversial because rights to bodily integrity are not controversial. Even the man who refused to donate a kidney to his son had his selfish refusal protected by a right. Why, in the face of the example of bodily integrity, would anyone reject the thesis that we have rights? Some critics of rights claim they presuppose selfishness and hostility between people, and they look forward to a world of better social relations, without rights.[41] Two quotations serve as a reply. Jonathan Wolff writes, 'A society in which we need to protect ourselves [from others] . . . is not the best society we can imagine, and surely we can hope for better. To which the defender of rights will reply: hope all you like, but don't give up your rights in the meantime.'[42] And Jon Elster writes, 'one

---

[38] Carl Wellman, *A Theory of Rights* (Totowa, NJ: Rowman and Allanheld, 1985), p. 185.
[39] Ibid.
[40] Recall the earlier point that rights are not the whole of ethics. They are not because having a right does not determine how one ought to exercise it.
[41] See Karl Marx, in 'On the Jewish Question', reprinted in Waldron (ed.), *Nonsense Upon Stilts*, and echoed by some communitarian and feminist writers.
[42] Jonathan Wolff, *Why Read Marx Today?* (New York: Oxford University Press, 2002), pp. 106–7. I would go further and say people retain their rights even in a society so fortunate that no one wanted to violate them. 'It is wrong to murder' would not be false simply because it never occurs to anyone to murder, and nor would the closely-related statement: 'People have a right not to be murdered.'

cannot assume that one will in fact approach the good society by acting as if one had already arrived there'.[43]

CONCLUSION

The ethics of acquiring organs for transplantation turns on our rights over our own bodies. This chapter has explained and defended the idea of moral rights, and argued that we have rights of bodily integrity and personal sovereignty. However, the tacit assumption has been that we are considering the rights of people who are alive whereas many of the ethical problems are about how to acquire organs from the dead. How could it make any difference what is done to the dead? How could they have posthumous rights? These are the subjects of the next two chapters.

---

[43] Jon Elster, 'The Market and the Forum: Three Varieties of Political Theory', in Jon Elster and Aanund Hylland (eds.), *Foundations of Social Choice Theory* (Cambridge: Cambridge University Press, 1986), p. 119.

3

The Possibility of Posthumous Harm

Some people want to donate their organs after their deaths, even carrying donor cards or having their status displayed on their driving licences. Yet their families might refuse to allow their organs to be taken. Whose wishes should prevail? Some people want their organs not to be taken. But people who are dead obviously have no further need for their organs in any biological sense, whereas plenty of living people would want them. Again, whose wishes should prevail? Thomas Paine said, in a somewhat different context: 'The vanity and presumption of governing beyond the grave, is the most ridiculous and insolent of all tyrannies.'[1] Why should the wishes of the dead be given weight?[2] If they should be given any, how much? These are tricky questions. Answering them in anything like an intellectually satisfying way requires drawing on and applying the substantial philosophical literature on the possibility of posthumous harm, and that is what this and the next chapter do.

Much of the literature on the ethics of taking organs from the dead is rather shy of the philosophical problems. One fairly common move among those who think priority ought to be given to the wishes of the dead is to say something like 'in our society, we give priority to individual autonomy over benefit to the community' or 'in our society, we respect the wills of dead people about their property, so we should respect their wishes about their bodies'.[3] These are points worth making, but they hardly amount to a demonstration. Any reflective person would wonder whether respecting the autonomy of the dead is quite like respecting the autonomy of the living, or even if it makes sense at all. And the trouble with consistency arguments, such as the one from wills, is that they can go both ways: given the puzzles about respecting the wishes of the dead, perhaps we should not respect their wills either. Of course, arguments have to start somewhere, but these ones for respecting the wishes of the dead can and should be pushed back further. The same can be said of some of the arguments for following the wishes of the family or meeting the needs of potential recipients even against what the dead person had wanted. A common argument here starts with the truism that dead people cannot think, feel, or act autonomously and ends with the conclusion that their autonomy

---

[1] Thomas Paine, *Rights of Man* (Harmondsworth: Penguin, 1969), pp. 63–4.

[2] 'The wishes of the dead' is short for 'the wishes of people while alive who are now dead'.

[3] These are paraphrases of arguments by Robert Veatch, *Transplantation Ethics* (Washington, DC: Georgetown University Press, 2000), pp.146–7 and Michele Goodwin, *Black Markets: The Supply and Demand of Body Parts* (Cambridge: Cambridge University Press, 2006), pp. 144–5.

or interests cannot be affected by posthumous events.[4] The truism is another point worth making, but it is hardly conclusive. Apart from a lack of charity to those who think the wishes of the dead should prevail, some of whom must realize the dead cannot think, feel, or act, there are plenty of other sensible ways of understanding both autonomy and posthumous harm. Again, we have to go deeper. The philosophical questions cannot be avoided if we are to discuss the ethics of removing organs from the dead in a serious and complete way.

This chapter will defend the view that people can be harmed by events after their deaths. The aim here is to elaborate and defend the view and ask what it implies. I do not want to say, or not yet anyway, that the only way to justify respecting the wishes of the dead is to accept this view. The next chapter will consider other reasons to respect the wishes of the dead.

For convenience, this chapter focuses on events that might reduce well-being rather than increase it. Suppose someone now dead had opposed the taking of her organs. We might say that, given her desire, the person would be *harmed* if her organs were taken. Mostly, I shall use 'harm' as roughly equivalent to reductions in well-being, and also speak in terms of people's interests as what can be set back, where to have an interest set back is to be harmed. The account of harm I use is not meant to beg any questions; it only follows Joel Feinberg's well-known account.[5]

I assume that death is either the end of the person or at least that nothing, including nothing experientially, happens to people in an afterlife as a result of what happens to their mortal remains.[6] This assumption is for the sake of argument: the challenge is to explain how posthumous harm can be possible even if is correct. My account is non-religious rather than anti-religious and its essentials may be accepted by atheists, agnostics, and believers. This shared acceptability would give the account an advantage as a basis for transplant policy, but I shall make no more of it here.

Throughout, we should be willing to accept at least some awkwardness in whatever view we come up with. Death and posthumous interests are strange topics anyway, and arguably the very language in which we think of them has been affected by the historical belief that people survive death in some form or other.[7]

The major question is how someone can be harmed at all by events after her death. The best-known philosophical account of how posthumous harm is possible has been given by George Pitcher and Joel Feinberg.[8] My account follows theirs, except in one significant way. The essentials of my account are as follows. People

---

[4] Stephen Streat, 'Moral Assumptions and the Process of Organ Donation in the Intensive Care Unit' *Critical Care* 8 (2004); John Harris, 'Law and Regulation of Retained Organs: The Ethical Issues' *Legal Studies* 22 (2002).

[5] Joel Feinberg, *Harm to Others* (New York: Oxford University Press, 1984), esp. ch. 1.

[6] I do not assume that we go utterly out of existence upon death, only that death is the end of us as persons. After all, our bodies remain for a while after our deaths. See Fred Feldman, 'The Termination Thesis' *Midwest Studies in Philosophy XXIV* (2000).

[7] Julian Lamont makes this plausible-sounding claim of many cultures in 'A Solution to the Puzzle of When Death Harms its Victims' *Australasian Journal of Philosophy* 76 (1998), p. 209.

[8] George Pitcher, 'The Misfortunes of the Dead', in John Martin Fischer (ed.), *The Metaphysics of Death* (Stanford: Stanford University Press, 1993); Joel Feinberg, *Harm to Others*, pp. 79–95 (reprinted in Fischer's anthology as ch.10).

have goals and the fulfilment of their goals has moral significance because it affects their well-being or the quality of their lives. The fulfilment of people's goals in many cases logically requires other people to do certain things or the impersonal world to be a certain way. Two key problems face the idea that people can be harmed by what happens after their deaths. The first problem states an 'experience requirement' for harms: to be harmed, one's experiences—meaning mental states—must be adversely affected.[9] But this problem is avoided on the account given here, where the non-fulfilment of goals harms the people whose goals they are even though their mental states are not altered. The second problem is known as 'the problem of the subject' and it says 'After death, the person does not exist and so cannot be harmed'. The account given here says the person before death can be harmed, a person who is clearly a proper subject. Against the objection that the account presupposes backwards causation, the reply is that the harm is the non-fulfilment of the person's goals, which is logical, not causal.

INTUITIONS ABOUT POSTHUMOUS HARM

The idea that posthumous harm is possible has some intuitive backing. Many people think we have at least some reason to uphold wills, thereby respecting wishes about the disposition of property after death. Many also think that defaming a dead person is wrong. It is, though, not clear what lessons should be drawn from wills or defamation of the dead. Sceptics about posthumous harm say our intuitions in these cases can be explained in other ways, for instance that the wrong of over-turning a will lies in its effects on the confidence of the living about what will happen to their property after they die.[10] It is unlikely that any intuitive cases will persuade a sceptic and, given the philosophical problems of posthumous harm, the cases on their own should not persuade anyone. Nonetheless, it is worth approaching the philosophical discussion with a set of cases designed to make the reader look sympathetically on the possibility of posthumous harm. Here are the cases.

In Case A, an agronomist devotes his life to developing cheap, productive, disease-resistant grains because of a deep commitment to his helping eradicate world hunger. For a time, his grains are so successful that everyone uses them and world hunger abates. Then a new disease evolves that kills his grains and, because his are the only ones used, it causes a vastly worse famine than ever before. Despite his best efforts, he has made the world a much worse place and the famine means

---

[9] 'Experience requirement' is James Griffin's term in his *Well-Being* (Oxford: Clarendon Press, 1986), p. 13.

[10] James Taylor argues that what is wrong with slandering a dead person is that it insults the autonomy of the living listeners, which might be so, but does not explain what would be wrong with breaching a promise of confidentiality to the dead and telling the listeners the truth. See Taylor, 'The Myth of Posthumous Harm' *American Philosophical Quarterly* 42 (2005), p. 318. Even if the explanations given by the sceptics are insufficient to explain all the intuitions, they do suggest ways to justify respecting the wishes of the dead that might be relevant to transplant policy, and these will be discussed in the next chapter.

his goals are utterly defeated. Quite apart from its effects on everyone else, the famine caused by his grains is a disaster for the agronomist.[11]

The conclusion that the famine is at least a serious setback to the agronomist's interest, and thus a harm, is relatively uncontroversial. Just to make it clear, the harm is the defeat of his major goal that he help reduce world hunger. Perhaps he feels terrible about what he has done, and that might be another bad thing, but this is not the harm in question. The harm to him is that his goal is defeated because his creations cause hunger.

Case B is the same, except for this: the crops fail shortly before the agronomist dies. His friends do not tell him (but do not lie) and he dies believing that he has achieved his goal. But he has not. His goal was not to believe he had achieved his goal or otherwise feel contented with himself; it was actually to reduce world hunger, at which he has been worse than useless. Intuitively we think that, even though he does not know it, he has been harmed by the famine his grains have caused.

Case C is the same as B, except for this: the crops fail just after the agronomist dies. As in A and B, he has utterly failed to fulfil his leading goal. His goal was to reduce hunger but he has made things worse. Why should we not say he has been harmed by the failure? If we accept the conclusion in B, we accept that he has been harmed even though he does not know about it. What difference does his being dead in C make, apart from merely ensuring he never finds out?[12]

These cases give us some reason to start taking seriously the possibility that people can be harmed after their deaths. They give those who would deny posthumous harm some explaining to do. But we also need some theoretical account of how people can be harmed without knowing about it and how people can be harmed after their deaths. This account will be developed through considering the philosophical difficulties that stand in the way of attributing posthumous harm.

THE EXPERIENCE REQUIREMENT AND THEORIES OF WELL-BEING

The first problem for the view that people can be harmed after their deaths arises from an experience requirement for harms. This requirement says that people's mental states must change if their well-being is to change. If a harm is a reduction in well-being, it is a necessary condition of a person's being harmed that her mental states change. Since a person's mental states cannot change after death, her well-being cannot change after death. Therefore, a person cannot be harmed by what happens after her death. While people may fear events that occur after their deaths and be adversely affected by their fear, the events themselves could not harm them.

The experience requirement has been widely discussed and largely dismissed in the philosophical literature. Here is a version of a common counter-argument.

---

[11] The agronomist case is adapted from Larry Temkin's example, *Inequality* (Oxford: Clarendon Press, 1993), p. 264. The A, B, C, format is a variant of Feinberg's, *Harm to Others*, p. 88.

[12] Derek Parfit, *Reasons and Persons* (Oxford: Clarendon Press, 1984), p. 495.

Imagine a person who greatly values her friendships, something it is entirely rational to value, and consider two imaginary cases. In the first case, she has genuine friends, that is, people who really do care about her. In the second, they do not care about her at all, but deceive her into believing that they are her friends. We can suppose that her mental states are identical in the two cases. What does not seem identical is her well-being. In the case where she is deceived, she does not get what she values, which is friendship and not just the feeling of friendship. That she does not get what she values follows from a truth about friends: people who do not care about you are not your friends. In other words, whether people are your friends depends partly on them and not entirely on your beliefs about them. Thus if a person's friends were to change into successful deceivers, the person's well-being would be reduced and this would be a change that occurs without her mental states altering.

The case of deceiving non-friends is just one of many in the literature. Many philosophers say that events can be intrinsically bad for people even if the events do not change their mental states for the worse. If all that counted were mental states, then people should be willing to sign up forever to a machine that will give them better experiences than they get in real life.[13] We should not feel the pity we do for an adult reduced through a brain injury to the level of a contented infant.[14] And we could not justifiably say that the agronomist is harmed, in Case B, when the crops fail but he does not find out.

The claim I want to make is that well-being is partly a matter of the fulfilment of one's goals. Goals are more than merely desires or wishes. To be a goal, they must guide a person's actions and have had some effort invested in them. The fulfilment of goals extends beyond the person's own body and mind. Fulfilling my goal to write a well-received book certainly requires that I do something, but it also requires others do something as well. The book goes out into the world and the world receives it well, or not. I have a goal for my children to prosper; whether that is fulfilled depends on whether, when they become adults, my children prosper.[15] The fulfilment of these goals is not just a matter of what I do or think at any time, just as it was not in the example of the agronomist whose goals were defeated by a new disease.

The claim about the significance of goals is made here partly because I think it right and partly to show how a highly plausible view of well-being would be ruled out if the experience requirement were correct. The crucial point, however, is that well-being partly depends on other persons and also on the impersonal world. This point need not be put in the terminology of goals, since 'projects' or 'aims' would do. The point need not even rely on the concept of goals. Some think love and friendship matter in well-being whether or not they are goals. These loves and friendships refer to other people. Some take well-being to be the broader concept of desire fulfilment. The fulfilment of a desire is a logical relation requiring that the

[13] Robert Nozick, *Anarchy, State, and Utopia* (Oxford: Basil Blackwell, 1974), pp. 42–5.

[14] Thomas Nagel, 'Death', in Fischer (ed.), *The Metaphysics of Death*, p. 65.

[15] The view that the fulfilment of worthwhile goals is essential to well-being is set out by Joseph Raz in *The Morality of Freedom* (Oxford: Clarendon Press, 1986), ch. 12. See also his account of what goals are at pp. 290–1.

world conform to what is wanted, and people can get what they desire whether or not their mental states change. The crucial point is that some elements of well-being—loves, friendships, goals—are, in a word, relational.

Nonetheless, the experience requirement for well-being cannot be refuted. There are always ways of explaining away the moral intuitions and counter-examples and there are always some difficulties with opposing views. Some will simply reiterate their intuition that people's well-being just cannot be affected by what they do not know. Some will claim that a change in a person's well-being must be a change in her; that a person is a body and mind; and so changes in her well-being must be changes in her body or mind.[16] We cannot reasonably hope for conclusive demonstration in deciding on accounts of well-being. But we can nonetheless select the most plausible account. For this reason, it would be desirable to show that some of the rival intuitions could be accepted without giving up the essentials of the account given here.

One suggestion Shelly Kagan has made is to distinguish well-being from the quality of life. Changes in well-being require real changes in the person, which supports the experience requirement for well-being. But the intuitions about the deceived spouse and the unlucky agronomist cannot be flatly ruled out and, in Kagan's view, the quality of the person's life can suffer due to events outside her experience. For our purposes here, we need not decide whether Kagan is right in thinking well-being and the quality of life are two irreducible concepts. We could simply translate the account given here into his terms. Thus we could agree that posthumous events cannot cause real changes, and so in Kagan's terms cannot affect well-being. If 'harming' is defined in terms of a reduction in well-being, then we could not say that someone has been harmed by posthumous events. But nothing stops us saying posthumous events can reduce a person's quality of life and we could redefine 'harm' so that it included reductions in the quality of life, or find a word other than 'harm' to capture the reduction. The point is that events after a person's death can have moral significance because of something rooted in the claims of that person, whether claims to well-being or quality of life. It is only of secondary importance to the account here how exactly this something is conceived.

THE PROBLEM OF THE SUBJECT AND THE ANTE-MORTEM PERSON

The problem of the subject is perhaps the most serious one facing any attempt to show the possibility of posthumous harm. In essence, the problem is that some subject must exist to be harmed: interests cannot be 'free-floating', the interests of nobody.[17] Even

[16] Shelly Kagan, 'The Limits of Well-Being' *Social Philosophy and Policy* 9 (1992); 'Me and My Life' *Proceedings of the Aristotelian Society* 94 (1994). There is a question, on this view, whether changes in the body are sufficient for changes in well-being. If so, an entirely new route opens up for arguing that taking organs from a dead person could affect well-being. Taking organs obviously affects the body.
[17] A point made by Ernest Partridge, 'Posthumous Interests and Posthumous Respect' *Ethics* 91 (1981), and accepted by Feinberg, *Harm to Others*, p. 83. John Harris, however, claims that interests

though the dead body and its organs exist in the cases we are considering, they do not have interests. They are in that respect like furniture; while one can, in a stretched sense, harm furniture, the furniture itself does not have interests that can be set back. There is some constraint on the sort of thing that can have interests, consciousness being one criterion. Dead bodies and organs are not conscious and nor is the person whose organs they were. With, and after, death, the *person* ceases to exist and there is no consciousness. There is, to be sure, controversy over the criteria for death, such as whether the death of the whole brain is either necessary or sufficient to be dead. But it is widely accepted that death, however elaborated, entails the permanent loss of consciousness, and that people who are correctly declared whole-brain dead are not conscious and never will be again. Hence the problem of the subject: how can dead people have interests when they do not exist as persons and are not and can never be conscious.[18]

The problem of the subject, as stated, has ignored the possibility that living people can be directly harmed by what happens to them after death. This possibility is the essential part of the Pitcher/Feinberg approach, well-known to those who write in this area. Pitcher and Feinberg say that persons can be described both ante-mortem and post-mortem. We can describe the person as she was while alive: kind, funny, five foot tall; and the person as she is while dead: a corpse, or a skeleton, or, in the end, nothing. The ante-mortem person can be a subject of harm and is Pitcher's and Feinberg's solution to the problem of the subject. Their solution will be adopted here. Note that 'ante-mortem' has a technical meaning: the living person as described after that person's death. I am living while I write this; I am not now an 'ante-mortem person' in the technical sense although obviously I am writing this at some time before my death. After I am dead, a description of me as I wrote this would be a description of me, the ante-mortem person.

Both Pitcher and Feinberg claim that the only proper subject of posthumous interests is the ante-mortem person. The post-mortem person does not have interests.[19] Neither says much to defend this claim, but it seems obviously correct. If we set aside the fact that dead human bodies were once live human bodies, and consider them just as they are, we have no more reason to ascribe them interests than to ascribe interests to furniture.

can persist without their fulfillment or frustration affecting the well-being of the person who held them. See his *Clones, Genes, and Immortality* (Oxford: Oxford University Press, 1998), pp. 122–3 and 'Organ Procurement: Dead Interests, Living Needs' *Journal of Medical Ethics* 29 (2003).

[18] It is sometimes argued that the objections from the experience requirement and the problem of the subject apply equally to the view that premature death is bad for the person who dies and that, since premature death is indeed bad, there must be something wrong with the objections. See Feinberg, *Harm to Others*, pp. 81–2. This is a mistake. Death could be merely instrumentally bad in causing a person to have a lower total of happiness (understood as a mental state). To say that well-being is determined by the total level of happiness is consistent with both the experience requirement and providing a proper subject, but inconsistent with the claim that posthumous events affect well-being. For this response, see Fred Feldman, 'Some Puzzles About the Evil of Death', in Fischer (ed.), *The Metaphysics of Death*, p. 318; John Broome, *Ethics Out of Economics* (Cambridge: Cambridge University Press, 1999), pp. 172–3.

[19] Pitcher, 'Misfortunes of the Dead', p. 161; Feinberg, *Harm to Others*, pp. 89–90.

According to some critics, if the Pitcher/Feinberg approach establishes that the ante-mortem person can be harmed, then it establishes only that a living person can be harmed. It is not then the dead who are harmed, and the idea of 'posthumous harms' is not vindicated.[20] On the face of it, this is a merely verbal quibble, since surely what counts normatively is not whether dead people are harmed but whether what happens after someone's death can have the normative significance of harm. If the Pitcher/Feinberg view is correct, events after death are normatively significant in virtue of their harming a living person.

The objection can be taken in another way.[21] Let us agree that interests require at least consciousness and that the dead, not being conscious, cannot have interests. I have said that the ante-mortem person is a conscious subject who can have interests. The objection to using the ante-mortem person as the subject of posthumous harm might be this: in order to have an interest at time t one must be conscious at t. People who are dead are not conscious at the time events after death occur so they cannot have interests at the time the events occur.

The claim that one must be conscious at t to have interests at t is immediately open to the counter-example of the unconscious. Do they not have interests, for example in not being raped, despite being unconscious at the time? It could be replied that, unlike the dead, the unconscious will become conscious again. But if people must be conscious at t to have interests at t, why is it relevant that they will be conscious at $t + 1$?

The claim would have to be reformulated: to have interests at t one must either be conscious at t or conscious at $t + 1$. This claim ought to be controversial in its own right. (It casts doubt on whether any weight should be given to the advance directives of people never expected to regain consciousness.) In any case, why accept it? The thought is that people who are unconscious can be affected by what happens to them, even if they do not find out, because they will be later conscious. The difference between the dead and the unconscious is that the dead are conscious only earlier whereas the unconscious can be conscious both earlier and later. But how does this difference explain why the unconscious can have interests but the dead cannot? Once we have given up the claim that interests must be contemporaneous with consciousness, why does later consciousness make someone an interest bearer but not earlier consciousness? To attach such significance to later consciousness seems an unsupported attempt to differentiate between the unconscious living and the dead.[22]

---

[20] Joan Callahan, 'On Harming the Dead' *Ethics* 97 (1987), p. 346. Cécile Fabre, *Whose Body Is It Anyway? Justice and the Integrity of the Person* (Oxford: Clarendon Press, 2006), pp. 22–3.

[21] Which might be what Fabre is getting at in her denial of the coherence of posthumous interests.

[22] We must set aside the reply that, unlike the dead, the unconscious might be upset when they find out what happened to them (which anyway need not happen). As Fabre says of her objection, the problem is supposed to be independent of the objection that people cannot be harmed by what they do not know. See *Whose Body Is It Anyway?*, p. 23, n. 17. Fabre has a different set of arguments against posthumous rights in her 'Posthumous Rights', in C. Grant, B. Holburn, A. Hatzistavrou, and M. Kramer (eds.), *The Legacy of H. L. A. Hart: Legal, Political and Moral Philosophy* (Oxford: Oxford University Press, 2008). I do not have the space to show it, but I think the arguments in this chapter and the next collectively meet her criticisms in 'Posthumous Rights'. For example, she

The claim of this section is that the ante-mortem person is an interest-bearer, and interests can be set back after the person's death. There is, then, a subject. But positing the ante-mortem person as a subject raises fresh problems. How does the ante-mortem person get affected by what happens later, and when? How can the ante-mortem person be a subject without presupposing some indefensible doctrine of backwards causation?

BACKWARDS CAUSATION

The idea of the ante-mortem person as the subject of posthumous harm raises the problem of backwards causation. Backwards causation occurs when effects precede causes in time. Suppose someone dies in 2007 and in 2010 some event occurs which it is claimed harms him. One natural way to take the claim is as saying that the later event, in 2010, caused a harm to the man at least as far back as the earlier time of 2007. But that is to say a later event caused an earlier one, a claim of backwards causation.

While not universally rejected, backwards causation has been thought by many to be either conceptually impossible, because it is part of our concept of causation that causes must precede effects, or physically impossible, or, more weakly, something that does not in fact occur.[23] It does seem that if an account of posthumous harm depends on the existence of backwards causation, then it is in serious trouble. The claim in this section will be that posthumous harm does not involve backwards causation because the harm is not a matter of cause and effect. The explanation builds on the Pitcher/Feinberg account. It not only avoids backwards causation but also allows us to give a plausible answer to the question of when harm occurs.

Pitcher's strategy is to argue that posthumous harm does not rely on a claim of backwards causation because it does not rely on a causal claim at all. He writes:

> On my view, the sense in which an ante-mortem person is harmed by an unfortunate event after his death is this: the occurrence of the event makes it true that during the time before the person's death, he was harmed—harmed in that the unfortunate event was going to happen . . . the occurrence of the post-mortem event is responsible for the ante-mortem harm. The sense of 'make true' and 'responsible,' here is non-mysterious. If the world should be blasted to smithereens during the next presidency after Ronald Reagan's, this would make it true (be responsible for the fact) that even now, during Reagan's term, he is the penultimate President of the United States.[24]

claims that although one may be unwittingly harmed by having experiences not true to one's life (in her term, experiences that are not 'veridical'), posthumous events could not make the ante-mortem person's experiences non-veridical, and so could not harm the ante-mortem person in that way. The ideas in the next section, on backwards causation, suggest this response: contrary to Fabre, posthumous events could make the ante-mortem person's experiences non-veridical by making those experiences untrue to life. The making would not be causal. It would be like the continued existence of the world non-causally making it false to have said, in 1800, 'The End is Nigh'.

[23] S. D. Rieber, 'Causation as Property Acquisition' *Philosophical Studies* 109 (2002).

[24] Pitcher, 'Misfortunes of the Dead', p. 168. Feinberg's arguments are much the same. See *Harm to Others*, pp. 89–91.

This quotation is significant in giving an explanation of how 'making true' need not be causal. But how does the explanation apply to harm? Pitcher considers the backwards causation objection and writes of harming a living person after his death: 'The idea that it must involve such a process rests on the wholly misleading picture of being harmed as a kind of alteration in one's metaphysical state.'[25] He then gives the example of a Mr Black, who is harmed just at the time his son is killed miles away, even though (as we have to add to Pitcher's example) he does not know. Pitcher says that the harming is non-causal, the idea of instantaneous causation being rejected.

If harming is not causal, then posthumous harm would not require backward causation. But how could harming not be causal? It is in one sense clearly possible to cause harm. I hit you on your nose and your nose hurts; this is cause and effect, and the pain in the nose is one of the harms you suffer. However, while the physical effects are indeed the result of a causal process, whether they should be considered a harm is another matter. Like benefiting, affecting well-being or anything else with value relevance, there is more to the concept of harming than just physical causation. Whatever the extra is, it is not causal.

Although harming has a non-causal element, it would be too quick to say that harming is therefore not causal and so could not require backwards causation. The problem of backward causation remains because changes in value plausibly supervene on the physical world (where the physical includes the mental): only if the physical world changes does the value of the world change. So while the judgement that it is bad that you suffer pain because your nose has been hit is not a causal judgement, what is bad occurs because of an underlying causal process. Because it relies on a causal process, we cannot say that the bad thing, pain, has happened before you have been hit without invoking backwards causation.

What we may say is that not everything that affects a person's well-being affects it by causing changes in him or her. We have already seen one example. Pitcher's Mr Black is harmed just as his son is killed. That his son is killed is the result of a causal process. But the harm to Mr Black is not causal. This example is an instance of a general point, which is that some aspects of well-being do not require changes in the individual concerned in order for that individual to be affected. Recall the view that well-being includes the fulfilment of goals. In this sense of fulfilment, the fact that a goal is fulfilled is a fact about the world, not about the person's mind. A goal could be fulfilled without any change to the mental states of the person whose goal it is. A causal process might have to occur for a goal to be fulfilled, but that the goal is fulfilled is logical.

Some aspects of well-being, then, do not depend on causal effects on the person. Because they do not, it is open that a person's well-being can be changed non-causally. When a person's well-being is changed non-causally, the change would not be the result of backwards causation. To bring all this closer to organ transplantation, if my goal requires that I be buried intact after death, then having my

[25] Pitcher, 'Misfortunes of the Dead', p. 164.

organs taken frustrates that goal. Of course, that someone takes my organs involves a causal process but its relation to the frustration of my goal is a logical relation, not a causal one, and therefore does not involve backwards causation.

The view just given can be put differently, using the idea of Cambridge changes in contrast to real changes. If I cut myself shaving, that is a real change in me. It is also a change in Confucius, it now being true of Confucius that a certain number of years after his death, I cut myself shaving.[26] But this is not a real change in Confucius, merely a Cambridge change. David-Hillel Ruben explains the distinction between real and Cambridge changes in terms of an asymmetry, where Cambridge changes depend on real changes but real changes do not depend on Cambridge changes.[27] The Cambridge change in Confucius could not have occurred without the real change in me when I cut myself shaving, whereas the real change in me of my cut could have occurred even if Confucius had never existed, and so did not undergo the Cambridge change. As Ruben himself says, the idea of Cambridge changes can be applied to the problem of posthumous harm. If posthumous harm did not require a real change but a Cambridge change, then posthumous harm would be possible.[28] And this is the idea expressed in the previous paragraphs. Well-being has aspects that can be changed without these involving real changes in the person but, for these changes to occur, something must have really changed. If after I die you remove organs from my body and thereby go against my wishes, you have undergone a real change and my body has undergone a real change, but the harm done to me is a Cambridge change. This is the solution offered here to the problem of backwards causation. But it leaves one significant question: when was I harmed?

WHEN DOES POSTHUMOUS HARM OCCUR?

The Pitcher/Feinberg account says that people are harmed while alive once they have acquired an interest that will be defeated after death. From the time it is true that their interests will be defeated, people are harmed all along. They have doomed interests and suffer shadow misfortunes. I think these claims are the least plausible part of the Pitcher/Feinberg account.[29] Their idea that one is harmed whenever one's interests are doomed implies that we are always in a harmed state since inevitably some of our interests will be set back later. As Lamont says, 'A view that involves the very counterintuitive claim that a murderer harmed his victim twenty years (or whatever) before he killed her should only be adopted when all other

---

[26] Parfit, *Reasons and Persons*, p. 494.
[27] David-Hillel Ruben, 'A Puzzle About Posthumous Predication' *The Philosophical Review* 97 (1988).
[28] Ibid., n. 20.
[29] Why did Pitcher and Feinberg want to assert the 'harmed all along' claim? They seem to think that if they say a person is harmed only when the harming event occurs, they would be committed to backwards causation. But why would they be if, as they also assert, harming is not causal? See Pitcher, 'Misfortunes of the Dead', p. 168. Feinberg, *Harm to Others*, p. 90.

positions have been explored and found worse.'[30] One could stipulate a meaning for harm that includes shadow misfortunes and doomed interests. But even if one does *call* the dooming of an interest 'a harm', it does not seem to provide the right link to not being well-off since there is nothing at all strange about saying that people are well-off now even though the interests they now have will be set back in the future.[31]

We still have the problem of saying when posthumous harm occurs. There are various suggestions in the literature, such as arguing that posthumous harm is timeless, but if the idea of posthumous harm as a Cambridge change is accepted, nothing seems to stand in the way of the most simple solution to the timing problem. This solution is to say that the ante-mortem person is harmed at the time when the harmful event occurs. Thus while I am alive, I am not harmed by anything after my death because it has not yet happened. After my death, a harmful event occurs. Only from that time am I harmed. The 'I' who is harmed is the ante-mortem person, and the ante-mortem person is, contrary to the Pitcher/Feinberg account, harmed for the first time. To say that the ante-mortem person is harmed is not to say that the living person was harmed at the time he was living; 'ante-mortem' is, as was said earlier, the term to describe living people from a vantage point after their deaths. To say that the ante-mortem person was harmed for the first time after death is not to invoke backwards causation; the change that occurs is not a real change, it is a Cambridge change. Hence we can say that a person is harmed at the time the harm occurs.

The great virtue of the simple solution is that it makes posthumous harms continuous with other harms. If you hit me on the nose, you harm me, and I am harmed only from the time my nose is hit. I am not harmed in advance by the shadow misfortune of the hitting, contrary to Pitcher and Feinberg, and nor am I harmed timelessly, or at least not in an interesting sense.[32] What we say about ordinary harms to living people we should also want to say about posthumous harms. The simple solution allows this: people are harmed posthumously at and not before the point at which the harmful event occurs.

THE IMPORTANCE OF POSTHUMOUS HARMS

It might be claimed that any harm-as-Cambridge-change must be utterly trivial. It is obviously an entirely trivial fact about Confucius that it is true of him that a certain number of years later I cut myself shaving. The suggestion that Cambridge changes are trivial is lent some colour by Ruben's other description of them as

---

[30] Julian Lamont, 'A Solution to the Puzzle of When Death Harms its Victims', p. 205 (footnote suppressed). Lamont also argues that it is not only awkward but mistaken to claim that people were harmed all along if the harms are not fully determined and thus might not happen.

[31] Judith Jarvis Thomson, 'Feinberg on Harm, Offense, and the Criminal Law' *Philosophy and Public Affairs* 15 (1986), p. 392.

[32] This paragraph is essentially Lamont's argument in 'A Solution to the Puzzle of When Death Harms its Victims'.

'phoney changes'. But although some Cambridge changes are undeniably trivial from any normative point of view, as are some real changes, not all of them are trivial. Ruben himself says:

> To predicate a Cambridge change of an object may be to predicate of it a phoney change, but notice that it is to predicate of the object a perfectly good property. To say of some person that he has acquired a new cousin upon the birth of a child to his aunt or uncle, is to ascribe a perfectly genuine property to that person, but is *not* to ascribe to him a perfectly genuine change.[33]

Nothing then in the idea of a Cambridge change requires it to be trivial and so if a posthumous harm is a Cambridge change, it need not be trivial. Consider another example: Mary shoots Joe just as Joe shoots Mary. Mary dies from Joe's shot just before Joe dies from Mary's shot. Joe's death, which occurs after Mary's, makes it true that Mary is a killer. This making it true is not causal and the change in Mary is not a 'real' change; yet being a killer seems an important feature of any assessment of Mary's life.[34]

It might still be wondered whether all this discussion of Cambridge changes, however ingenious as a way of avoiding the problem of backwards causation, is really connected to harm. Pitcher provided the example of the penultimate President as an illustration of how what happens later can make propositions true of a person at an earlier time—but being a penultimate President does not seem to have much to do with harm. Even becoming a killer, significant though that might be as an element in one's biography, might not be thought to be a harm or a benefit.[35]

The reply to these doubts is to remind ourselves of the significance of relational elements in well-being. The success or failure of people's goals, loves, and friendships, to take a partial list, all depend to some degree on what happens outside their own bodies and minds. If what happens is failure, then this is bad for them even when the failures are Cambridge changes. On the definition used in this chapter, where harm is the rough equivalent of a reduction in well-being, these changes are also harms. Alternatively, for writers such as Kagan, mentioned earlier, who take well-being and harm to refer only to changes in the body and mind, we could think of the relational elements as aspects of the quality of life. What reason is there to deny the normative significance of the relational elements when they extend beyond a person's body and mind? I do not know of any that should cause us to disregard the value of goals, loves, and friendships.

It could nonetheless be true that the posthumous interests that are relevant to transplantation are trivial or otherwise without much weight, but that would be because of the interests and the context involved, and not simply because they involve Cambridge changes.

---

[33] Ruben, 'A Puzzle About Posthumous Predication', p. 224.

[34] Dorothy Grover, 'Posthumous Harm' *The Philosophical Quarterly* 39 (1989).

[35] Taylor, 'Myth of Posthumous Harm', p. 315 complains that the analogy between penultimate presidents, killing, and harm has not been made out, although he does not give reasons for thinking it could not be.

ORGAN RETRIEVAL AND THE INTERESTS
OF THE DEAD

I shall close this chapter by briefly relating posthumous interests to transplantation. Consider some reasons why people might care what happens to their organs after they die. They might want to donate because of the good it would do, or out of a sense of religious duty. They might want to refuse because of a cultural view of the importance of intact burial or out of a different sense of religious duty. They might refuse because they fear donors get worse medical care or end up being used to entertain medical students in anatomy classes. Not all of these reasons are good ones. How do they relate to the view of posthumous interests set out in this chapter?

I explained posthumous interests in terms of achieving one's goals. Goals are an element of well-being that is subjective in the sense that a person actually has to endorse a goal for it to be hers. However, on any view of well-being bar the crudest subjectivism, people can make mistakes about where their interests lie. Some mistakes involve obvious errors of fact. For example, people in New Zealand do not become subjects of an anatomy class without their and their families' explicit written consent, so it is a mistake to refuse to donate organs in New Zealand out of fear of anatomy. People's goals can be based on less obvious mistakes too. If some people want to donate because they think God wants them to and others refuse because they think God opposes organ retrieval, some of them must be wrong.

We are assuming people can have posthumous interests. If people are wrong about what would promote their interests, what follows? Should the state then work out what those interests require independently of what people actually think their interests require? We are in the territory of large debates in political philosophy about paternalism, perfectionism, and state neutrality. I shall be arguing, in the next chapter, that people's own decisions about their posthumous interests should be taken as the decisive representation of what those interests are. My reason will be respect for personal sovereignty: the decisions about their own interests are ones people ought to take for themselves, a conclusion which is consistent with both affirming and denying that people can be mistaken about their interests.

I do not say it is generally the case that people's mistaken decisions about their interests should be respected. Living people may make disastrous mistakes about their lives and health which perhaps should be prevented even at a cost to their personal sovereignty. In a case where people want to donate organs while alive, we might worry about whether they should be allowed to make the sacrifice. Biological self-interest is an important component of well-being. But it is not an important component of well-being for the dead because they no longer have any requirements of biological self-interest. They do not need their organs as organs any more. In the case of the dead at least, we respect their interests by doing what they wanted.

Insofar as we aim to respect the interests of the dead, we should not take the organs of people who opposed retrieval, even if they opposed it for false or silly reasons. But the interests of the dead can compete with the interests of the living. How far, then, should we aim to respect the interests of the dead? This is the subject of the next chapter.

4

The Moral Claims of the Dead

For what reason and to what extent should the use and disposal of people's dead bodies be governed by what they wanted while alive? This is hardly an esoteric question. Dead bodies can be used not only as a source of organs, but for anatomy teaching, in tissue banks, in archaeological research and display, in vehicle safety testing, and a whole host of other ways. Every day people must decide whether to bury, cremate, or otherwise dispose of their relatives' bodies. The question of respecting the wishes of the dead is, however, particularly difficult in transplantation. Unlike burial or cremation or the use of bodies in research and teaching, organs for transplant are both scarce and matters of life and death for the people who need them. If we will not take the organs from someone who has refused, the cost will be high. If, in addition, we will not take organs from those who neither refused nor agreed, the cost will be much higher. We need to know whether people do have rights to control what happens to their bodies after they die, and what respecting these rights requires.

Chapter 2 gave an account of people's claims over their bodies. It argued that people have moral rights of bodily integrity and personal sovereignty. This account was, however, about the rights people have over their live bodies. Chapter 3 set out the reasons for thinking that people's interests can be affected by what happens after their deaths. This chapter puts together the material from chapters 2 and 3 to try to determine the claims people have over their bodies after they die.

As we discuss the moral claims of the dead, let us recall some assumptions. We are assuming, for the sake of argument, that no afterlife exists or at least that nothing, including nothing experientially, happens to people in the afterlife as a result of what happens to their mortal remains. On the basis of chapter 3, we can assume we have avoided the problems of the subject and the experience requirement. Can we then simply take the ideas of bodily integrity and personal sovereignty and apply them to the dead? Should we simply say that just as the living have rights over their bodies, so too do they have these rights over their corpses?

I shall argue that personal sovereignty does apply to the dead. We have a basic intuition that people ought to be able to control what happens to their bodies after they die. In the early part of this chapter, I explain what follows in the way of rights. I then contrast the intuition with other attempts to justify posthumous rights, via bodily integrity, religious freedom, honouring bequests, and respecting the sensibilities of the living. I turn next to the objections. One argument points out that a posthumous wish involves caring earlier about a later event. Why should caring at an earlier time about a later event matter when caring later about an earlier event does not? Another argument relies on a choice theory of rights, which holds that all rights must be waivable. The objection is that, as the dead cannot waive rights, they cannot have rights. The third argument observes that people do not suffer physical harm or bad experiences after death whatever is done to their bodies, and claims this observation undercuts posthumous rights. I reject the objections.

The chapter is incomplete in one respect, namely determining the strength of posthumous rights.[1] A full test requires comparing the interest of the dead in bodily control with competing interests, for instance, those of the family or potential transplant recipients. The comparisons are done in subsequent chapters.

PERSONAL SOVEREIGNTY AND POSTHUMOUS RIGHTS

This section applies the personal sovereignty model of chapter 2 in the context of organ retrieval from the dead. Essentially, one has a right to control what happens to one's body after death because it is one's body. Consider the vivid instance of Gladstone, who bossily arranged for his sister, Helen, to be buried as an Anglican even though she had been a Catholic for many years.[2] In burying his sister thus, using as a pretext the slenderest of evidence of her wishes, Gladstone treated her deepest wishes as of no consequence in themselves but merely a sign of someone unable to think clearly. (Gladstone had a long record of interfering in the affairs of his relatives.) If one can disrespect the dead, Gladstone disrespected his sister.[3] The point is not that someone is respected when just any of her deep wishes are ignored. If Helen had had a deep wish for a Catholic revival, ignoring this wish would be no disrespect. The point is, her wish was about her own body and the ending to her own life, and ignoring that wish did disrespect her.

Disrespect in one of its forms presupposes a sphere in which one should have the power to decide. One is disrespected when one's decisions are ignored, if they are the decisions one ought to be able to make. In Helen's case, the disrespect presupposes that she should have had the power to determine the disposal of her remains. This power seems closely related to personal sovereignty. Personal sovereignty is about 'self-rule' and while the body is not the self, and people disagree about how the body relates to the self, body and self are at the least very closely related and self-rule implies bodily control. The value of control extends past biological life. Someone may want some good to come from her death, to have

[1] I need not consider how long after someone's death people are constrained by her rights because organ transplantation only involves what are sometimes referred to as the 'newly dead'. For a discussion of duration, see Daniel Sperling, *Posthumous Interests* (Cambridge: Cambridge University Press, 2008), pp. 84–6, and my 'Last Rights: The Ethics of Research on the Dead' *Journal of Applied Philosophy* 19 (2002).

[2] Roy Jenkins, *Gladstone* (New York: Random House, 1995), p. 246n, p. 431.

[3] F. Kamm, *Morality, Mortality*, vol. 1 (New York: Oxford University Press, 1993), pp. 209, 219. Kamm's main argument is that the family's power to override the individual is objectionably inegalitarian, but I do not think it inegalitarian at all.

the end of her life do good for others. Her wish to shape her life can be fulfilled only after she dies and, if she dies in certain circumstances, it could be fulfilled by organ donation. Someone else may have lived by religious beliefs that preclude donation. Shaping one's life in accordance with such beliefs can also be fulfilled only after death. When it comes to shaping one's life, death is not the end. What happens after death matters too.

It is, I think, a widely shared and basic intuition that my body is mine and I should decide what happens to it. The intuition expresses a basic value, a value that one cannot justify in terms of some other value, such as well-being or the Millian independent autonomous life. While the right to control what happens to one's body does form part of well-being or an independent life, that is because control is important anyway. Many writers explicitly extend the idea to cover decisions about one's dead body[4] and it best explains the right in law virtually everywhere to veto the retrieval of organs from one's own dead body—even though we all realize the power of veto may cost lives.

Because the value of control is basic, what can be said in support is limited. One cannot appeal to other values. But one can sharpen the supporting intuition, show it at work in examples, distinguish it from other intuitions, explain how the value fits within wider normative views, and respond to objections. I shall do some of these tasks now and more throughout the book.

One piece of sharpening is to qualify the idea of 'control'. Sandra Ilene West may have had a right to be buried in a blue Ferrari while wearing a designer gown,[5] but only assuming the car and gown were hers. In one sense, the right to bodily control gives the right to be buried as one wishes, but not in the sense of giving a right to a Ferrari and a gown. The right is negative. The right to bodily control includes a right against being prevented from offering one's organ for transplant, but not the right to have the offer accepted. If someone offers an organ, others may have a reason to accept the offer, but no one has a duty to take organs just because they were offered. What if the organs are useless? In particular cases, one may have a right to get what one wants in a positive sense, for instance as the result of a promise or contract or, as in the case of Sandra West, when one's property rights combine with the right to determine the disposal of one's body. But such cases are largely irrelevant in the context of transplantation.

If we follow the personal sovereignty model, the intuition can also be sharpened by thinking of it in terms of a self-regarding sphere in which people should be free to make decisions that affect them. This freedom should be protected by rights. It is a familiar objection that a self-regarding sphere does not exist and no non-trivial decision affects only the person making it. The reply is that decisions are self-regarding, and thus properly to be made by the individual, when they concern

---

[4] Govert den Hartogh, *Farewell to Non-commitment: Decision Systems for Organ Donation from an Ethical Viewpoint* (The Hague: Centre for Ethics and Health, 2008), p. 23. David Price, *Human Tissue in Transplantation and Research: A Model Legal and Ethical Donation Framework* (Cambridge: Cambridge University Press, 2009).

[5] Sperling, *Posthumous Interests*, p. 143.

matters of greater significance for the individual than for others, or they affect the individual more directly, or else they do not affect the interests, as opposed to mere dislikes, of other people. So if we ask why the decision about donation of the body is in the personal sphere and the effects on others are to be excluded, the answer is because the decision is about the person's own body, and what could be more self-regarding than that?

People may have a moral obligation to donate even if they have a right not to. The right limits the freedom of others to use their organs; it does not tell people how to exercise their right. It is often said that to agree to donate is to act like a Good Samaritan.[6] At a small cost to oneself, one could save the lives of others or at least greatly improve their quality. It is not morally optional to behave like a Good Samaritan; one would do wrong if one behaved otherwise. Now whether or not the Good Samaritan argument is sound, and exceptions do have to be made for people who greatly care about their mortal remains, its conclusion is entirely compatible with personal sovereignty. So long as the moral duty is not enforced by coercive law or excessive social pressure, it is consistent with a right to decide otherwise—a right, indeed, to do wrong.

What a self-regarding sphere contains, and so what is protected by a right, is not all and only what matters to a given person. A Catholic revival may have mattered more to Gladstone's sister than being buried as a Catholic, but a Catholic revival is not in her sphere of decision-making. And it may not greatly matter to a person what happens to her body after she dies but, if she cares enough to have a wish, it is in the self-regarding sphere and protected by a right. Some people breezily say they do not care what happens to their bodies after they die. Even though the right to choose is one they may not value, they still have the right, just as people apathetic about politics have a right of free expression and people uninterested in clothes have the right to choose what to wear. In any case, the breezy comments need not be taken at face value. Even those who do not want to exercise a right often want to be free from interference. Those who say they do not care about their dead bodies may not want to have the decision taken out of their hands. They may also be unaware of the range of uses to which dead bodies can be put, some of which—such as being used in skin treatments for the ageing rich—they may dislike.

By the earlier assumptions about the afterlife, what happens to people's bodies after they die would not affect their experiences. How could it matter much or at all if posthumous wishes are flouted when flouting could not cause any suffering for the people who had had the wishes? This is an important question which I answer more fully at the end of the chapter. A partial reply is that, my body being mine, it is mine to decide what to do with. I will not have bad experiences after I die, but according to the basic intuition, I am the one whose wish should be decisive. The right is based on my relationship to my body, not the experiences having a right would protect me from.

---

[6] Den Hartogh, *Farewell to Non-commitment*, section 7.

People may make mistakes about their own interests. However, the right of personal sovereignty is the right to run one's own life, including past one's biological death, and this right limits paternalistic or perfectionist attempts to make people do what someone else thinks they ought to do, even when the someone else is correct. We do not have to agree with Catholicism to believe that Gladstone's sister ought to have had her wishes about burial respected. In the case of living people, some difficulties can arise when they wish to do something that seems likely to harm their physical or mental health. Should we respect their personal sovereignty in such cases? However we answer that question, it does not arise in the case of the dead. Their biological self-interest is no longer a consideration. People may make mistakes about their posthumous interests, but the right of personal sovereignty protects even their mistaken decisions. Insofar as we are taking into account the interests of the dead, we should do what they wanted, not what they ought to have wanted.

If we accept the right of the individual to decide, we must qualify the superficially plausible thought that the interests of the living are more important than the interests of the dead. A dead person may not have cared greatly about organ retrieval and is in no position to be upset at being overruled, but the decision about donation is the deceased's to make, even if it comes at some cost to the living. But how much cost? As critics of liberalism like to point out, 'No man is an island', and respecting the right of the deceased may have bad consequences for others. Perhaps the right is so weighty the consequences are a price worth paying, but we need an argument for why. Or perhaps while the deceased may have a right to decide, others—like the family or potential transplant recipients—have a competing right. Even though control over one's own body seems a self-regarding matter, more needs to be said to show that the decision should be one's own. What we eat seems to be the paradigmatically self-regarding matter of what we put in our own bodies, but it may not be when we want to eat smelly cheese or durian[7] on public transport. While a decision over one's dead body is prima facie in the self-regarding sphere, and so one's own to make, something needs to be said about why the effects on others do not take it out. And something will be said, in subsequent chapters.

OTHER FOUNDATIONS FOR POSTHUMOUS BODILY CONTROL

Our judgements in a case may support a right of individual decision, but can we be sure it is because of the personal sovereignty intuition and not some other view? This section considers different foundations for posthumous bodily control: bodily integrity, religious freedom, respect for bequests, and taking account of the sensibilities of the living. In trying to show that personal sovereignty justifies individual decision-making about our own bodies, I do not have to disagree with the other

[7] Durian is a fruit whose pungent smell is considered by some to be fragrant and many others to be vile. It is widely banned on public transport and in hotels in South East Asia.

views. There can be more than one route to the same conclusion. However, I think personal sovereignty is the best foundation for posthumous control; the others I now discuss do not justify a right of the same scope or weight as does personal sovereignty, if they justify any right at all.

Bodily integrity

Consider the idea of bodily integrity. A right to bodily integrity is a source of autonomy. Self-rule, although broader than protection from unconsented-to invasions of one's body, is partly made up of such a protection. Moreover, many think the right to bodily integrity is justified independently of autonomy, for instance as a precondition of having any rights at all, which are in turn justified because humans are not bees in a hive but rather have inherently individual interests.[8] The fundamental contribution of my body to my identity means that I have a right not to have my body intruded on without my consent while I am alive. An assault on my body is an assault on me.

It is sometimes claimed that bodily integrity applies to intrusions after death.[9] I am doubtful about this claim. It would be highly problematic to conclude that we have a right against posthumous invasion without consent given that many die without consenting or dissenting to anything, a point I say more about in chapter 6. Here I concentrate on the underlying reason of bodily integrity, which I think mistaken.

Here are two reasons to think the right to bodily integrity does not apply after death. First, many think that living people should not be able to waive entirely their rights to bodily integrity. Specifically, and relatively uncontroversially, the living cannot waive their right by giving or selling their hearts, entire livers, both lungs, or other organs necessary for life. But also relatively uncontroversially, these organs can legitimately be retrieved after death with consent. That shows that, at least in common thinking, the requirements of bodily integrity are altered by death. Second, suppose someone asks to be buried after death but in fact his family has him cremated for spiteful (and thus non-financial) reasons. To burn a living person without consent would be, amongst many other bad things, a violation of a right to bodily integrity. We may think, in the case of the dead man, that the spiteful family has done wrong, even wronged the man. But I cannot believe we would think his right to bodily integrity has been violated. That suggests that there is no posthumous right of bodily integrity.

Here is a more philosophical reason for scepticism about a posthumous right of bodily integrity. Interference with the body after death occurs when the deceased

---

[8] See Judith Jarvis Thomson's influential discussion in her book *The Realm of Rights* (Cambridge, MA: Harvard University Press, 1990), pp. 218–23.

[9] Walter Glannon, 'Do the Sick Have a Right to Cadaveric Organs?' *Journal of Medical Ethics* 29 (2003), p. 153. Robert Audi, 'The Morality and Utility of Organ Transplantation' *Utilitas* 8 (1996), p. 147. According to den Hartogh, 'Under Dutch law, the right to decide on what is done with my mortal remains is interpreted as part of the right to physical integrity recognised under Art. 11 of the Dutch Constitution.' *Farewell to Non-commitment*, p. 23, n. 3.

person is no longer there. So if there is to be a violation of the person, it must be a violation of the ante-mortem person. But while we can make sense of the ante-mortem person's concern for reputation extending beyond death, or her interests in her privacy, or the completion of her projects, it is hard to make sense of her bodily integrity so extending. At least, if bodily integrity does so extend, it seems so different in force as to be different in kind. Consider an example that Joel Feinberg cites: a paralysed patient is injected with a tranquillizer even though he shrieks 'Don't stick that fucking thing in me!' Feinberg writes: 'the forceful violation of his bodily autonomy that follows is a dramatically shocking event, akin to watching a rape on stage'.[10] I do not think we would feel anything comparable if we watched an injection into a dead person who had objected. What seems fundamental about bodily integrity is the closeness of the person to her body—that persons are embodied. But persons are not embodied after death, because the person is no more. So the main ground for a right to bodily integrity does not apply posthumously. Bodily integrity can be violated only when the person and the body are concurrent.[11]

Religious freedom

Some people have religious or cultural beliefs that lead them to oppose the retrieval of their organs after they die. To take one example, some Maori treat life as a journey where, as we come into the world intact, so we should go out intact, and they take this to preclude organ retrieval: 'The circle of life demands that all life is derived from the earth and returned to the earth complete.'[12] Many Jehovah's Witnesses, Orthodox Jews, and Chinese, amongst others, want not to donate their organs, sometimes very strongly. I consider in this sub-section whether religious or cultural views justify a right not to donate at all and, if so, in any distinct way.

It is often pointed out that all the major religions at least permit, and in some cases recommend, their adherents to donate.[13] So we should not be misled, from the way the objection to donation has just been set up, into thinking that organized religion in general opposes organ donation. However, although official leaders do not oppose donation, this does not mean religious opposition should go unprotected. Unless for some reason the state should treat the official views as authoritative

[10] Joel Feinberg, *Harm to Self* (New York: Oxford University Press, 1986), p. 354. The example is from Brian Clark's play *Whose Life is it Anyway?*
[11] Margaret Brazier and Daniel Sperling separately defend posthumous bodily integrity against John Harris's objection that bodies inevitably disintegrate after death, but what they mean by 'bodily integrity' differs from what I mean. See Harris, 'Law and Regulation of Retained Organs: The Ethical Issues' *Legal Studies* 22 (2002), pp. 547–8; Brazier, 'Retained Organs: Ethics and Humanity' *Legal Studies* 22 (2002); Sperling, *Posthumous Interests*, p. 14, n. 14.
[12] Tariana Turia, 'Speech: The Circle of Life—the Human Tissues Bill', 14 November 2006. The conclusions Turia draws about organ retrieval from the dead are by no means uniformly held among Maori and Turia herself seems to see views changing with education and debate. Speech accessed from <www.maoriparty.com> October 2007.
[13] Robert Veatch, *Transplantation Ethics* (Washington, DC: Georgetown University Press, 2000), ch. 1. Organ Donation Taskforce, *The Potential Impact of an OptOut System for Organ Donation in the UK* (London: Department of Health, 2008).

declarations of belief—which would be contrary to the usual interpretation of religious freedom as an individual right—then unofficial views within a religion should not cease to be protected simply because of what the leaders say.[14]

Note that the argument for being free to refuse to donate is an argument of religious freedom, not an argument based on the truth of the religious belief. An argument that is some variant of 'God forbids organ donation' implies that no one, not just the believer, should donate. Atheists and many religious people (including the representatives of official religions) think such a belief is false; and, in any case, arguments relying on the truth of religious beliefs are not suitable for public reasoning in an impartial or free state. But even someone who disagrees with people's beliefs can think they should be free to act on them, and thus it might be said that it is a denial of religious or cultural freedom not to have rights of control over one's dead body.[15] However, while we have a clear sense of religious freedom as freedom from certain kinds of interference, such as freedom from persecution, how does religious freedom justify control rights over bodies?

It is plausible to argue that one should be able to control what happens to one's own body and one could then exercise control in accordance with one's religious beliefs. But religious freedom is not then doing any work in justifying control. Control depends on another justification, such as personal sovereignty.[16] To see this point further, consider a religious person who objects to donation by people who are nothing to do with his religion. We would surely want to exclude this outsider from even having a say in whether organ retrieval should occur. Moreover, in excluding the religious outsider, we would not be infringing on his religious freedom—it is not as if his right yields to the claims of others. His right to religious freedom does not include the right to say what happens to other people's bodies.

In the example, I stipulated that the people who wanted to donate were not part of the religion of the outsider. What if they were? What if members of some religious or cultural community wanted to donate in opposition to the wishes of the majority or the leaders? Should individuals be entitled to take the decisions about their bodies or should these be made by their wider grouping? Clearly, the personal sovereignty model would say that the decisions are the individuals' to make, in whatever consultation they choose with others. But even enthusiasts for group control tend to think groups should control only their own members.[17] And this is

---

[14] S. McGuiness and M. Brazier, 'Respecting the Living Means Respecting the Dead Too' *Oxford Journal of Legal Studies* 28 (2008), pp. 308–9.

[15] James Muyskens, 'An Alternative Policy for Obtaining Cadaver Organs', in M. Cohen, T. Nagel, and T. Scanlon (eds.), *Medicine and Moral Philosophy* (Princeton, NJ: Princeton University Press, 1981), p. 194; Joel Feinberg *Freedom and Fulfilment* (Princeton, NJ: Princeton University Press, 1992), p. 113. McGuiness and Brazier, 'Respecting the Living Means Respecting the Dead Too'.

[16] McGuiness and Brazier, 'Respecting the Living Means Respecting the Dead Too', p. 311, offer a religious freedom objection to organ conscription, although one that seems in the end to come down to personal autonomy.

[17] Are there any such enthusiasts? Consider Turia again, in her speech 'The Circle of Life': '[T]he Maori Party wants to place on record, our concern at the proposal in this Bill that the wishes of an individual can over-ride the collective process of whanau [family] decision-making.' (Although she was wrong about the effect of the Bill.)

to make my point: what comes first is working out who should control bodies. Once we have the answer, we can say who is entitled to decide what happens to a body on the basis of their religious or cultural beliefs.

Wills

Do we need all this philosophical discussion of posthumous interests, personal sovereignty, and rights? Is it not obvious that we should follow the wishes of the dead about organ retrieval, just as we respect wills for property?[18] But once we go deeper into the alleged analogy between bequests and bodies, we will find both disanalogies and unsettling similarities. Consider these:

(1) Respecting wills could have good consequences, for instance by reassuring people or giving them an incentive to pass resources to subsequent generations rather than go on a pre-death consumption splurge.[19] The different consequences of respecting individual decisions about organs may not support individual decision-making. It is hard to believe that, in a society without rights of bequest over one's body, people would go on a pre-death consumption splurge of their organs.

(2) Rights of bequest vary across jurisdictions but, in some at least, individuals do not have unlimited rights to dispose of their property as they wish.[20] They often have to provide for their dependent families, for example. However, it is hard to see how the family could have a claim on the individual's body analogous to their dependency claim on the estate, except, perhaps, when a dependent family member needs a transplant and could use the relative's organ.[21]

(3) Many oppose rights of bequest on the grounds that they cause unjustified economic inequality. But these grounds do not apply to decisions over organs. Moreover, one might criticize a right of bequest by disputing the legitimacy of private property acquisition, but these problems of acquisition do not really apply to control over one's own body. Hence another disanalogy.

(4) Relatedly, estates are taxed in many jurisdictions, a point bizarrely overlooked in many of the arguments invoking wills. Perhaps an argument could be constructed that, just as a percentage of material property is taxed, so a percentage of bodies

---

[18] The wills argument is suggested by Michele Goodwin, *Black Markets: The Supply and Demand of Body Parts* (Cambridge: Cambridge University Press, 2006), p. 144; T. May, M. Aulisio, and M. DeVita, 'Patients, Families, and Organ Donation: Who Should Decide?' *The Milbank Quarterly* 78 (2000), p. 333; Veatch, *Transplantation Ethics*, p. 176. The argument is common in public discussion.

[19] This idea is developed in Richard Epstein, 'Justice across the Generations', in P. Laslett and J. Fishkin (eds.), *Justice Between Age Groups and Generations* (New Haven: Yale University Press, 1992), pp. 89–93.

[20] Readers familiar only with the rules on bequest in England and Wales, the US, and similar jurisdictions may be surprised to learn that in continental Europe, a big part, often around half, of an estate must be equally divided between surviving children. See *The Economist*, 'Where There's a Will There's a Row', 17 October 2009.

[21] Andrew Moore mentioned this example to me.

should be.[22] Thus, by analogy, it may be permissible to take organs without consent, which should unsettle those who favour the deceased's right of control.

(5) If bodies are like bequests, perhaps intestacy rules should apply. In the case of transplantation, where the deceased have often not made clear decisions, perhaps the analogy justifies an entitlement for the next-of-kin to decide. But to go yet further, perhaps unclaimed bodies should be disposed of as the state sees fit, a conclusion that would be resisted by those who think some consent is needed before organ retrieval.

(6) We might doubt the analogy altogether on the grounds that a body is not property, and the rules for the disposal of one need not apply to the other.

I shall say no more about wills or the related idea of property rights in the dead body.[23] Even if one could construct an illuminating analogy between individual powers of bequest and control over bodies after death, what would be of primary interest is what is illuminated. The most obvious reason why people should have a right to dispose of their bodies given a right to dispose of their material property is that both properly come with a personal sphere—in other words, we have a restatement of a personal sovereignty view.

The sensibilities of the living

It is often said that the sensibilities of the living are the sole reasons for respecting the wishes of those now dead. People are worried about what will happen to their bodies after they die. They would not find out, of course, but if they see the corpses of other people being misused, then they would live in fear, or at least apprehension. Preventing fear is the reason to respect posthumous wishes. The reason is not the harm done to the people whose bodies they were but the harm done to the people who find out. A somewhat different view involves respect for the dead, a value common in many cultures despite the very different ways in which it is expressed. For example, the law may be used to prevent people disrespecting the dead by exhuming bodies, and the reason given for the law is to prevent offence to the living.

Pointing to the effects on the living of abusing the dead need not be an alternative to the personal sovereignty view. Both could be right. However, philosophers who deny there can be posthumous harms often say the effects on the living are what lie behind the intuitive view that the wishes of the dead should be respected. In other words, they want to debunk the idea that the claims of the

---

[22] This is Cécile Fabre's argument in *Whose Body Is It Anyway? Justice and the Integrity of the Person* (Oxford: Clarendon Press, 2006). Points 3 and 4 about wills are discussed further in chapter 7.

[23] See Andrew Grubb, '"I, Me, Mine": Bodies, Parts and Property' *Medical Law International* 3 (1998). For some reasons to bypass property in dead bodies, see T. M. Wilkinson, 'Parental Consent and the Use of Dead Children's Bodies' *Kennedy Institute of Ethics Journal*, 11 (2001), pp. 343–4. For a powerful criticism of the idea of ownership in living people, see Jim Harris, 'Who Owns My Body?' *Oxford Journal of Legal Studies* 16 (1996).

dead have force in their own right. Ernest Partridge, for example, gives a rule consequentialist argument for respecting wills. He says that if people while alive do not believe their wills will be respected after they have died, they will be less happy and have an incentive to use up their property. A practice of respecting wills would have better consequences even though, once people have died, failing to respect their wishes would not harm them. Respecting their wishes is necessary to send a message to others that wills would be respected, deathbed promises kept, and so on.[24]

One way to take the debunking idea is as saying that the sensibilities of the living justify all that the personal sovereignty view does, but without the metaphysical baggage of posthumous interests and rights. In other words, the conclusion about respecting wishes remains but the foundation changes.[25] Another way to take it is as debunking the idea that we ought to respect the wishes of the dead—there are no posthumous interests, only the sensibilities of the living, and these really are too feeble to justify giving up the value of extra organs the dead can supply.

The more radical debunking view is right to say that the sensibilities of the living are rather feeble reasons to respect the wishes of the dead, at least in the case of organ transplantation. Without the foundation of something like the personal sovereignty view, it is hard to see how assuaging people's fears could alone justify letting others die for want of transplanted organs. Suppose transplantation itself frightens people, even though the practice is to respect scrupulously individual wishes. Their fears would not be enough to ban organ retrieval outright.

Avoiding bad feelings is not a plausible foundation of a right of posthumous bodily control, but it may contribute to its weight. It is plausible that a right has more weight when people care about it than when they do not. While rightholders would not feel distress at or after the time of infringement because they would be dead, they could plausibly feel distress beforehand, if they fear infringements will occur. If they would feel distress, it would plausibly be more important to respect their right than it would if they did not feel distress. Hence the sensibilities of the living could be relevant to a right over one's own body; but they are not its foundation.

As for avoiding giving offence, I think this is largely irrelevant in the context of organ transplantation. The idea was that some culturally required practices of respecting the dead may be enforced because of the offence to the living that a breach would cause. Avoiding offence may justify laws against desecrating graves, exhuming bodies, or necrophilia (even when the deceased had consented). I doubt that avoiding offence would justify laws against organ conscription any more than a it would justify prohibiting the use of cadavers in road crash testing.[26] The gains are too great to be outweighed by offence. In any case, the idea of offence seems poorly suited to being a basis of individual rights of decision. In most countries, organ retrieval is allowed when the dead had consented and forbidden when they had

---

[24] Ernest Partridge, 'Posthumous Interests and Posthumous Respect' *Ethics* 91 (1981), pp. 259–61.
[25] This is Partridge's view in ibid.
[26] Feinberg, *Freedom and Fulfilment*, pp. 113–14. Mary Roach, *Stiff* (New York: W. W. Norton, 2003), p. 92, cites a 1995 article that calculated that since 1987 8,500 lives per year have been saved through the use of dead bodies in vehicle safety research.

dissented. By contrast, in typical cases of offence, the consent of the participants makes no difference. Consensual sex in a public place is still offensive, for instance. While offence may be felt at the breach of a cultural practice of letting people decide what happens to their bodies after they die, people would be offended because they have the basic intuition about bodily control. The reason we should respect their intuition is not because people would be offended if we did not; it is because the intuition is correct.

OBJECTIONS AND REPLIES

I should be the one to decide what happens to my body after I die, as you should be for yours, because of the special relationship between our bodies and us. This special relationship, I have argued, should be protected by a right. But because the underlying intuition is basic, it cannot be demonstrated. How, then, could one persuade those who doubt we have a right to control what happens to our bodies after we die? Obviously, it depends on why they doubt. If it is because they think nothing after death could affect people's interests, then I refer them to chapter 3. If it is because they do not like the idea of rights in the context of transplantation, preferring to think in terms of gift and altruism, then I say they are confusing rights with selfishness, and being rather naïve about gifts.[27] If it is because they do not like the idea of rights at all, then I refer them to chapter 2. If it is because they have philosophical doubts about posthumous rights, then I refer them to the rest of this chapter.

Autonomy and time

John Harris accepts that people have autonomous wishes about what happens to their bodies after death, but he denies it follows that frustrating their wishes infringes on their autonomy. He writes, 'I wish that certain things had not happened to me whilst I was a child. At the time I was not autonomous and had formed no views about them. Did these things frustrate my autonomy because I now wish that they had not been done? Equally with things I now wish will not happen after I lose my autonomy.'[28] Harris's argument is both intriguing and brief. It could be developed in many different ways. All I can do here is raise problems for the argument as stated.

Harris implicitly concludes from his argument that there cannot be posthumous autonomy.[29] How would this conclusion follow from his example of wishes about childhood? My death and my childhood are similar in two ways: I am autonomous in neither state and neither state is in the present. The two similarities suggest two

---

[27] See chapter 2 on rights and selfishness and chapter 9 on gift and altruism.

[28] Harris, 'Law and Regulation of Retained Organs, p. 535.

[29] The evidence for Harris's intended conclusion is in the immediately following part of his article, where he proceeds as if his case against posthumous autonomy were complete.

arguments against posthumous autonomy: only while one is autonomous can one's autonomy be frustrated; and autonomy can only be frustrated if one's wish and the frustration coincide in time. On both arguments, frustrating posthumous wishes could not affect autonomy because the dead are not autonomous and they have no wishes at the time the frustration occurs.

It is question-begging to claim that one's autonomy can only be frustrated while one is autonomous. While it is a trivial truth that one must have certain capacities to act autonomously, which the dead lack, one's autonomy could extend past the time at which one had these capacities. Many people think, in opposition to Harris, that autonomy can be affected by what happens in a later non-autonomous state. They think that expressed wishes about future dementia should be respected because of respect for earlier autonomy.[30] We may accept Harris's view that wishes about our childhood are irrelevant to our autonomy, but future dementia differs from childhood: childhood is in the past. Harris gives no reason why the past and future should be treated the same.

The second argument states that autonomy can be affected only if one still has the wish at the time it is frustrated. Putting arguments about time in terms of 'earlier, later, now' gets confusing, so let me reformulate Harris's argument using t, $t + 1$, and $t - 1$. As I interpret Harris's argument, he thinks something like this is obvious:

My autonomous wish at t about $t - 1$ is frustrated. At $t - 1$ I do not have the wish. The frustration at t does not infringe on my autonomy at t (or any time).

He then extends this to:

My autonomous wish at t about $t + 1$ is frustrated. At $t + 1$ I do not have the wish. The frustration at $t + 1$ does not infringe on my autonomy at t (or any time).

On this interpretation, it does not greatly matter that Harris's example is about childhood. The force of Harris's argument is in the more general premise that frustrated wishes about one's past do not frustrate one's autonomy. Suppose I now have wishes about my past, but my past when I was twenty and autonomous rather than whilst a child. Suppose I autonomously chose a career at t that at $t + 1$ I autonomously regard as a mistake. The frustration of my $t + 1$ wishes surely does not infringe on my autonomy.

Must we then conclude that the fulfilment of wishes about the future also does not affect autonomy? I think not. If we ask why fulfilment of wishes about the past does not affect autonomy, the reason does not carry over to the future. Suppose we take autonomy in the sense of personal sovereignty. Personal sovereignty is a basis for what I ought to be able to do. I cannot make decisions about the past because my past is fixed. 'Cannot' implies 'not ought' so it is not an infringement of personal sovereignty that I cannot shape my past. But I can shape my future, so

---

[30] See e.g. Ronald Dworkin, *Life's Dominion* (London: Harper-Collins, 1993), ch. 8.

the possibility that I ought to be able to shape it is not ruled out. Wishes about the past, whether childhood or not, are not 'equally' like wishes about the future.[31]

Harris may reply that can we make autonomous decisions only in the present and it is only in the present that autonomy can be infringed upon. Thus the non-fulfilment at $t + 1$ of an autonomous decision at t is not an infringement of autonomy. This view is suggested by Harris's own claim that there is no reason of autonomy to respect people's autonomous advance directives.[32] If Harris thinks autonomy is only in the present, he has an unusual view that he ought to, but does not, defend.

However, Harris's view is not wholly misguided. Arguably, my past wish does not give me a reason for action. If at t I want to be a soldier at $t + 1$ but, at $t + 1$, I have changed my mind, I do not have a reason to become a soldier at $t + 1$ just because I wanted it at t. In a sense, autonomy is in the present in that, if I change my mind, my present desires take priority over my past desires when deciding how to act. But although the present may have priority, we need not conclude that past decisions are irrelevant to autonomy. The absence of a present decision leaves the past decision. My wishes about my body after death can be countermanded by me later in life. But if they are not countermanded—for anything Harris has said—they remain in force.

We are left with the nagging question of when my autonomy is infringed upon if earlier wishes are frustrated. If my wishes at t about $t + 1$ are frustrated at $t + 1$, when was my autonomy infringed upon? Perhaps we may apply the solution offered in chapter 3 to the problem of when posthumous events can be harms: autonomy is infringed upon when the frustration of the wishes occurs.

Benefit and choice theories of rights

The argument has been that, in virtue of personal sovereignty, living people have rights over what happens to their bodies after death. Some writers, however, believe posthumous rights to be conceptually impossible. They say it is part of the concept of rights that rights are waivable and, because the dead necessarily cannot waive their rights, so the dead cannot have rights.[33]

The claim that all rights are waivable forms part of a much larger dispute amongst theorists of rights. On one side are benefit theories, sometimes called 'interest' theories of rights, which say that rights protect those aspects of a person's well-being important enough to hold others to be under a duty.[34] On the other side, choice

---

[31] A wish at t about $t + 1$ becomes a past wish when $t + 1$ arrives. But it is not a wish about the past, and it is being a wish about the past that is supposed to be irrelevant to autonomy.

[32] Harris, 'Law and Regulation of Retained Organs', p. 536.

[33] One limb of Harris's argument for organ conscription is that the dead cannot have rights, on a choice theory of rights. See 'Law and Regulation of Retained Organs', pp. 534–9. The other limb is that the dead do not have benefit theory rights either, although not for conceptual reasons. Fabre also says the dead do not have benefit theory rights because they cannot be harmed. See her 'Posthumous Rights', in C. Grant, B. Holburn, A. Hatzistavrou, and M. Kramer (eds.), *The Legacy of H. L. A. Hart: Legal, Political, and Moral Philosophy* (Oxford: Oxford University Press, 2008).

[34] Joseph Raz, *The Morality of Freedom* (Oxford: Clarendon Press, 1986), p. 166; Jeremy Waldron *The Right to Private Property* (Oxford: Clarendon Press, 1988).

theories of rights, sometimes called 'will' theories, say rights protect not well-being but autonomy.[35] Because rights protect autonomy, rights must be waivable.[36]

The benefit and choice theories are highly abstract, but it is often thought that the difference between them matters when they are applied to the dead. The benefit theory allows the dead to have rights. If people's interests can be affected by posthumous events, then it makes sense conceptually, on a benefit view, to say they have rights. By contrast, a choice theory appears to say that the dead could not have rights, even if they could have interests, because they could not waive their rights. The relative merits of choice and benefit theories of rights are not to be settled by what they say about the rights of the dead. The decision between them is a large one, indeed, one sometimes described as 'a standoff'.[37] Clearly, it would be wise in writing on applied ethics to avoid choosing between these theories if at all possible—why make an ethical conclusion depend on a fundamentally controversial view of rights if it is not necessary?

One way to avoid choosing may be to say we have duties towards the dead but they do not confer rights.[38] That view would require quite a bit of working out and defending. Suppose a doctor promises to save the life of a patient and to do so would have to take an organ from a dead person who had refused. Promises create rights; would the patient's right outweigh the non-rights-based duty to the dead? Instead of non-rights-based duties, I would like to say that people have rights over their dead bodies without having to reject the choice theory of rights. It is worth looking harder at why a choice theory is supposed to be incompatible with these rights. It turns out that the choice theory may well be compatible with posthumous rights after all.

Let us consider the main reasons offered for a choice theory of rights. Wayne Sumner's major reason is that the choice theory marks the distinction between autonomy and well-being.[39] This reason is consistent with the view of posthumous rights I have defended, since the rights are based not on well-being but personal sovereignty (which is an interpretation of autonomy). People are free, while alive, to waive their rights. That is, indeed, one way to understand what happens when people agree to donate their organs after death: they waive their rights against the retrieval of their organs. Hillel Steiner's major reason for the choice theory is that the function of rights is to resolve deadlock when moral principles conflict, which he takes to support a choice theory rather than a benefit theory. He thinks conflicts between choices can be avoided in principle, and choices between benefits or interests cannot.[40] Like Sumner's reason, Steiner's reason for the choice theory is

---

[35] See e.g. H. L. A. Hart *Essays on Bentham* (Oxford: Clarendon Press, 1982); L. W. Sumner *The Moral Foundation of Rights* (Oxford: Clarendon Press, 1987); Hillel Steiner *An Essay on Rights* (Oxford: Basil Blackwell, 1994). The dispute between benefit and choice theories is long and complicated, much too long and complicated for a book on transplantation to cover properly. Those who want to find out more could see Matthew H. Kramer, N. E. Simmonds, and Hillel Steiner *A Debate over Rights* (Oxford: Clarendon Press, 1998).

[36] For a statement of this requirement, see Steiner, *An Essay on Rights*, pp. 57–8, 61.

[37] Sumner, *Moral Foundations of Rights*, p. 51.

[38] Sumner envisages duties that do not confer rights at ibid., p. 204.

[39] Ibid., pp. 47, 97.

[40] Steiner, *An Essay on Rights*.

consistent with rights for the dead. What avoiding deadlock requires is knowing in advance who is allowed to do what and, as far as posthumous rights are concerned, knowing in advance just requires setting out the duties of others and the conditions under which they can be waived. Where, then, is the incompatibility between the choice theory and posthumous rights?

Steiner makes one detailed argument against posthumous rights. He focuses on the right of bequest and he thinks that if he can show the right of bequest makes no sense conceptually, then he will have shown that no posthumous rights make sense. His argument goes like this. Bequest is the transfer of property after a person's death, not a gift within life. Direct transfer from a dead person to a living is not possible, since people who are dead cannot transfer things. Some executor is required. However, the right of bequest requires that the executor has a duty to the dead person, in part because otherwise the executor could give the property to whomever she chose. Dead people necessarily cannot waive duties to them, so the duty to the dead person is not waivable. But rights-based duties must be waivable, according to the choice theory. So the conclusion seems to be that there cannot be a choice theory right to bequeath. There is one more move: to invent a fiction, which Steiner thinks the law does, and say the executor is the dead person, and so can transfer property. But there are no fictions in the state of nature so, morally speaking, the rest of the world has no duty not to appropriate the dead person's property.[41]

Steiner's argument could be easily generalized to rights to give or withhold organs after death. At or after the point of death, one cannot transfer or withhold organs. No one can have a duty to transfer organs based on the right of the dead person because the dead person cannot waive the duty. There would have to be some legal fiction, but there are no fictions in the state of nature, and so the organs are unowned (if one accepts Steiner's independent theory of property acquisition). A law conscripting organs would not infringe on a pre-legal right.

Clearly there are numerous questions one can ask of Steiner's argument, some of which, such as the significance of a state of nature, are dealt with at length in his book and which I cannot explain or explore here.[42] Here is a question we can ask: What if someone says 'take my heart after I die, but not before'? This is gift-giving with an indeterminate date. A person in advance waives a right against organ retrieval. Why is advance ability to waive not enough to satisfy the waivability condition of choice theories of rights? Steiner says that when people normally give gifts, they acquire new duties as a result of their gift. Before the gift, everyone except the owner had duties towards the owner in respect of his property, but now the erstwhile owner has the duty towards the person to whom he gave the gift. But a dead person cannot have duties to keep off his old property because he is dead and cannot have duties. Therefore, Steiner says, the normal process of gift-giving does not work in the case of the dead.[43]

---

[41] Steiner, *An Essay on Rights*, pp. 250–8.
[42] Just to make it clear, my aim in criticizing Steiner is not to defend rights of bequest but to argue for the possibility of posthumous rights which may, but may not, include rights of bequest.
[43] Steiner, *An Essay on Rights*, pp. 253–4.

The crucial premise here, that ex-owners must acquire new duties after giving, seems unmotivated. The best explanation I can give is that it rests on a fallacious slide between 'If he existed, the gift-giver would have new duties' and 'Any gift-giver must acquire new duties, which means he must exist'. The first version is right, but why should we believe the second? And if we do not, nothing seems left of Steiner's argument. People could have rights against organ retrieval which they could choose to waive before they die.

We should take stock. I hope that posthumous rights are compatible with both benefit and choice theories. The supposed problem is that choice theories insist that all duties are waivable and that the dead cannot waive their duties. We have yet to see why the ability of people to waive their rights while alive is not enough to satisfy the waivability condition. Why, in other words, must the waivability condition obtain at the time at which the fulfilment of the alleged right is in question? I leave this as a question noting, finally, that if a choice theory really is incompatible with posthumous rights, then the conclusion might be 'so much the worse for the choice theory', rather than 'so much the worse for posthumous rights'.

Rights and experience

In his book *Consent to Sexual Relations*, Alan Wertheimer asks what is the harm and wrong of rape.[44] The explanation he gives is that the distinctive harms of rape, over and above any physical effects caused by assault, are partly physical, in the risk of sexually transmitted infections or pregnancy, and partly experiential.[45] Moreover, these are the primary explanations for what is wrong with rape. Women—all of us—have rights of bodily integrity; but these are founded on the avoidance of damage to the physical organism and avoidance of distress. The details of Wertheimer's account of the harms of rape need not concern us here, but his claims imply that to go against the wishes of people about their bodies after they die would not infringe on their rights. The dead would not suffer physical harm if, say, their organs are retrieved against their wishes, and nor would they suffer mental distress. Wertheimer's view thus conflicts with this chapter's conclusion in favour of posthumous rights, and this sub-section argues against his view.

What would Wertheimer's account say about the rape of a woman who is unconscious, who suffers no physical harm, and who never finds out about it? Are we to say this case of rape does not infringe on the woman's rights? To say so would be so counterintuitive as to call Wertheimer's account into serious question. He considers this case and makes the following reply: if, contrary to the stipulation, the woman did later find out, she would be harmed by the earlier rape. His view of the harm of mental distress does not require that the distress occur at the same time as the act.[46] He is, however, willing to say that, if the woman never finds out—and again bearing in mind the stipulation that she suffers no physical harm—she would

[44] Alan Wertheimer, *Consent to Sexual Relations* (Cambridge: Cambridge University Press, 2003).
[45] Ibid., pp. 100–2, 107–12.   [46] Ibid., pp. 110–11.

not be harmed. 'Has she been harmed? My intuition is to say yes, but I think the correct answer is no.'[47]

However, Wertheimer thinks that although the woman is not harmed, she is wronged and her rights are violated. He claims it is crucial to distinguish the wrongness of someone's actions and the harm to a victim in a particular case. Roughly speaking, wrongness is a function of the harm that can be expected to occur, the culpability of the wrongdoer, and perhaps the size of any actual harm. People could thus act wrongly and still be legitimately punished even though what they did caused no harm. Attempted murder where a gun misfires is one example: the expected harm is very high and we can suppose that the would-be murderer is culpable, so a serious wrong has been committed even though no harm has been done. Another could be the case we are considering, of the rape of the unconscious woman. Wertheimer says the woman may in fact suffer no harm, but since people usually find these things out, the expected harm would be very great and, if we add the expected harm to the culpability of the rapist, the act would be wrong.[48] Not only would the rapist act wrongly, he would violate the woman's rights. In Wertheimer's view, rights function as prophylactics. Rights protect not just against actual harm but against the serious risk of serious harm.

If Wertheimer's view that rights protect against physical harm and aversive experience can explain away the apparent counter-example of raping the unconscious, what about organ retrieval from the dead? Consider a case where a person strongly opposes, and is known to oppose, her organs being taken and her organs are taken nonetheless. Would Wertheimer's account say this is a wrong or the violation of the person's rights? It is hard to see how. Wertheimer argues that the basis for rights is either physical harm or mental distress. In the case of this dead person, no physical harm or distress could occur. Nor are these absent harms matters of probability. On the assumptions of no afterlife or relevant afterlife, there is no expected harm either, so Wertheimer's account has no basis for judging those taking the organs to have acted wrongly.[49]

Since I argue for posthumous rights, I have to confront Wertheimer's claim that rights must be justified experientially if they do not protect against physical harm.[50] He writes,

> if humans were constituted like turtles, which are immune from certain forms of attack, there would be no point to the moral principle that it is wrong to attack other humans. Consider the rights of prisoners. As Simon Blackburn notes, 'Keeping prisoners in the cold, or the dark, or deprived of sleep, or fed on rotten meat, is abominable

---

[47] Alan Wertheimer, *Consent to Sexual Relations* (Cambridge: Cambridge University Press, 2003), p. 111, n. 78.

[48] Ibid., pp. 96–7, 102, 111.

[49] Perhaps earlier distress could justify the right on Wertheimer's view. But see my doubts in the previous sub-section on the sensibilities of the living.

[50] In the section 'Should we accept the experiential view?', pp.107–12, Wertheimer offers various other arguments that seem rather off the point of his own question. In particular, his claims that rights are not foundational premises but must be supported and that rights protect benefits is consistent with saying that rights protect against more than aversive experiences.

because of our biological need for warmth, light, sleep, and a proper diet. If we had other natures, like polar bears or cockroaches, it might not be so bad.' Similarly, if humans did not typically experience distress in response to invasions of our privacy or sexuality, then there would be no point to insisting that we have a right that others not engage in such behaviours.[51]

This is a somewhat puzzling passage. Clearly it cannot validly be argued that, because some of our rights depend on our vulnerabilities, which in turn depend on our natures, all rights depend on experience. Perhaps the lesson of the turtle shell argument is simply that rights have to have a point and a right would be pointless if the interest it protected could not be set back. However, the interests of the dead can be set back, so the lesson is not that posthumous rights are pointless.

Wertheimer says it would be pointless to have rights protecting privacy or sexuality if invasions did not typically cause distress. This idea must be distinguished from another, that if we did not typically care about the invasions, there would be no right against them. Wertheimer equivocates across the two ideas at various places.[52] The distinction between them matters because people can and do care about things other than their own distress. People will typically feel distress at acts they care about (in a negative sense), if they know these acts have occurred. If the acts occur without their knowing, they will not feel distress at the acts; but that does not mean that they are indifferent to whether the acts occur. The important point is this: perhaps we only have rights when we care about them and would be distressed if we knew of their violation. That does not mean we only have the rights whose violation would cause actual, not just hypothetical, distress.

We are, however, left with a challenge: what is the point of having rights over one's body if they are not based on the distress one would typically feel at infringements? This challenge is easily met. Even in the case of sexual violation that concerns Wertheimer, one may well care about intimacy and control over revelation in sex over and above caring about the aversive experiences one has when one lacks control over them.[53] In the case of taking organs after death, the point is the one already given: what happens after death can fulfil goals that people have; fulfilling the goals affects personal success even if the person does not know about the fulfilment; and when the goals fall within the sphere of personal sovereignty, they are protected by moral rights. I realize that I have not here shown that Wertheimer's view is wrong, only that his arguments are not enough to support it. Perhaps in the end there is just a fundamental clash of intuitions, although Wertheimer himself says 'It does seem that a purely experiential view cannot be right.'[54]

---

[51] Ibid., pp. 100–1. The quotation from Blackburn is taken from his *Ruling Passions* (Oxford: Clarendon Press, 1998), p. 151.

[52] See his view that rights protect what we care about, in *Consent to Sexual Relations*, p. 108, and his inference from the imaginary woman who does not object to rape that she does not know about at the time, p. 111.

[53] Although this is not to cast doubt on Wertheimer's evolutionary explanation of the psychic harms of rape.

[54] Wertheimer, *Consent to Sexual Relations*, p. 95, n. 27.

NEXT STEPS

This chapter has set out and defended an account of personal sovereignty that extends past death. People have a negative right to control what happens to their bodies after they die. The task now is to apply this in the context of transplantation. While people may want to donate their organs, their families may want to withhold them. While people may refuse to donate their organs, sick people desperately need them. The right of personal sovereignty needs to be set against these competing interests. Furthermore, people often die without consenting or refusing to donate their organs. What then must others do if they are to respect personal sovereignty? These are the topics for the next three chapters.

5

The Dead and Their Families

This chapter is an enquiry into the ethics of family decision-making about the retrieval of organs from the dead. The family's role in the decision to donate is of great practical importance. Organs will not be taken if families withhold consent, as they do in 40–50 per cent of cases in the US, UK, and other countries.[1] The family has the power, in withholding, to override the consent of the deceased to donate. The power of veto is not restricted to countries with 'opt in' systems of organ donation. Even in 'opt out' countries, medical staff will not take organs when the family object.[2] Of course, families do not only object. They also consent to retrieval, often when the deceased has made no formal declaration of intent or expressed any clear wishes. Whereas the family's power of veto has been politically controversial, the role of the family as a default decider is largely assumed to be unproblematic, if it is even noticed.[3] The role of default decider should be more controversial than it is, since it amounts to the power to donate when the deceased did not consent and the power to withhold badly needed organs when the deceased did not dissent.[4]

Family decision-making could be put into practice in different ways. The family could be asked for informed consent, where the consent would have to meet the usual standards of adequate understanding of the relevant facts and where, without consent, retrieval would be blocked. The family could be asked for consent with, as before, the absence of consent being equivalent to a veto, but where the consent need not be informed. The family could be asked if they have objections, where the burden would be on them to raise objections if they are to veto retrieval, but where their views have at least been solicited. And the family could be left to raise objections without these being solicited but where, if they do raise them, organ

---

[1] One large study found that in the US, family consent was not given in 46 per cent of cases of potential donors. See Ellen Sheehy et al., 'Estimating the Number of Potential Organ Donors in the United States' *New England Journal of Medicine* 349 (2003). For the UK, the figure is around 40 per cent refusal. See UK Transplant *Potential Donor Audit: Summary Report for the 24 Month Period 1 April 2007–31 March 2009* available at <www.uktransplant.org.uk> (last accessed August 2010).

[2] As chapter 6 explains, many wrongly believe that countries with opt out systems simply take organs from those who fail to opt out. In practice, families usually have the power to veto retrieval.

[3] As chapter 6 also explains, many wrongly believe countries with opt in systems do not take organs from people who had not consented while alive.

[4] Several writers have been sharply critical of the family's role in practice. See e.g. David Price, *Human Tissue in Transplantation and Research: A Model Legal and Ethical Donation Framework* (Cambridge: Cambridge University Press, 2009) and Govert den Hartogh, *Farewell to Non-commitment: Decision Systems for Organ Donation from an Ethical Viewpoint* (The Hague: Centre for Ethics and Health, 2008).

retrieval is vetoed. The different grounds for family decision-making may turn out to be grounds for different types of decision-making.

If we ask why the family should have any decision-making authority, public debate and the literature offer three lines of justification. First, families should decide so as to give best effect to the claims of the deceased. The arguments here are over whether the deceased transferred authority to the family or whether families know better than others what the deceased wanted. Second, families have a legitimate claim in their own right to decide. The arguments here concern the family's distress, respecting family bonds, and religious and cultural diversity. Third, families should decide because the alternative of overriding them would have excessive social costs. In particular, overriding families would cause a net drop in the supply of organs. This chapter argues that we often do not know—but could do more to find out—whether families give best effect to the claims of the deceased; that the family does have a claim in its own right, but only not to be distressed, a consideration of limited scope and weight; and that the family should have a power of veto given the likely effect on the supply of organs.

FAMILY DECISION AND THE INDIVIDUAL'S WISHES

The first line of justification for family decision-making is based on the claims of the dead over their own bodies. The least controversial justification is direct transfer by individual consent, that is, when the deceased consents to the family's deciding. The family then acquires a right to decide from the right of the deceased. Assuming the consent is adequate, after being properly informed for instance, the family would have as strong a claim to decide as the deceased did. But people rarely consent to delegate the decision even where there are formal mechanisms to delegate. Indeed, several countries, including the UK and New Zealand, do not offer formal options of delegating to the family.

People may not consent to their families' deciding and yet want them to nonetheless. Let us assume that, to respect the claims of the deceased, we should do what they wanted.[5] Whether a deceased person, or the deceased as a class, want their families to decide is a factual question. The question could be answered by asking the family what the deceased wanted, but it could also be answered, perhaps more accurately, by survey data. I have not found any such data, but asking people whether they would want their families to decide would be a useful research exercise.

One argument for the family to decide is that the deceased wanted them to. A different argument says that families are best placed to report on the deceased's wishes. According to this argument, families should make a substituted judgement on behalf of the deceased. When living patients are incompetent, one common

[5] In chapter 6, I argue that consenting is not the same as wanting, still less presumed wanting, and that the deceased's consent should not be required before taking their organs. If the deceased's consent were necessary and sufficient for organ retrieval, the family would not need to be consulted.

standard for deciding on treatment is to choose as the patient would have done if competent, and families are usually given the role of deciding.[6] In the case of donation, families would then be asked to decide as they think the deceased would have done. The source of the family's decision-making authority would be the interests of the deceased combined with the family's alleged accuracy in stating them.[7]

Assuming we should do what the deceased wanted, are families actually best placed to say what the deceased wanted? The accuracy of families could be tested empirically. I have not found any research testing their accuracy at predicting whether their relatives would want to donate, but there is related evidence about family accuracy in making substituted judgements about end-of-life treatment. For instance, hospice patients have been asked whether they would want to receive antibiotics if they became incompetent, and their answers were compared with their families' predictions. Taking the average of all the available eligible studies, a systematic review found that families were accurate only 68 per cent of the time.[8] Interestingly, the review found no evidence that surrogate decision-makers were more accurate either when chosen by the patients rather than, say, designated by state law, nor that prior discussion between patients and surrogates about treatment preferences improved accuracy. This last finding casts some doubt on the idea, common in discussions of transplantation, that people should talk to their families about donation if they want their preferences acted upon.[9]

However, the argument was only that families know better than anyone else what the deceased wanted, not that families are infallible. Do families know better? The systematic review did find that surrogates were more accurate than doctors, but since families are not particularly accurate, the possibility arises that a better method could be developed to guess the deceased's wishes. Families are only one source of evidence, which could be combined with other sources, such as data about what people generally want, in an algorithm more accurate than families alone.[10] A better method would undercut the argument that asking the family is the best way to find out whether the deceased wanted to donate. And even if asking families is the best way to find out the wishes of the dead, it will be wrong in many cases.

---

[6] The substituted judgement standard is more commonly used in the US than the UK or Canada. Daniel Sperling, *Posthumous Interests* (Cambridge: Cambridge University Press, 2008), pp. 70–1.

[7] In Germany, families are instructed in the relevant statute to decide as they believe their relative would have. In the Netherlands, they are encouraged. See den Hartogh, *Farewell to Non-commitment*, p. 24.

[8] D. Shalowitz, E. Garrett-Mayer, and D. Wendler, 'The Accuracy of Surrogate Decision Makers: A Systematic Review' *Archives of Internal Medicine* 166 (2006).

[9] Although there is some evidence that families are more likely to donate if they *think* they know the deceased wanted to be a donor. See Laura Siminoff and Renee Lawrence, 'Knowing Patients' Preferences about Organ Donation: Does it Make a Difference?' *The Journal of Trauma* 53 (2002), pp. 759–60. An advertising campaign to encourage people to tell families their preferences may increase the supply of organs whether or not families are actually right about the preferences.

[10] See also the article 'Logical Endings: Evidence-based ethics' in *The Economist* (17 March 2007), reporting psychological research suggesting that computer programs are currently as accurate as families at predicting the decisions people would make about their own end-of-life care in intensive care units.

To sum up, if the deceased consented to the family deciding, the family have the right the deceased had. The family should then be put in a position to make an informed choice, and their choice should have the same force as the deceased's. But transfer by consent is rare, and likely to remain rare even if the option to transfer became formally available. If the deceased's consent is not required and their wants count too, letting the family decide could give best effect to the deceased's claims. In some cases, the deceased would have wanted their families to decide. In other cases, the family would be best placed to report on what the deceased wanted. But these arguments turn on facts as well as on the moral claim that, in the absence of consent or dissent, we ought to respect the wishes of the deceased. Do the deceased want their families to decide? Quite possibly, but where is the evidence? And families are not particularly reliable guides to what the deceased wanted. In many cases, we will not know whether it does give best effect to the deceased's claims if the family decides. But of course there are other arguments for family decision-making besides fulfilling the deceased's wishes, and I now turn to them.

THE CLAIMS OF THE FAMILY

This section is about the claim of the family in its own right to permit or prevent organ retrieval from a dead relative; that is, a claim not derived from the interests of the relative or anyone else. What is it about the family that could justify its authority to decide whether organs may be taken from its dead relative in opposition to either the relative's claims or the needs of the sick? We cannot answer the question simply by pointing to other cases where we accept family decision-making because they differ in obvious ways from organ donation. For example, the family generally has a duty to dispose of the bodies of relatives, which requires certain rights to exclude others.[11] However, the historical reason for the duty was to prevent the cost of disposal falling on the community, which is no reason to allow families to dispose of scarce organs. Families are also involved in deciding on medical care for incompetent (living) relatives, but the major reasons are to protect their relative's biological interests, to tell medical staff what the patient wanted, or because the patient would have wanted the family involved. In the case of organ donation, the dead have no biological interests to protect, and while there is nothing wrong in principle with the family deciding so as to give best effect to the interests of the deceased, it is not the idea that the family should decide in its own right.

One general point can be made now, since it applies to all the reasons offered for the family's deciding in its own right. All the reasons could be outweighed. Consider what happens in apparently parallel cases. On the one hand, most potential organ donors die in intensive care units and, in many cases around the world, intensive care doctors will not override families who refuse to donate their relative's organs. The doctors will not override out of a concern for the family's

---

[11] Although English law gives the duty to the deceased's estate, not the family. See M. Brazier, 'Organ Retention and Return: Problems of Consent' *Journal of Medical Ethics* 29 (2003), n. 31.

interests, however exactly they would express that concern. On the other hand, organ donation is not the only matter in which families in intensive care units have strong opinions and in other cases, families' wishes are overridden. Sometimes families want medical care even in cases where the prognosis for a patient is hopeless. Sometimes families want artificial ventilation maintained even when the patient is brain-dead, and therefore dead, according to the legal and medical norms of all countries where organ transplantation occurs. Intensive care doctors often do not in these cases go along with the families for long, especially not in cases of brain death.[12] Doctors will cease non-palliative care for patients against the family's wishes either for the sake of the patient or to free up scarce resources so that other patients can be admitted to intensive care. The parallel with organ donation is obvious. Why not override the claims of the family for the sake either of the interests of the deceased or to acquire organs for the sick?

Although I have not seen it answered, this challenge may not be unanswerable. Something about organ donation may set it apart from withdrawing support for the brain-dead or in so-called futile cases, or perhaps practice in those cases should be revised so that it is consistent with practice in organ donation. So let us go into the reasons for the family to decide in its own right about organ donation.

I begin with the need to avoid distressing the family. Avoiding distress is morally important, I argue, but it may not support family decision-making and, even if it does, it is not important enough on its own to override the claims of either the deceased or the sick. If the family is to have justifiable decision-making authority, some reason must be found in addition to distress. I then consider the bonds of family. We may have a sense of the importance of these bonds, but it is hard to explain how they justify having families decide on organ donation. Finally, I consider, and reject, an argument from respecting religious and cultural diversity. With the exception of avoiding family distress, the section concludes there is little justification for the family to have a claim to decide in its own right.

Distress

Perhaps the most obvious reason for giving the family decision-making authority is to do with the distress family members suffer at a tremendously difficult time.[13] Most of those who are suitable donors die in intensive care and prematurely. The decision about donation has to be made quickly, and families may well find they cannot agree to it. Overriding the family could, and likely would, cause them to feel

---

[12] Stephen Streat describes what happens in Australasian intensive care units in cases of very severe brain damage. After explaining the situation to the families, '[w]e then usually proffer a firm medical consensus recommending that intensive therapies be withdrawn and invite family discussion and agreement with that recommendation. We seek consensus with that opinion, but we do not "ask for permission" to withdraw therapies.' See Stephen Streat, 'When Do We Stop?' *Critical Care and Resuscitation* 7 (2005), p. 230.

[13] See David Price, 'From Cosmos and Damian to van Velzen: The Human Tissue Saga Continues' *Medical Law Review* 11 (2003), pp. 18–19; Paula Boddington, citing Australian guidance, 'Organ Donation After Death: Should I Decide, or Should My Family?' *Journal of Applied Philosophy* 15 (1998), pp. 69–81, 70.

powerless, angry, insulted, or indignant. Some writers, who are critical of the family's power of decision (and, often, the individual's power), attempt to discredit the family's reactions. They say the family are being squeamish or irrational, for instance because they overestimate the visual damage done by removal of organs.[14] However, the families' stated reasons might well not be the real basis of the distress, but rather rationalizations of a much more basic psychological reaction and, in any case, the basis of the distress is beside the point. Distress is a bad thing in itself.[15]

In principle, an argument from distress could do more than support a family veto. It could also support the family's having the power to donate and override the individual's refusal. The family may, for instance, want something good to come of their relative's premature death and be distressed if it were unable to donate the organs because of the deceased's refusal. Insofar as the goal is to reduce the distress of the family, or avoid causing more, distress could support the family's having the power both to withhold and donate. But in practice, I suspect that families would be more likely to feel distress if their wish to withhold is overridden.[16]

Several writers argue that considerations of distress are not in fact good reasons for the family to decide.[17] Some ambitiously claim that removing the family's power of decision would remove a burden from them, so reducing their distress. Reducing distress would thus be a reason against the family's having a say. Less ambitiously, the claim is that families would get used to a policy that took the decision from them, so that, over time, they would not be much more distressed by such a policy than if they had the power to decide.[18] These claims about distress raise empirical questions which cannot be decided here and which might well have different answers in different times and places. At best, though, considerations of distress only offer contingent support to the view that families should decide.[19]

Even if the family should decide so as to spare them distress, it is a further question whether they should be asked to give informed consent. Suppose the only reason to seek family consent is to avoid further distressing them. Then the process of getting permission should be designed with a view to distressing families as little as possible. The process should not be designed to elicit informed consent, unless

---

[14] John Harris has made these points in a number of places. See, for instance, his *Clones, Genes, and Immortality* (Oxford: Oxford University Press, 1992), pp. 123–5, and 'Organ Procurement: Dead Interests, Living Needs' *Journal of Medical Ethics* 29 (2003). Eric Rakowski agrees with Harris in *Equal Justice* (Oxford: Clarendon Press, 1991), p. 170.

[15] F. M. Kamm, *Morality, Mortality*, vol.1 (New York: Oxford University Press, 1993), pp. 220f. gives reasons why people quite reasonably might not want to donate the organs of their loved ones.

[16] As Stephen Streat, an intensive care doctor, suggested to me.

[17] Thomas May, Mark P. Alusio, and Michael A De Vita, 'Patients, Families, and Organ Donation: Who Shall Decide?' *The Milbank Quarterly* 78 (2000), pp. 329–30; Aaron Spital, 'Mandated Choice for Organ Donation: Time to Give it a Try', in A. Caplan and D. Coelho (eds.), *The Ethics of Organ Transplants* (Amherst, NY: Prometheus Books, 1998), p. 150.

[18] Harris, *Clones, Genes, and Immortality*, p. 125.

[19] A British taskforce describes taking the decision from families to reduce their distress as a form of paternalism 'at odds with the ethos of today's NHS'. Organ Donation Taskforce, *The Potential Impact of an Opt Out System for Organ Donation in the UK* (London: Department of Health, 2008), p. 17. The taskforce may think that families should decide for reasons besides minimizing distress. If, however, the *only* reason for the family to decide were to spare them distress, it would be self-defeating to have them decide if doing so would make them more distressed.

that happens to be the way to minimize distress. To see the difference, recall the requirements of informed consent. If someone's consent is to be informed, then the salient facts must be disclosed and the person must, at the time of deciding, understand and perhaps care about those facts and her decision. The aim of informed consent is normally to protect the autonomy and well-being of the person, not to minimize distress. Indeed minimizing distress may conflict with informed consent. It is usually a (possibly justifiable) derogation from informed consent not to tell patients about their condition if doing so would upset them.

Now to apply this to our case. Suppose the point of getting the family's permission is to avoid distressing them rather than to get genuinely informed consent. It is sometimes objected that families cannot give genuinely informed consent shortly after learning of the death or imminent death of their relatives because they are too distraught to be able to take in the information. The conclusion may be drawn that the bodies should not be used if consent is only sought and given at that time. If the aim is only to minimize distress, that conclusion would not follow, and it would not matter if families could not take in the information, unless they later thought they had been badly treated and were upset by that. Furthermore, because it would not matter, empirical information about people's capacity to process information after experiencing the death of a loved one would not be directly relevant to assessing the legitimacy of family consent. The sort of information needed would be about how to ask them in a way that minimizes their distress and whether they subsequently regret their decision.

Consider now failing to disclose or glossing over details of the transplant process which would be likely to put families off agreeing. That would also derogate from informed consent but again not be objectionable if the aim is to minimize distress, unless families were subsequently to feel that they had been duped. Indeed, as far as avoiding distress is concerned, there is no direct reason against taking organs secretly. That said, it is hard to believe secret taking would go undetected, and neither doctors nor the state should exercise power without accountability, which is generally incompatible with secrecy. But the point remains: considerations of distress offer only contingent support to informed choice.

How important is it to avoid distressing the family? It is surely uncontroversial that there is a reason to avoid distressing the family. This reason would justify asking the family even if doing so had some minor costs in convenience and time. But what if a choice must be made between either distressing the family or fulfilling the needs of the sick or interests of the dead? Remember the parallel between organ donation and withdrawal of care in intensive care units. The claims of the family are often overridden in other cases by the interests of the deceased or the needs of sick people for access to intensive care, so why not in organ donation?

Let us first compare the distress of the deceased's family with the needs of the sick. In arguing against the conscription of organs, Margaret Brazier says that relatives ought to be protected from distress. She imagines a woman from a religious family whose father's organs would be taken under conscription. Brazier asks 'Were she distraught to the point of illness at the invasion of her beloved father's physical integrity, would that distress count for little?'[20] But while her distress counts for something, why put it above the distress of the families of people who need a transplant, let alone those people's interests in having one? The families of potential recipients would be distressed if their relative dies from want of an organ, or must remain semi-attached to dialysis, or must struggle with failing organs. If distress is simply a bad thing of which there ought to be less, Brazier has not made a case against conscripting organs.

Brazier claims that the criminal law (in the UK presumably) now says: '[i]nflicting psychiatric harm on others deliberately and knowingly constitutes an offence'.[21] The implication is that distressing the family of the deceased is, or is relevantly like, a criminal offence. However, how could the rule against deliberately and knowingly inflicting psychiatric harm tell against a policy of conscription? 'Knowingly' inflicting distress cannot sensibly be criminalized (if 'inflicting' means 'cause'). If an intensive care doctor tells family members their relative is dead, she may knowingly cause distress, but telling them could hardly be made illegal. Perhaps this is why Brazier adds 'deliberately' to 'knowingly'. But 'deliberately' is vague; if it means 'intentionally', then the objection does not apply: taking organs against the wishes of the family would not be with the intention of making the family distressed. The intention is to get the organs, and distress would be a regrettable by-product. Again, Brazier has not made her case.

One may think that the family has a right not to be distressed. If so, this right could outweigh the greater good of more organs. But distress is not in general a free-standing basis for a right. The distress I may feel if you take back the book you lent me does not give me a right to have the book, not even one outweighed by your property right. We quite plausibly have a right not to be terrorized, but that is because the threats, if carried out, would violate rights we already have, such as a right against physical harm.[22] The family's distress on its own does not justify a right's protection.

Let us now compare the distress of the family with the interests of the deceased in the, perhaps rare, case when the deceased decided to give or withhold their organs in conflict with their families' wishes.[23] If we follow chapter 4, rights protect personal sovereignty even after death. People have a right to control what happens to their bodies, which includes a right to veto retrieval and to offer their organs free from interference. These rights are not absolute, however, so the question is whether they are defeated by the family's distress. I think not.

People's rights to determine what happens to their bodies while alive (and competent) override the feelings of their family. If a 20-year-old woman wants a tattoo, her family may not stop her no matter how upset they would be. The decision involves the woman's body, so it is hers to make. My parents may not force

---

[20] Margaret Brazier, 'Retained Organs: Ethics and Humanity' *Legal Studies* 22 (2002), p. 566.

[21] Ibid., p. 567.

[22] See Judith Jarvis Thomson, *The Realm of Rights* (Cambridge, MA: Harvard University Press, 1990), ch. 10, and Anthony Ellis, 'Thomson on Distress' *Ethics* 106 (1995).

[23] Brazier considers only cases where 'the deceased herself has not clearly articulated her wishes'. See Brazier, 'Retained Organs', p. 567. Her argument about distress is therefore seriously incomplete.

me to have lifesaving medical treatment, just as no one may, because I have a right to control what happens to my body. The claim that people have rights against the world, including their families, is not very controversial. To be sure, a family in which people non-jokingly insist on their rights against each other is not a happy family, but then some families are not happy families, and they are often the ones whose members need rights.[24] For the reasons given in earlier chapters, personal sovereignty applies past death so, by extension, people's decisions to donate or withhold their organs should not be overridden by family distress. If it comes to a choice between the personal sovereignty of the deceased, which is protected by a right, or not distressing the family, which is not, the deceased's interests should prevail.

The distress of the family is not the trivial matter it is claimed to be by some supporters of organ conscription. But nor is it the decisive consideration it is argued to be by some writers and policy-makers. If distress is considered on its own and not as a back-up reason to respect other claims, it should yield to respecting the claims of the deceased over their own bodies or to the needs of potential recipients and their families.

The bonds of family

What may underlie some beliefs that the family ought to decide about donation is a sense of the importance of family life, a sense that, to paraphrase one writer, families should be able to grieve in their own way, come to terms with death, and go through their rituals of laying their relative to rest.[25] However, although family life is generally taken as of great importance, I have not seen a rigorous and detailed attempt to explain how it justifies the family's deciding about donation when the deceased had a contrary view or the organs are badly needed. This absence of rigour and detail is rather frustrating, because simply saying 'family life is important' does not explain why, or how important it is that, the family should decide. Perhaps the idea is only the one already discussed: that families would be distressed if not permitted to decide. But many who cite the importance of the family clearly think they have an extra argument. What are they getting at?

As a start, we should remind ourselves of the variety of the relations within families. Even within a nuclear family, spouse could decide for spouse; mother, father, or both could decide for children of various ages; adult children could decide for parents; and siblings could decide for sibling. When one adds the complications of extended families, divorced spouses, long-term lovers, or distant relatives who suddenly appear, then the reasons often given for family decision may be off the mark. It is one thing to say that parents should decide what happens to their dead infant. One may appeal to the value of the family unit or parental rights. Neither applies to an estranged daughter or loathed spouse deciding for a 50-year-old man.

---

[24] Jeremy Waldron, 'When Justice Replaces Affection: The Need for Rights' in his *Liberal Rights* (Cambridge: Cambridge University Press, 1993).
[25] Brazier, 'Retained Organs', pp. 560–1.

The strongest case for family decision-making can be made for parents deciding for their young children. Many will agree with Robert Nozick when he wrote: 'There is no bond I know stronger than being a parent.'[26] Unlike in other cases, the children would be young enough to have made no valid decision for themselves and to have no posthumous interests to compete with their parents.[27] That parents should decide is surely a widespread and strongly held view. Some may feel it is so basic it cannot be justified, but others have tried to argue for parental decision-making on the basis of the strong bonds between parents and their children. The Scottish Independent Review Group on the Retention of Organs summarized their case for parental authorization before post-mortem by saying: 'Recognition of the intimate bond between parent and child, and the privacy of the family unit, reinforces the priority of parental decision making for their infants and young children even after death.'[28] The Scottish group rejected arguments for requiring parental authorization based on the best interests of children, property, or possession, and 'turned, therefore, to an analysis of the family unit and in particular to the obligations and powers which flow from the notion of parenting itself'.[29] In stating their view of family bonds, the Scottish group echoed enquiries in England set up following scandals in the UK, notably at Alder Hey Royal Liverpool Children's Hospital in 1999.[30]

I think the parental bond argument has not been made out, and I shall raise some problems for it, but I do not mean to justify the practices at Alder Hey, which were bizarre as well as repugnant (and did not involve transplantation). The strength of the parental bond is the basis for only one reason for parental decision-making and there are other reasons. That said, I admit that I find it hard to see what other reasons there are, besides avoiding distress. I must also admit that I share the intuitive view that the parents of young children generally ought to decide whether to donate their organs if they die even though I find this view hard to justify.

What is it about the parental bond that supposedly justifies parental decision-making? Consider Edgar Page's argument from the value of parenthood and Ferdinand Schoeman's argument from intimacy, which the Scottish report cited in support of its view, although neither considered parental rights over the bodies of their dead children.[31] Page argues that parents want to shape their children's lives, to fix their basic values and broad attitudes, to lay the foundations of their lifestyles. Parental rights to consent to medical treatment, determine a child's religion, and so

---

[26] Robert Nozick, *The Examined Life* (New York: Simon and Schuster, 1989), p. 28.

[27] Chapter 7 elaborates this claim.

[28] Independent Review Group on the Retention of Organs at Post-Mortem, *Final Report* 2001, recommendation 4 available at <http://www.sehd.scot.nhs.uk/scotorgrev/Final%20Report/ropm.pdf> (last accessed 8 August 2009).

[29] Ibid., section 1, par. 15.

[30] *The Royal Liverpool Children's Inquiry Report* (London: The Stationery Office, 2001). The hospital had 2,500 pots containing the tissue of dead children, taken at post-mortems often not only without proper consent from parents but sometimes with deceit.

[31] Edgar Page, 'Parental Rights' *Journal of Applied Philosophy* 1 (1984). Ferdinand Schoeman, 'Rights of Children, Rights of Parents, and the Moral Basis of the Family' *Ethics* 91 (1980). Scottish Independent Review Group, Section 1, Par 15.

forth serve parents' interest in shaping their children. But he argues that the parents' interest alone is not enough to justify parental rights. Parental rights must define a valuable practice of parenthood. Schoeman argues that rights of parenthood are justified by the contribution they make to intimacy in relationships. If the state tried to regulate families, it would drive out inner commitment, undermine trust, and deny parties the space they need to construct their own relationships. The challenge is to explain how a view about relationships between the living applies once one of the parties is dead.

Page bases parental rights on an interest in shaping children's lives. But this interest is not affected by the use of dead children's bodies because the use is not an aspect of their lives, not even metaphorically speaking. In this respect, small children differ from older children and adults. In thinking of how older people's lives went, we should take into account the manner of their deaths and what subsequently happens to their bodies, and, in a metaphorical sense, we could think of the use of their corpses as an aspect of their lives. But this is just a variant of the idea of posthumous interests. Young children cannot have posthumous interests and using their dead bodies is not an aspect of their lives. So the interest in shaping young children's lives does not apply after they die. Still less does Schoeman's idea of intimacy apply after death. There cannot be intimacy between the living and the dead because the dead have no selves to share.

So far, I have asked about how and why the parental bond gives a reason for parents deciding about organ donation. I do not think any clear reason has been given. The most obvious way in which the bond between parents and children is relevant is to think how parents would feel if their wishes about their dead child were ignored or overridden. But this is the argument from distress again, and the parental bond argument was supposed to provide an extra reason.

If such a reason existed, its weight would be in question too. To test its weight, assume that parents would not donate organs so we can see whether the parental bond outweighs the needs of sick children and their families. Why would respecting the bond outweigh meeting the needs of sick children for organs? If the parental bond is so important, what about the bond between the sick children and their parents? Some of the children would die without an organ, which is not only very bad in itself, but also bad for their parents. Indeed, how do parental bonds function as reasons for third parties? Having a bond affects the parents' reasons. It is a socially valuable bond, so it would also be in some way a reason for the state and other third parties. But the parents of the dead child whose organs could be used are not the only parents there are. Why should this bond be protected by a right when the bonds of other parents are not (until their children die, when they too would have a right to decide how to dispose of them)? I do not say these questions could not be answered. But they have not been.[32]

---

[32] Does it matter how strong the bond is? Not all parents have strong bonds with their young children. And what if parents disagree with each other? These are hard questions which I shall not pursue.

The family bond argument is at its most persuasive in the case of parents and young children. It is unpersuasive when it comes to other family bonds.[33] Let us not be sentimental about families. An old joke in intensive care units has it that 'Where there's a will, there's a relative'.[34] Some families are motivated by 'guilt from previous events' or swayed by the 'prodigal son coming from far away'.[35] Families are not monolithic. Some members may wish to donate their relative's organs and others object. What then would respect for family bonds require? Some jurisdictions try to resolve conflict with a legal pecking order of decision-making,[36] trying to impose legal order on family chaos. Why should the hated spouse take priority over the same-sex lover, or even a close friend? But without a pecking order, the most vociferous—especially those most vociferously opposed to donation— may get their way.

Many families are close and many families are not. If the accident of birth was unaccompanied by any closeness, trust, or love, it is hard to see why it should confer decision-making authority. When family bonds are strong, it is easier to see that the family's wishes are important. But perhaps the family's wishes are important because the deceased cared about the bond, and the reason to respect the bond is because it is what the deceased would have wanted. In other words, either the bond was not close, in which case it is no reason for relatives to decide, or else it was, in which case the reason to decide follows from the interests of the deceased. The family bond is not then a reason in its own right for the family to decide.

As with the argument about parental bonds, the question arises why family bonds are reasons for third parties and what reasons they are. One can see how the bonds of family are reasons for family members and, in the context of organ donation, perhaps they ought to think about their relatives' feelings. But the state and medical staff are third parties. If family bonds are important, why should they give priority to the bonds of the family before them, and not the family bonds of people who need organs? This is another unanswered challenge to those who would defend family decision-making.

Religious and cultural disagreement

Some families have religious or cultural beliefs that lead them to oppose the retrieval of their relative's organs. Chapter 4 discussed such beliefs in the context of deciding about one's own body. It said neither the truth of the beliefs nor a right of religious freedom is a sound basis for rights to control what happens to one's own body. Still less does the truth of the beliefs or religious freedom justify the family's having control over someone else's body. Recall the religious outsider who would be outraged if a family consented to the retrieval of organs. The outsider's religious

---

[33] The Scottish inquiry said that priority over their families' wishes should be given to the wishes of adults and mature children. Scottish Independent Review Group, p. 16.

[34] Daniel Sperling's case of the family that pocketed the money left to pay for the burial is one of many to make this point. Sperling, *Posthumous Interests*, p. 173.

[35] Streat, 'When Do We Stop?', p. 230.

[36] Including the UK and New Zealand, in their new Human Tissue Acts.

freedom would not be interfered with if retrieval proceeds because the right of religious freedom does not give the right to control bodies.[37]

What about cultural sensitivity? New Zealand's Ministry of Health may have had this in mind when it pointed out that New Zealand is culturally diverse and different groups will have different responses to organ and tissue donation.[38] Characteristically for government documents, it failed to draw any substantive conclusions from these claims but it may be said—and is in other contexts[39]— that not all cultures are as individualistic or materialistic as the mainstream Western tradition, that the individual's wishes do not override the family's in some cultures, and that it would be inappropriately culturally insensitive to insist that they do.[40]

It is not worth spending much time on the cultural sensitivity argument, but let me make a few comments. It is unclear how individualistic or materialistic Western culture is in the matter of organ and tissue donation, since it is commonplace to allow the family to override the individual. So the argument may be wrong about cultures. Moreover, the argument potentially undercuts an individual right of veto (one found in the law of very many countries, whether Western or not) where cultures do not regard the deceased's wishes as decisive. Is dispensing with the right of veto the desired conclusion of the argument? How is cultural sensitivity to be applied in a diverse society? If someone from an 'individualistic' culture marries someone from a 'collectivist' culture, whose cultural view should prevail if one of them dies? Why does cultural sensitivity matter anyway? The only persuasive argument I know is to avoid giving offence, an obviously limited consideration.[41] Essentially, its force is in avoiding making things worse for the family at a terrible time, something we have already discussed in the sections on distress.

Let us see where we are up to. Families should decide on organ donation either because the deceased wanted them to decide or because the family know what the deceased had wanted. The trouble is that we often do not know whether the deceased did want their families to decide and that families are unlikely to be very accurate at reporting the deceased's wishes. Families should also in some cases decide so as to spare them extra distress, although what those cases are depends on whether their deciding would reduce their distress and what would be lost if they did decide. Those are the two main reasons for the family to have decision-making

---

[37] S. McGuiness and M. Brazier, 'Respecting the Living Means Respecting the Dead Too' *Oxford Journal of Legal Studies* 28 (2008), p. 311, argue that the religious freedom of the family rules out conscription, but they do not consider conflict within the family so they avoid having to face up to cases where the family's alleged right of religious freedom is tested when it conflicts with the right of bodily control.

[38] New Zealand Ministry of Health, *Review of the Regulation of Human Tissue and Tissue-Based Therapies: Discussion Document* (Wellington: Ministry of Health, 2004), p. 4. See also the Australian National Health and Medical Research Council, *Donating Organs After Death: Ethical Issues* (Commonwealth of Australia, 1997), p. 1.

[39] H. M. Chan, 'Sharing Death and Dying: Advance Directives, Autonomy and the Family' *Bioethics* 18 (2004).

[40] Boddington sympathizes with this argument in 'Organ Donation After Death: Should I Decide, or Should My Family?', pp. 77–9.

[41] T. M. Wilkinson, 'Individualism and the Ethics of Research on Humans' *HEC Forum* 16 (2004), pp. 12–13.

authority. The third is that, if families' decisions were overridden, bad social consequences would follow. The argument is found in discussion of the family veto, which I now consider.

THE FAMILY VETO

In most countries, doctors will not take organs from a dead person whose relatives object. In so-called opt in countries such as the US, UK, and New Zealand, doctors refuse organs not only from people who never stated a view but even from people who explicitly consented, if their relatives object.[42] In opt out countries such as France, where organs may legally be taken unless the deceased explicitly refused, families are still given the power by doctors to veto retrieval. Even Spain, the most successful country in terms of retrieval of organs from the dead, gives the family the power to veto retrieval.[43] The power of veto is a medical, not a legal, creation. In many of these countries, the law does not require family consent before retrieval, at least in cases where the deceased has consented. Rather, doctors will not exercise their legal power to retrieve organs when the family object. Japan and Singapore are outliers. Japan is unusual in legally requiring not only the consent of the deceased but also the consent of the family.[44] Singapore is unusual because it not only has a law permitting retrieval when the deceased did not object, it has enforced the law against the wishes of the family, as we shall see.[45]

Critics of the family veto seem to have a mental picture of a dead person who adamantly wanted to donate, but whose disliked curmudgeonly distant relative protests about donation and ensures it is blocked. The critics think donation is nothing to do with the curmudgeon and giving relatives the veto interferes with people's claims over their own bodies and wastes organs. In fact, the curmudgeonly relative picture is overdrawn. The family veto in practice often cannot be taken as either an infringement of the deceased's claims or a waste of organs. Let me explain.

In many jurisdictions, an agreement to donate cannot be interpreted as an adamant wish to donate regardless of the effect on the family. To take one example, the typical indication in New Zealand of a desire to donate is a tick in a box on a driving licence application, which hardly constitutes either informed consent or

---

[42] The legislation of some 41 states in the US requires that individual consent to donation not be overridden by families, but in practice doctors still let families override. See Ashley Christmas et al., 'Organ Donation: Family Members NOT Honoring Patient Wishes' *The Journal of Trauma* 65 (2008), p. 1096.

[43] Lisa Hitchen quotes Rafael Matesanz, director of the National Transplant Organization of Spain: 'The families are always approached. They always have the last decision[.]' See her 'No Evidence that Presumed Consent Increases Organ Donation' *British Medical Journal* 337 (2008), 1614.

[44] See Alireza Bagheri, 'Criticism of "Brain Death" Policy in Japan' *Kennedy Institute of Ethics Journal* 13 (2003).

[45] Austria is also asserted to be a country that overrides a family's refusal to donate. According to McCunn et al., 'only the patient him- or herself can refuse'. See M. McCunn et al., 'Impact of Culture and Policy on Organ Donation: A Comparison between Two Urban Trauma Centers in Developed Nations' *The Journal of Trauma: Injury, Infection, and Critical Care* 54 (2003), p. 998.

evidence of a desire to donate no matter how upset one's family would be as a result. Ticking a box while waiting to acquire a licence is a casual affair for the many people who are not seriously contemplating sudden and early deaths. They do not know about the steps likely to be taken, such as the injection of hormones to ready their bodies for retrieval, and they do not think about the effects on their families.[46] Indeed, actually existing opt in schemes may well be thought to fall short of valid informed consent, unless we take a very relaxed view of validity. (Although it might then be said that these countries should have a better way of informing and recording wishes.) Nor is there good reason to think families usually override their relatives' wishes when they know them.[47] The family power of veto probably does not, in practice, amount to disrespect for the wishes of the dead and nor would it waste organs on a large scale.

While existing opt in schemes do not solicit clear informed consent, suppose a system were mooted where people could give informed consent to the retrieval of their organs while understanding that their families would not be able to override them. Such a system could not be objected to on grounds of the claims of the dead, but it is often argued that such a system may well have net bad effects, notably on the supply of organs. On this argument, the family should always have a veto.

Transplanters argue that the bad publicity that would inevitably follow overriding the family would cause a drop in supply.[48] Here is one common explanation of this claim. Some people fear that, if they became seriously ill, they would not receive thorough treatment if they had agreed to be donors, because doctors want their organs.[49] This fear—which is not well-founded, but need not be to have an effect—would increase if families were known to be overridden. People look to their families to protect them when they cannot protect themselves. Publicly overriding families would make people feel more vulnerable to doctors skimping on their treatment. They would be more reluctant to donate, and more likely to opt out when this is possible.

---

[46] Stephen Streat, 'Moral Assumptions and the Process of Organ Donation in the Intensive Care Unit' *Critical Care* 8 (2004).

[47] However, Christmas et al., 'Organ Donation: Family Members NOT Honoring Patient Wishes', found five of 25 families of registered donors vetoed retrieval. Siminoff and Lawrence's study, reported in their 'Knowing Patients' Preferences about Organ Donation', found that 10 per cent of families who thought the deceased wanted to donate nonetheless refused donation. But we do not know, in these cases, whether the deceased wanted to donate if that meant overriding their families.

[48] Stephen Munn, head of New Zealand's liver transplant unit, says (with some hyperbole), 'If we ever removed the organs against the family's wish that would be the last set of organs we would ever get.' See the quotation in Jenny Chamberlain, 'To Give or Not to Give?' *North and South* (March 2004), p. 36. Similar ideas are expressed by the Organ Donation Taskforce, *The Potential Impact of an Opt Out System for Organ Donation in the UK*. See also Michael Volk and Peter Ubel, 'The Impracticality of Overriding Family Rejection of Donation' *Transplantation* 86 (2008), pp. 1631–2.

[49] Laura A. Siminoff and Mary Beth Mercer, 'Public Policy, Public Opinion, and Consent for Organ Donation' *Cambridge Quarterly of Healthcare Ethics* 10 (2001), p. 384. The authors found in the US study that 51.9 per cent of non-white donor families expressed this fear, compared with only 20.8 per cent of white donor families. The Organ Donation Taskforce reported on deliberative events in the UK where this fear was expressed. See Organ Donation Taskforce, *The Potential Impact of an Opt Out System for Organ Donation in the UK*, p. 17.

While the common explanation is plausible, is there any evidence that overriding families would cause a drop in the supply of organs or have other bad effects? The argument about fewer organs has usually relied on proxy evidence, for instance about the effects of other scandals on willingness to donate.[50] Families are usually not overridden, so one cannot point directly to the bad effects of doing so. However, a case in Singapore in 2007 makes a number of points on behalf of the family veto. A man declared brain-dead was due to have his organs removed in accordance with Singapore's presumed consent law. As one news report put it,

> Sim's family had no objection to his organs being used for transplants but wanted doctors to wait one more day before turning off the life support machine. But as Sim's 68-year-old mother and about 20 other relatives knelt weeping before the doctors, begging them to wait, nine police officers entered the ward and restrained the distraught family while Sim's body was quickly whisked away. 'The hospital staff were running as they wheeled him out of the back door of the room. They were behaving like robbers,' said Sim Chew Hiah, one of Sim's elder sisters.[51]

After the case became public, people rushed for forms to opt out of donation.[52] In the face of a case like this, it becomes entirely understandable why doctors would not want to override the family. It would reduce the supply of organs and give medical care a poor name, itself likely to be bad for patients.

The argument about the effects of bad publicity makes some presuppositions. It presupposes that rigid conscription would be either wrong or infeasible. Under rigid conscription, nobody could opt out, so the bad publicity from overriding the family should not make much difference to supply. The publicity argument also presupposes that public fears cannot be successfully allayed without a family veto. If people realized that agreeing to donate had no effect on treatment, they need not react with fear if families are overridden. Still, the presuppositions are probably correct. Conscription without an opt out is probably infeasible and, as chapter 7 will argue, hard to defend, and attempts to allay fears have not succeeded so far. The argument that overriding the family would cause a fall in the supply of organs is probably correct.

Although the threat of a fall in the supply of organs is a powerful argument for the family veto, the conclusion is limited. It may be a bad idea to override the family because of the effect on supply, but it does not follow that families should be asked to give informed consent or even be asked at all for their views. The argument is about avoiding bad publicity, which may require not overriding the family but

---

[50] A 1992 French case is often cited. A 19-year-old's corneas were taken (legally) under a form of presumed consent law, causing hostile media coverage and damaging trust in organ donation. See Organ Donation Taskforce, *The Potential Impact of an Opt Out System for Organ Donation in the UK*, p. 23.

[51] Koh Gui Qing, 'Scuffle for Organs Sparks Donor Debate in Singapore' Reuters, 28 February 2007.

[52] Tan Hui Leng, 'More Seek Organ Donation Opt-Out Forms after Hospital Scuffle', TodayOnline (28 February 2007). The long-run effects on the organ supply are not known.

may also require nothing more. The argument does not show that families have a right to decide.

A remaining question is whether the deceased have claims that would be infringed upon if their families are given the power to veto their express consent to donate. Posthumous personal sovereignty does include a right to veto the use of one's body and the family should not have the power to donate the individual's organs against that person's wishes. But even a personal sovereignty right would not straightforwardly rule out a family veto on the individual's wish to donate. Whether it would depends on the source of the family's power. This is perhaps a surprising conclusion, and here is how it is reached.

Imagine initially there are only would-be donors, their families, and potential recipients. Personal sovereignty includes a right for the individual to offer organs for retrieval after death. But this is a right to make an offer; it is not a right to have the offer accepted. Clearly a potential recipient may turn the offer down. If, however, someone has a right to offer and someone else has a right to accept, it would infringe on both their rights if they were prevented from making this transaction. Thus giving the family a direct right in legislation to veto the transaction would infringe on the deceased's right. But it would not infringe on the deceased's right if the potential recipient—who has the right to refuse—were to accept, but only on condition that the family also consented. The family would then have acquired the power of veto without infringing on the right of the deceased. This is why, from the point of view of posthumous personal sovereignty, it matters how the family comes by the power of veto. A parallel might make the point clearer. I have a right to offer to marry someone, but not the right to have the offer accepted by anyone (no one has a duty to accept). If the state requires parental consent before the marriage of adult children, this would infringe on my right and the rights of potential spouses. If, however, my potential spouse insisted on parental consent before marriage, she would not infringe on my right. She would simply be conditionally exercising her right to refuse.

Let us now add the medical staff needed to perform the transplant to the would-be donor, family, and potential recipient. If medical staff also have the right to accept or refuse the offer from the deceased, similar conclusions follow. If medical staff make acceptance of the deceased's offer conditional on the family's consent, the family acquires a power of veto in a way that does not infringe on the personal sovereignty of the deceased. As it happens, I do not think that medical staff quite have the *right* to accept or refuse. The scope of their legitimate power is better thought of in terms of the authority they need to carry out their duties, including a duty to manage the transplant process. It surely is part of their legitimate authority to turn down the offer of an organ out of a justified fear of bad publicity and a consequent fall in the supply of organs. It is less clear that medical staff should have the authority to give the family a veto out of a misguided belief that the families' interests deserve it. But since the organ supply reason is probably a good one, I need not say more about a medically created veto.

CONCLUSION

In practice, families have the power to veto retrieval, even from dead relatives who have consented, and the power to consent in the common cases where the deceased did not dissent. These powers cannot be justified by the claims of the family in their own right. The power to veto the deceased's consent relies for its justification on the empirical claim that, without it, the supply of organs would fall. The empirical claim is probably true, but it does not justify a right to decide with its associated requirement of informed choice. Giving the family the power to donate or with-hold organs where the deceased neither consented nor dissented can only be justified if it gives best effect to the deceased's claims. It would if the deceased wanted the family to decide, for which we do not have strong evidence, or if families were accurate at stating the deceased's wishes, which they seem not to be.

In this chapter, I have avoided discussing the implications of missing consent or uncertainty about the deceased's wishes. The next chapter considers these implica-tions in the context of a choice between opt in and opt out systems of organ retrieval.

6

Consent and Uncertainty about the Wishes of the Dead

The preceding chapters have been concerned with the importance of the wishes of the dead and what to do when they are known to conflict with the wishes of their families. However, the sense among many involved in the practice of organ donation is that the wishes of the dead are usually not known. As is often said, people do not like to think of their deaths, still less the premature demise typical of organ donors, and their relatives often feel at a loss when they are asked to donate. On the assumption that the interests of the dead should count for at least something, the cases where their wishes are unknown pose something of a problem. What ought we to do with dead people's bodies when we do not know what they wanted?

This chapter defends a policy under which organs may be taken where (1) there is no good reason to think the deceased would have objected and (2) the family do not object. This policy is within a family of policies sometimes called 'opt out' or 'presumed consent'. But let me say the following immediately: the debates about opt out and presumed consent are usually a tissue of confusion and error and it is very important not to be put off (or attracted) by the labels. What I shall be arguing for differs little from practice in most countries, including those, such as the US, UK, the Netherlands, Australia, and New Zealand, that take themselves to be opt in countries. In fact, the discussion of presumed consent and related ideas tends to be so misleading I shall postpone my own discussion until the second part of the chapter. That is where I shall substantiate my remarks about confusion and error, as well as say more constructive things about the effects of an opt out system on the organ supply, the ethics of an opt out system, and the ethics of the currently fashionable idea of 'framing' requests to the family in such a way as to make them more likely to donate. For now, focus on this question: How should we respect the wishes of the dead when we are uncertain what those wishes were? The first part of the chapter tries to answer this question without getting tangled in preconceptions about presumed consent and opting in or out.

UNCERTAINTY AND THE CLAIMS OF THE DEAD

This first part begins with the suggestion that uncertainty about dead people's wishes does not matter because their organs should not be taken without their consent and whether they consented will usually be knowable. I argue that the deceased's consent is not required by respect for their interests. Respecting their interests instead requires doing what they wanted. We may, however, not know what they wanted, perhaps because the dead never had a determinate wish to be known or perhaps because their determinate wishes were not communicated to those deciding on organ retrieval. When we do not know what they wanted, we should follow the best guess about their wishes, which might be for or against taking their organs.[1] I discuss and reject the claim that taking the organs of a person who opposed it is morally worse than failing to take the organs of a person who wanted to donate. This first part of the chapter concludes with a reason to take organs based on the interests of potential recipients.

Is consent necessary?

If we want to respect the wishes of the dead, not knowing what they wanted is clearly a problem. But the problem could be bypassed if the deceased's consent were required before their organs may be taken. Assuming consent is a public act of will, such as entering a register, other people will generally know or could easily find out whether the deceased had consented. If they had consented, it would do them no wrong to take their organs. If they had not consented, they would be wronged if their organs were taken. Either way, no one need guess what they did or might have wanted.

Requiring consent would help avoid enquiring into what the deceased wanted only if consenting and wanting are distinct. Many, although not all, writers believe they are distinct. Even if you want an injection and your doctor knows you want it, the doctor may not simply stab you with the needle when your back is turned. She must get your consent first. Even if a surgeon knows you want to be sterilized, the surgeon may not simply sterilize you during an operation for something else. Again, she must get your consent first. One lesson from these examples is that wanting is not consenting. Wanting is a state of mind whereas consent is a public act. Another lesson is that mere wanting does not license invading the body in the way consent does. People have a right to control what happens to their bodies, and consenting exercises control in a way that wanting does not. Consenting, but not mere wanting, removes the duties when consent waives the right of bodily control.[2] Waiving by consenting does not mean that consent must be formal, still less written. As we shall see later in the chapter, even doing or saying nothing can be genuine tacit consent in the right circumstances. Nonetheless, wanting is not consent and does not have the force of consent.

Much more would have to be said to show that, as I believe, wanting is distinct from consenting. However, I can be brief here because I need not insist that

---

[1] Wishes might be more nuanced—'yes' to kidneys, 'no' to heart for instance. The arguments of this chapter can be straightforwardly applied to this complication: when people would not want their hearts taken but would want their kidneys taken, take the kidneys but not the hearts.

[2] Alan Wertheimer, *Consent to Sexual Relations* (Cambridge: Cambridge University Press, 2003), pp. 144–52; Judith Jarvis Thomson, *The Realm of Rights* (Cambridge, MA: Harvard University Press, 1990), pp. 348–50; Allen Buchanan and Dan Brock, *Deciding for Others* (Cambridge: Cambridge University Press, 1990), pp. 115–17.

they are distinct. I shall argue that taking organs after death does not directly infringe upon the rights of people who did not consent but did want to donate, even though wanting is not consenting. If wanting is consenting, we get to the same conclusion, that taking from those who wanted to donate would not infringe on their rights.

Assuming that consent is distinct from wanting, to require the deceased's consent before retrieval would be a radical step. As the chapter later explains, very few countries require the deceased's consent, family consent generally sufficing when the deceased did not dissent. It is just as well, from the point of view of acquiring organs, that the consent of the deceased is not required. Many people die without giving anything that amounts to consent, let alone informed consent,[3] so requiring their consent would likely make available only relatively few organs.

However, perhaps existing practice is wrong and the deceased's consent should be required before retrieval. When the deceased consent, they waive some right or claim over their own bodies and, as the previous chapter showed, the family does not have the same right. We should not thoughtlessly assume that, when the deceased's consent is missing, the family's consent will do instead. Although in the end I disagree with it, I think we should take seriously the view that when the deceased's consent is missing, their organs should not be taken. One argument for the view says that the rights of the dead directly require consent; another—more plausible—argument says that, although not directly required, requiring consent is the best way to protect those rights.

Is consent directly required by our right to control our own bodies? On one argument, we have a negative right against invasions of our bodies and we must consent before others are permitted to invade. Because the right is important, infringing is usually wrong. The right is a barrier to permissible invasion which can only be lifted by consent.[4] E.-H. Kluge is one writer who appears to endorse the direct consent requirement. He writes, 'the very concept of presumed consent is fundamentally misguided: It undermines the principle that unless we have given explicit consent to interference with our person, our body remains inviolate.'[5]

To test whether consent is directly required by a right of bodily control, and to make sure we are not misled by worries about whether we really know what people wanted, assume we do know people wanted to donate. Requiring consent would rule out organ retrieval from people who are known to have wanted to donate organs but who did not consent, a conclusion many will find implausible. Requiring consent is even more implausible in the different situation of treating temporarily incompetent people in an emergency.[6] Consider a common case: an

---

[3] Stephen Streat, 'Moral Assumptions and the Process of Organ Donation in the Intensive Care Unit' *Critical Care* 8 (2004).

[4] An interpretation I owe to Govert den Hartogh from correspondence and from unpublished work he generously shared.

[5] E.-H. Kluge, 'Improving Organ Retrieval Rates: Various Proposals and their Ethical Validity' *Health Care Analysis* 8 (2000), p. 286.

[6] See also Michael Gill, 'Presumed Consent, Autonomy, and Organ Donation' *Journal of Medicine and Philosophy* 29 (2004), pp. 49–51.

unconscious patient is brought to the emergency department with a head injury, is treated, makes a full recovery, and is grateful and pleased. Although she did not in fact consent in advance, she would have agreed if she had been asked and she retrospectively endorses her treatment. It is hard to believe that she has had a right infringed upon, even justifiably infringed upon, just because she did not consent. In other cases where people's rights are justifiably infringed upon, they leave 'traces'. We feel they should be compensated, or at least receive an apology.[7] I doubt anyone—including the rightholder—would think that compensation or an apology are owed in the common emergency case; so we have some reason not to see this as a case where a right is infringed upon.

What if we said that the unconscious patient's right was infringed upon because she had not lifted the barrier to bodily invasion before she was treated? Then we would have to say that the absence of her consent was the equivalent of her dissent. Assuming people have a right to refuse treatment, the absence of consent would thus make treatment wrong. That is to say it would be wrong to treat an unconscious patient who would have wanted to be treated just because she had not consented. This conclusion is absurd. But if a living person's rights do not directly require consent before invasion, why would a dead person's?[8]

A rule requiring prior consent may, however, be indirectly justified. We may say, to those who would take a dead person's organs, 'you should have asked before', and perhaps we should be suspicious if they have not. Perhaps more should be done than often is to inform and seek people's views.[9] A rule requiring consent could protect against deliberate or careless sidelining of the deceased's wishes or it could be fairer than not requiring consent, if it were reasonable to place the burden of getting agreement on people who want to take and use the organs.[10] In sum, even if not directly required by rights, consent could be indirectly required as the best or fairest way of protecting the deceased's interests. However, protecting rights imposes costs which need to be taken into account when deciding the level of protection. It is clearly out of the question to make maximal efforts to inform and discover each person's view about every use after death when we realize that maximal efforts might require armies of trained counsellors to visit everybody. Moreover, the costs of requiring consent do not fall only on those who would benefit from the organs. They also fall on those who would want to donate. A rule requiring prior consent may in some cases be justified, but only when the costs have

---

[7] Judith Jarvis Thomson, *Rights, Restitution, and Risk* (Cambridge, MA: Harvard University Press, 1986), ch. 4.

[8] I give a fuller discussion of the parallel between the unconscious patient and the non-consenting dead in my 'Consent and the Use of the Bodies of the Dead' *Journal of Medicine and Philosophy* (forthcoming).

[9] F. M. Kamm claims that deliberately not making efforts to ask people before they die and relying on their families to consent is a way of circumventing their wishes. See *Morality, Mortality*, vol .1 (New York: Oxford University Press 1993), pp. 212, 214. But how much effort should go into asking people before they die?

[10] Marie-Andrée Jacob, 'Another Look at the Presumed-Versus-Informed Consent Dichotomy in Postmortem Organ Procurement' *Bioethics* 20 (2006).

been properly accounted for.[11] I leave it open, until the second part of the chapter, whether a prior consent rule would be justified in the case of organ retrieval.[12]

The interests and wishes of the dead

Obviously, the dead are not now competent to make decisions for themselves. It is other, living, people who have to decide for them, including whether to take their organs. Organ removal is, however, somewhat different from other cases of decision-making for the incompetent. People who are dead no longer need their organs as organs. The category of what is sometimes called their biological self-interest is empty. Unlike cases where a once-competent person's wishes about her treatment conflict with her biological self-interest, as in the hackneyed case of an unconscious Jehovah's Witness who gave instructions against a blood transfusion, no such conflict is possible in the case of taking organs from the dead. Insofar as it is dead people's interests we should be concerned with in deciding whether to take their organs, and because biological self-interest is irrelevant, their wishes should be decisive.

Some people will have either consented or dissented. Of those who have done neither, some people will have wanted to donate and others will have wanted not to donate. Some other people will not have had wishes about donation but will have had clear enough beliefs and desires to imply that, if they had thought about it, they would have either wanted or wanted not to donate. We could, for instance, reasonably infer that a person would want her organs not to be taken if she wanted to be buried intact and distrusted modern medicine. But in some cases, it will be impossible to do what the dead wanted either because they had had no wishes to be known or because their wishes are incoherent. Consider trying to follow the wishes of someone who wanted to help others but who loathed modern medicine. We could not say what a person with such wishes wanted because the wishes pull in opposing directions.

Cases of consent or dissent are easy. Taking organs from those who consented does not infringe on their rights; taking organs from those who dissented does infringe on their rights. In cases without consent or dissent, it seems reasonable to say that taking the organs from someone who is known to want to donate does not infringe on her right. After all, the right does not directly require consent and, as her interests are determined by her wishes, it is in her interests to donate.

What of people who had no desires but whose desire can be inferred? If it is agreed that taking organs does not infringe on the rights of people who wanted to donate, then it seems a natural step to say that taking organs does not infringe on the rights of people who would have wanted to donate. A similar conclusion is commonly accepted in other cases of deciding for the incompetent, for instance in

---

[11]   What if not enough is done to seek prior consent, however 'enough' is reckoned? Would it always be wrong to take organs from any dead person in countries which do not ask properly or keep an adequate register? A really dedicated defender of consent may say so, but I doubt the view would be widely shared.

[12]   The considerations mentioned in this paragraph are relevant to other topics such as taking sperm from the dead or dying for posthumous reproduction or doing research on the dead or incompetent. See my 'Consent and the Use of the Bodies of the Dead'.

various doctrines of substituted judgement. Leaving aside practical questions about how the inferring should be done, how reliable it has to be, and who is supposed to do it, we can say that, in principle, taking dead people's organs does not infringe on their rights when they did want or would have wanted to donate.

Although consent may not be required, it is not open season for taking the organs of everybody who did not actually dissent. If taking organs does not infringe on a right when and because the deceased wanted to donate, surely taking organs would infringe upon their rights when and because the deceased wanted *not* to donate. And if we may treat those who would have wanted to donate the same as people who actually wanted to donate, then we should also treat those who would have wanted *not* to donate the same as those who actually wanted not to donate. Taking organs from those who are known to have wanted not to donate or those whose desire not to donate may be inferred would infringe on their rights. Thus I am not arguing that the absence of dissent should be treated like consent.

We are left with those who are known to have no actual or inferable wishes about their organs. If one accepts that dead people's interests for or against their organs being taken are determined by their wishes, they do not have an interest for or against. Decisions about whether to take their organs have to be based on criteria other than their interests.

Uncertainty

In some cases, no one knows what the dead wanted because they had no, or no coherent, wishes. The not knowing is not due to a lack of information; rather, there is nothing to be known. But in other cases, the deceased's wishes are not known because of a lack of information, perhaps because they were not disclosed or because no one knew the deceased very well. Here it is possible to go against the interests of the dead. In these cases, so this section claims, decision-makers ought to follow the best guess about what the dead people wanted.

A best guess will be partly based on evidence about whether the deceased would have wanted to donate. Opinion poll data about popular support for organ donation is sometimes cited as evidence. If opinion polls show that 70 per cent of the general population are willing to be organ donors, and we had no information about a dead person other than that she was a member of the general population, then we are somewhat more likely to follow her wishes if we take her organs. If 70 per cent oppose donation, we are somewhat more likely to follow her wishes if we do not take her organs. It must be said, though, that a guess based on the actual polls that have been carried out could well be criticized on the basis of doubts about the questions asked, the value of the opinion poll methods, and the statistical accuracy of drawing inferences about individuals from general population data.[13] General population

[13] For such criticisms, see among others Streat, 'Moral Assumptions and the Process of Organ Donation in the Intensive Care Unit'; M. D. D. Bell, 'The UK Human Tissue Act and Consent: Surrendering a Fundamental Principle to Transplantation Needs?' *Journal of Medical Ethics* 32 (2006), p. 284; Gill, 'Presumed Consent, Autonomy, and Organ Donation', p. 40.

data is just that: a generalization. We might have grounds for being more specific, for instance with population subsets such as Maori in New Zealand or Muslims in Singapore who are often thought to be more reluctant to donate than the general population. It is, however, the family who would typically provide much more individualized data about what a specific dead person had thought.[14]

Evidence about whether the deceased would have wanted to donate is only one consideration in trying to follow their wishes. We should also consider how bad it would be for them if we were to make mistakes. The underlying idea is familiar in writings about decision-making under risk and uncertainty. Suppose, as an example, 51 per cent of the population support donation, but only have a mild preference for it. Suppose 49 per cent are vehemently opposed. With no further information, we are more likely to do what a given dead person wanted if we take her organs; but still we should not, given the intensity of preference and associated cost of error.

The best guess about a person's wishes need not be reliable or well-informed— just better than the alternatives. It is obviously possible and indeed likely that if best guesses are followed, mistakes will be made. Some people who would have opposed donation would have their organs taken and some people who wanted to donate would have their organs not taken. Many critics of opt out schemes think taking organs from someone who opposed donation is worse than failing to take from someone who wanted to donate. If they were right, this would be an argument against following the best guess—but, I shall claim, they are not right.

No safe side to err on

When it is not known what the dead had wanted, errors are inevitable. The focus in this section is the claim that taking organs in error is in itself worse. There is no good reason to think so, as we see when we explore its possible justifications.[15]

Let us take first the idea of posthumous autonomy. On one mainstream view of autonomy, people should be able to decide what happens to their bodies after they die because this decision is within their sphere of decision-making. This view does not support the conclusion that mistaken taking is worse than mistaken not taking. If others fail to follow people's wishes about their bodies, they could be taken to infringe on autonomy, but mistakenly not taking fails to follow wishes just as much as mistaken taking.[16] Clearly, given particular preferences, it could be worse for one dead person to

---

[14] Chapter 5 discussed the idea that the family should be asked so as to follow the deceased's wishes.

[15] Gill, 'Presumed Consent, Autonomy, and Organ Donation', pp. 44f. also argues that errors on either side are symmetrical. Part of his ingenious argument is that the body must be interfered with anyway, since it cannot be left where it is, so one cannot reject retrieval of organs on the grounds that it constitutes interference. This argument is not persuasive as it stands. There might be degrees of interference, and retrieval of organs could be more interfering than disposing of the body. Moreover, there are reasons of hygiene for the safe disposal of bodies that might justify interference to prevent a dead body threatening others, and these reasons do not apply to organ retrieval.

[16] James S. Taylor argues that respect for posthumous autonomy cannot require successfully following the deceased's wishes but must instead involve following a fallible procedure. See his 'Personal Autonomy, Posthumous Harm, and Presumed Consent Policies for Organ Procurement'

have organs taken against her wishes than it would be for another to have them not taken when she wanted to donate. But contingent particular preferences do not give a general reason why mistaken taking is worse than mistaken not taking.

The strongest argument I know for thinking mistaken taking to be especially bad is based on a view of our right to bodily integrity. Responding to opinion poll evidence that 70 per cent of the population want to donate, Robert Veatch and Jonathan Pitt write, 'In a society that affirms the right of the individual not to have his or her body invaded without appropriate consent, procuring organs on the basis of a presumption of consent will violate that right at least 30 percent of the time.'[17] Taking organs from a body is an invasion of it, so to take organs from a dead person who has not consented is to infringe on her right against invasion. However, not taking does not infringe on the right since no invasion occurs. Mistaken taking infringes on a right; mistaken not-taking does not. Hence, the argument concludes, mistaken taking is morally worse.

Like Veatch and Pitt, I accept we have a right against invasion, for the reasons given in chapter 4. However, when the wishes of the dead are unknown or unclear, it is not at all obvious what the right requires or permits. It is not even obvious what Veatch and Pitt think the right requires or permits. They imply that the right conflicts with unconsented or inappropriately consented invasion, which sounds as if they think the right directly requires consent, a view I criticized earlier. But they also imply that it is only the 30 per cent opposed who have their right violated. Do they think those members of the 70 per cent in favour who did not consent also had a right infringed upon? Or do they think that merely being in favour is appropriate consenting? Perhaps instead they think the right is a right against unwanted, not unconsented, invasion. Whatever their interpretation of the right, I do not think invading someone's dead body against that person's wishes need infringe on a right. Specifically, no infringement occurs when the invasion is a result of following a reasonable best guess about the person's wishes.

Consider a version of the case, often cited in discussions of presumed consent, of the treatment of the unconscious.[18] Suppose a class of unconscious people have a life-threatening condition that can be treated only with a very expensive drug. People have a negative right not to be treated against their wishes but, let me stipulate, they have no positive right to this drug because it is so expensive. Suppose, though, that a generous person has donated a supply of the expensive drug. We do not know whether a given unconscious person would want the treatment, but we do know that only a few—but a few nonetheless—in the general population would oppose it. If we believe the

---

Public Affairs Quarterly 20 (2006). Taylor's view is similar to my later claims about respecting rights under uncertainty.

[17] Robert Veatch and Jonathan Pitt, 'The Myth of Presumed Consent', in Robert Veatch, *Transplantation Ethics* (Washington, DC: Georgetown University Press, 2000), p. 172. See also their further claim about negative rights on p. 215.

[18] It may help to say how the aim in presenting this emergency case differs from the aim in the earlier one. The earlier emergency case tested whether consent was required for taking organs when the person is known to have wanted to donate. This emergency case tests whether there is anything worse about mistaken taking than mistaken not taking when it is not known what a person wanted.

Veatch and Pitt objection to presumed consent, we should have to say that the mistaken treatment of those who would have opposed it violates their rights, while failing to treat those who would welcome it would not violate their rights (since they do not have a positive right).[19] Since Veatch at least takes a stringent view about respecting rights,[20] he ought to conclude that treatment would be wrong. But of course he does not because it obviously is not wrong.[21] How, then, could one reconcile the view that treatment is ethically permissible with the view that people have a right not to be treated against their wishes?

One option is to say that the rights of the few who would oppose treatment are outweighed by the gains to the many being treated. Since the gains to the many are, by hypothesis, not protected by a right, this option gives up the stringency of rights, which would be problematic. Another option is to say that the people who are mistakenly treated do have their rights infringed upon but are compensated by the benefit of the treatment. Its benefit may well help explain why treatment is permissible, but this answer still involves giving up the stringency of rights since, by hypothesis, the rights of those treated against their wishes are infringed upon. In any case, it seems more accurate to say that the right needs stating more carefully. In this third option, it would not count as an infringement of a right if someone were treated in error against his or her wishes as a result of an honest and reasonable attempt to do what the person wanted. If we accept some version of that conclusion, then taking organs in honest error also need not infringe upon a negative right.

Is sex a counter-example? If we think sex is only permissible with consent, sex with an unconscious person who did not previously consent is impermissible. By analogy, taking organs without consent is impermissible.[22] In response, we might regard sex with an unconscious person as wrong using the same reasoning as can support taking organs even from those who had not consented. Consider the number of mistakes: most people would want not to have sex while unconscious. Consider the size of mistakes: those who would dissent to sex each lose more, especially psychologically, if someone has sex with them than those who would want sex would lose if they do not have it. Adding the number of mistakes to their size supports a rule against sex without consent. But it is possible and perhaps true that more people would want their organs used after their deaths than would not. And we still have no reason to regard taking in error as worse than erring by failing to take. There are no psychological costs, for instance, to dead people whose organs are taken. So it is entirely consistent to reject sex without consent but endorse taking organs posthumously without consent.

Intuitive cases aside, there does not seem much philosophical support for the view that taking in honest and reasonable error infringes on negative rights.[23]

---

[19] Veatch, *Transplantation Ethics*, p. 171.

[20] Veatch and Pitt in ibid., pp. 146–7.

[21] See Veatch's and Pitt's endorsement of treatment, ibid., p. 171.

[22] Kluge, 'Improving Organ Retrieval Rates', p. 286 draws this analogy.

[23] On an objective conception of wrongdoing, one could do wrong even if one reasonably believes one is doing right, so reasonable but mistaken treatment could perhaps be wrong. I cannot go into the debate about whether wrongdoing is objective or subjective, so let me just say (a) that from the doctors'

Consider theses about the priority of negative rights over positive rights or over producing better consequences. Some say negative rights should have priority because they are part of the design of a morality that gives us a status as individuals in our own right rather than cells in some organism.[24] Others say that negative rights have priority for conceptual reasons to do with the nature of rights.[25] These considerations are particularly apt when considering a conflict between the claims of potential recipients to receive organs and the negative rights of people not to have their organs retrieved against their wishes. But these considerations are not apt when considering how to follow a rightholder's wishes when those wishes are not known. One does not, for instance, treat people as cells in an organism when doing what one reasonably thinks they would probably want because they would probably want it—even if one turns out to be mistaken.

A pro tanto reason to retrieve organs

Consider now a case with no basis for a best guess either way because a person had no coherent wishes or because no one can find enough evidence about what they were. One rare example would be people who die without registering as donors and whose next-of-kin cannot be traced.[26] Since the wishes of the deceased, by hypothesis, do not give guidance, it seems reasonable to allow meeting the needs of potential recipients to be at least a tie-breaking reason for taking organs. In philosophical terms, meeting needs is a 'pro tanto' reason, one that is decisive unless outweighed.[27] Note that, unlike the arguments so far, this argument is based on a new consideration, the needs of potential recipients. The argument is thus not rooted in but also not against the likely interests of the deceased. The significance of the tie-breaking reason depends on how many cases there are where a tie needs to be broken, that is, where the evidence about the wishes of the deceased fails to determine a decision. Obviously, what could justify not taking, despite the pro tanto reason to meet needs, could be what this and the previous chapters have been about: the family's objection or evidence of the deceased's opposing interests.

Whether the pro tanto reason to meet needs actually is a reason to take depends on the effects on the supply of organs of taking from dead people who did not consent and who are thought neither to have wanted retrieval nor opposed it. If

---

point of view, mistaken failing to treat would be wrong too, so to point out that mistaken treatment could be wrong does not help them decide what to do and (b) as I suggest, perhaps our right is only a right to a certain form of reasonable consideration, rather than the treatment that could only be given by the omniscient.

[24] Warren Quinn, *Morality and Action* (Cambridge: Cambridge University Press, 1993), pp. 167–74; Thomson, *The Realm of Rights*, ch. 8; F. M. Kamm, *Morality, Mortality, vol.2* (New York: Oxford University Press, 1996).

[25] Hillel Steiner, *An Essay on Rights* (Oxford: Basil Blackwell, 1994).

[26] The UK has changed its law (wrongly, as this section claims) so that organs may not be taken from the small number of people in this category. My thanks to a donor coordinator in Manchester and David Price for pointing out the change.

[27] Shelly Kagan, *The Limits of Morality* (Oxford: Clarendon Press, 1989), p. 17. A tie-breaking reason is a pro tanto reason, but pro tanto reasons could be weightier than a tie-breaking reason.

taking from such people produced fewer organs than some alternative, perhaps by causing a backlash against transplantation,[28] then it would be more help to potential recipients not to take organs. But if the supply increased, then the pro tanto reason is a reason to take organs.

Readers who are familiar with debates about opt out and presumed consent should take care in assessing the pro tanto reason for taking. It is not a reason to presume consent. It is not a reason to take organs against the family's wishes. With small exceptions, such as the law on taking organs from people with no next-of-kin, it may be no reason to change the law or even existing practice. Indeed, it need not be a reason for the state or doctors alone, or even primarily, because the pro tanto reason is also a reason for the family. As we know, families are usually asked to decide on donation when the deceased have expressed no formal views, and they may feel that, when they do not know that the deceased wanted to donate, they should not donate. But if the arguments in this chapter are correct, they should not refuse to donate. From the point of view of the deceased, mistaken donating is generally no worse than donating, and the needs of recipients give a pro tanto reason to donate; so families in a position of ignorance should donate.

To summarize the first part of this chapter: if we consider only the claims of the dead, organs may be taken from people who are thought not to have opposed their organs being taken. This comprises those who consented, those it is thought wanted or would have wanted to donate, and those who had no known wish one way or other (and therefore had no known objection).

OPT OUT, PRESUMED CONSENT, AND THE CURRENT DEBATES

It is now time to apply the theoretical material to actual or proposed practice. In this part of the chapter, I discuss the ethical debates about whether, in the absence of clear wishes, the default should be to take or not take the organs. As I have said, the debates are characterized by confusion and error about current practice, so I begin with a skeletal description of it. I then explore the terminology of defaults and, in particular, of the term 'presumed consent' before turning to substantive questions about whether changing defaults would increase the supply of organs and whether taking organs without the deceased's consent is ethically permissible. I argue that taking without consent could be permissible, but I also argue that countries without formal opt out arrangements should introduce them. Finally, I consider the ethics of framing requests to families in ways that are designed to get them to agree to donate.

The following description is broadly accurate about the practice of most countries—including 'presumed consent' countries—with programmes to retrieve

---

[28] There was a backlash in Brazil, but this was against a law taken to exclude the family from decision-making. C. Csillag, 'Brazil Abolishes "Presumed Consent" in Organ Donation', *The Lancet* 352 (1998), p. 1367.

organs from the dead. If a deceased person consented, for instance by joining a donor register, the family nonetheless have a power of veto. If the deceased dissented, for instance by formally refusing, the organs will not be taken. If the deceased neither consented nor dissented, the family have the power to donate or withhold the organs. Within this broad description, details vary from country to country and sometimes region to region.[29] For instance, in some places, families have to give written consent before retrieval may occur while, in others, families have to object before retrieval will be blocked. For the purposes of this section, the most important aspects of the description are these: just like 'express consent' countries, 'presumed consent' countries in practice tend to give families the option of vetoing retrieval from a relative who did not opt out; and, just like 'presumed consent' countries, 'express consent' countries in law and practice do not require the deceased's consent before retrieval.[30]

I have put 'presumed consent' in scare quotes because, as a synonym for opt out, it is less than ideal. 'Opt out' suggests a system where organs are taken unless the deceased opted out, and it is a descriptive term that implies no particular justification. 'Presumed consent', by contrast, implies a justification, namely that consent may be presumed. However, an opt out system need not rely on presumed consent for justification, since it could be argued that when people were ambivalent or undecided and did or thought nothing amounting to consent, it is better to default to taking their organs than not. Moreover, presumed consent is a particularly poor justification because the presumption would be either unnecessary or false. It will usually be known whether people have consented or not. For those who have consented, the presumption would be known to be unnecessary; for those who have not, the presumption would be known to be false.[31] Usually, in this section, I shall use the neutral term 'opt out' rather than 'presumed consent'.

The choice between opt in or opt out systems has been of considerable political controversy. The debates, both political and academic, have focused on whether the choice makes any difference to the numbers of organs retrieved and whether an opt out system would be unethical. Perhaps the biggest problem in assessing the debates, and certainly the most frustrating, is that many of the disputants either do not make it clear what they are talking about, or their arguments and evidence do not fit their definitions. I shall give some examples, out of the countless number available, of error and lack of clarity and then turn to the arguments about the supply of organs and ethics.

---

[29] Organ Donation Taskforce, *The Potential Impact of an Opt Out System for Organ Donation in the UK* (London: Department of Health, 2008), p. 11.

[30] As David Price makes clear in his magisterial discussion of presumed consent and its supposed alternatives in his *Legal and Ethical Aspects of Organ Transplantation* (Cambridge: Cambridge University Press, 2000), ch. 2. One of the lessons in method Price gives is the importance of not conflating law, regulations, guidelines, and medical custom.

[31] I am grateful to Govert den Hartogh for making this point so clearly to me. The criticism of presumed consent would not apply to the unlikely case where records of consent have been lost and a presumption of consent may be justified. 'Presumed consent' is not a contradiction in terms, whatever its other defects.

Here is one example of error. Alberto Abadie and Sebastien Gay, in an otherwise careful academic article, want to assess the effect on the organ supply of legal defaults. They write, 'In many countries, including the U.S., Great Britain, Germany and Australia, cadaveric organ procurement is carried out under the informed consent principle. Under an informed consent law, cadaveric organ extraction requires the explicit consent of the donor before death, which is usually reflected on a donor registration card.'[32] The trouble is, their description is simply false. Not only in practice but also in law, the consent of the deceased is not required.[33] Countries that insist on consent almost invariably allow the consent of the family to substitute for the consent of the deceased when the deceased did not dissent.[34]

To take an example of being unclear, vague, and incomplete, consider the report of the UK's Organ Donation Taskforce. Their report characterized the UK as a 'soft opt in' country in these terms: 'Doctors can remove organs from adults who have opted in. It is up to each person to decide if they want to opt in. It is normal practice to let relatives know if the person has opted in and doctors can decide not to proceed if faced with opposition from relatives.'[35] Their description omits to mention what happens if people do not opt in. From some parts of the report, with its emphasis on individual gift and autonomy, one would think that organs are not taken without the individual's opting in.[36] But other parts of their report make it clear that, even when the deceased did not opt in, their organs may be taken with family consent.[37] What, then, is the difference between soft opt in and what the Taskforce calls 'soft opt out', of which they take Spain to be an example? The Taskforce describes in these terms the Spanish version of soft opt out: 'Doctors can remove organs from every adult who dies—unless a person has registered to opt out. It is good practice for doctors *to ask the relatives* for their agreement at the time of death.'[38] And if we ask what the difference is between soft opt in and soft opt out, one is that the opt out countries have a formal register to opt out, whereas the UK does not (and here the opt out countries do better than the UK, as I shall be arguing). The other difference seems to be that the families must give explicit

---

[32] Alberto Abadie and Sebastien Gay, 'The Impact of Presumed Consent Legislation on Cadaveric Organ Donation: A Cross Country Study' *Journal of Health Economics* 25 (2006), p. 600.

[33] Abadie and Gay, ibid., are commendably aware that practice and law do not match up exactly. Their mistake is about the law. A specific example occurs in Appendix C, where they cite the UK and New Zealand as informed consent countries on the basis of their respective 1961 and 1964 Human Tissue Acts. But those laws permitted retrieval of tissue not only when the deceased consented but also when the deceased did not, in the absence of known objection. On Abadie and Gay's classification, they should come out as presumed consent countries. See Price, *Legal and Ethical Aspects of Organ Transplantation*, pp. 93–6.

[34] Price, *Legal and Ethical Aspects of Organ Transplantation*, p. 93. Japan is apparently an exception. See Alireza Bagheri, 'Criticism of "Brain Death" Policy in Japan', *Kennedy Institute of Ethics Journal* 13 (2003).

[35] Organ Donation Taskforce, *The Potential Impact of an Opt Out System for Organ Donation in the UK*, p. 11.

[36] See ibid., e.g. sections 4.9 and 7.4. Clearly many who gave evidence to the Taskforce wrongly assumed the UK system would take organs only with individual consent. See e.g. section 13.9.

[37] See ibid., e.g. sections 7.5, 8.5.

[38] Ibid., p.10 (emphasis in original).

consent before retrieval in the UK whereas in Spain families are only asked, although they may then veto retrieval since they have the 'last decision'.[39] In the Taskforce's own terms, the differences between the UK's opt in system and soft opt out systems are slight indeed. How could they be expected to make a big difference in the number of organs retrieved? Why would a change to soft opt out, if change it be, require expensive public relations campaigns?[40] The question about so much of the argument about the ethics and effectiveness of opt out systems is 'how useful is the reasoning and evidence when based on misunderstanding or incompletely describing practice and law?' Bearing this question in mind, let us assess the arguments.

The main argument for an opt out system is that it would increase the supply of organs. That is what Gordon Brown, then British Prime Minister, argued in 2008 when he said that the UK should consider presumed consent to try to close the 'aching gap between the potential benefits of transplant surgery in the UK and the limits imposed by our current system of consent'.[41] However, the Taskforce, whose inquiry he instigated, found the evidence mixed.[42] As academic commentators often recognize, it is hard to say what the effects of an opt out system would be. Simply comparing the supply of organs in opt out countries with the supply in opt in countries is not very helpful. Opt out countries may have more organs because they also have more intensive care beds, more donor coordinators, or more road accidents, to take a few confounding factors.[43] Before and after comparisons are also of limited use. Perhaps the publicity that accompanies a change to an opt out system is what increased the supply of organs, not the change itself. In any case, what may work in one country may fail in another. A public with respect for state and medical authority may put up with an opt out system[44] whereas a less deferential public would not. However, some commentators do argue that, when disaggregated from confounding factors, opt out defaults have the independent effect of increasing the supply of organs.[45]

How could opt out increase the supply of organs? A common-sense explanation points to the disparity between popular support for organ donation, as measured by

[39] The report quotes Rafael Matesanz as saying that, in Spain, the family have the 'last decision'. Ibid., p. 22. The ambiguous term 'last decision' is also used by Abadie and Gay to characterize presumed consent in practice in 'The Impact of Presumed Consent Legislation on Cadaveric Organ Donation', p. 600.
[40] As the Taskforce suggested it would. Organ Donation Taskforce, *The Potential Impact of an Opt Out System for Organ Donation in the UK*, sections 1.11, 14. The Report largely sets aside, as infeasible for the UK, 'hard' opt out, where the consent of the deceased is not needed and the family may not veto retrieval.
[41] Quoted in a BBC report, 'Organ Donor System Overhaul Call', BBC News, 13 Jan. 2008.
[42] Organ Donation Taskforce, *The Potential Impact of an Opt Out System for Organ Donation in the UK*, section 11.
[43] Points often made to explain the high organ retrieval rates in Spain.
[44] A point often made about Austria, which, according to Richard Thaler and Cass Sunstein, has the extraordinarily low opt out rate of 1 per cent. See *Nudge: Improving Decisions about Health, Wealth, and Happiness* (New Haven: Yale University Press, 2008), p. 179. I have heard questions raised in discussion about the reliability of Austrian consent statistics.
[45] Abadie and Gay, 'The Impact of Presumed Consent Legislation on Cadaveric Organ Donation'; E. Johnson and D. Goldstein, 'Do Defaults Save Lives?' *Science* 302 (2003).

opinion polls, and the number of people who actually opt in to donation, as measured by entry on a register or carrying a donor card. According to common sense, people simply do not get round to opting in. An opt out system would then lead to more organs because people would instead not get round to opting out. Furthermore, many people would be pleased to be donors without having to put the effort into opting in, which is why opt out systems are sometimes thought of as 'consent for the disorganized'.[46]

The idea is a seductive one. As if we could not come up with countless examples in our own lives, a wealth of evidence from social psychology and behavioural economics demonstrates the force of inertia.[47] But as a reform proposal, the opt out default misfires badly. It is wrong about what it is reforming and its method is implausible. As I have said several times, people do not have to opt in before their organs may be taken, at least not in most countries and not in the US, UK, Netherlands, Australia, New Zealand, and other countries where opt out systems are widely proposed. Family consent is taken as a substitute. Because families are asked, the inertia explanation seems implausible. It is entirely understandable that people do not get round to opting in or out in the case of their own bodies; the chances that they would be candidates for donation are very low and people are often reluctant to think about their premature deaths. Hence the inertia explanation is plausible for them. But the families of the deceased are not in the same position. The chances of their relatives' being candidates for donation are 100% and they have little choice but to think about what should happen to their relatives' bodies. It is not as if the family would fail to get round to expressing their view because of inertia.

It might be said that the family should not be asked their views. What is sometimes called 'hard presumed consent' would combine an opt out system with the drastic change of setting aside family objections. But inertia is unlikely then to work its magic. As chapter 5 explained, overriding families' objections is likely to have such bad publicity that people will take the trouble to opt out, perhaps in droves. We should also remember that people do not only have preferences about whether to donate or not; they also have preferences about how their families are treated. Many people would not want their families suffering extra distress after they die and, if overriding their families would cause them distress, they would not want their families overridden. The point is important because people may then not be so inert at opting out if they see other people's families being ignored, which would undercut the inertia explanation of how opt out would increase supply. The point is also ethically important. Opt out systems are supposed by some to give people what they had wanted yet were too disorganized to do for themselves. But if the opt out system causes distress to families, it will give some people precisely what they had wanted not to happen.

---

[46] A term cited by the Organ Donation Taskforce, *The Potential Impact of an Opt Out System for Organ Donation in the UK*, p. 8.

[47] The evidence is summarized in Thaler and Sunstein, *Nudge*.

I have been setting out the inertia idea as it usually appears in the media and political discussion, and it is subject to fatal objections. There are other explanations of how an opt out system could increase supply. For instance, perhaps families could themselves have to opt out so that, rather than being asked for informed consent, they would have to volunteer objections on being told that donation was possible. Perhaps families would be more likely to donate if asked in such a way that consent appears to be the right answer. We know that how a decision is 'framed' makes a difference to decision-making in other cases, so perhaps framing would make a difference to the decision about donation.[48] Or perhaps not—parents presented with someone else's child at the end of the school day are unlikely to go home with their default option, and perhaps families will similarly feel strongly enough about donation that their views would come through whether they were asked for consent or whether they had to volunteer dissent. Still, opt out systems could increase the supply of organs, so let me now turn to the question of whether they would be unethical.

The ethics of opt out

Misunderstandings and lack of clarity make for confusing ethical debates too. Critics of opt out, which they usually call 'presumed consent', often do not explain what makes it worse than the systems that supposedly have express consent. It is puzzling, to say the least, to see how commonly 'presumed consent' is described in various ways as 'the most outrageously unethical of all possible policies for organ procurement' by writers who endorse, or at least do not criticize, the policies in their own countries that permit organ retrieval from dead people who have not consented.[49] Some of the hostility is clearly of limited applicability. For instance, the criticism of the term 'presumed consent' as a euphemistic and fraudulent misnomer has force, but is irrelevant if we call the policy 'opt out'.[50] Some writers object to the sidelining of the family, in which case it is properly directed only at

[48] David Price seems to think changing the default for families could increase supply. See his discussion of Belgium in Price, *Legal and Ethical Aspects of Organ Transplantation*, p. 91. See also Govert den Hartogh, *Farewell to Non-commitment: Decision Systems for Organ Donation from an Ethical Viewpoint* (The Hague: Centre for Ethics and Health, 2008), section 16. Den Hartogh thinks framing the request to the family in such a way as to expect consent could increase organ supply, although he believes it would require a law change in the Netherlands. See p. 79. I shall shortly raise ethical questions about framing which den Hartogh does not mention. He may not need to consider them if his ideal system comes to pass, because that system would be designed so that people who have not opted out would have genuinely consented to donate, leaving only the problem of persuading their families. But he ought to consider doubts about framing if his ideal system does not come to pass.

[49] See Veatch, *Transplantation Ethics*, p. 160 for the quotation and p. 148 for the endorsement/non-rejection. Anyone who thinks presumed consent is the *most* outrageously unethical of *all* possible procurement policies either has peculiar ethical views or a limited imagination. Is it not worse to kill the healthy for their organs?

[50] In addition to Veatch, see also the President's Council on Bioethics staff paper by Eric Cohen, 'Organ Transplantation: Defining the Ethical and Policy Issues', p. 27, available at www.bioethics.gov (last accessed 20 August 2009); Aaron Spital, 'Conscription of Cadaveric Organs for Transplantation: Neglected Again' *Kennedy Institute of Ethics Journal* 13 (2003), p. 171; C. Erin and J. Harris, 'Presumed Consent or Contracting Out' *Journal of Medical Ethics* 25 (1999).

hard opt out systems. Some of the hostility is to opt out by stealth, in which case it does not apply to well-publicized practices.[51]

A common complaint about opt out systems is that they fail to respect individual autonomy adequately and they suggest that bodies are owned by the state. The implication is that organs should only be retrieved with individual consent. Let us assess this conclusion against the theoretical material from earlier in the chapter.

First, an opt out system could, in principle, satisfy a consent requirement. Consider Active Donor Registration (ADR), a system described and largely recommended by Govert den Hartogh in a report to the Dutch Health Minister. ADR would be an extensively publicized easy opt out scheme, where people merely have to send back an annually posted reply-paid form.[52] The explicit consent of the deceased would not be necessary for retrieval, but den Hartogh believes silence in such conditions would be tacit consent.[53] Tacit consent is genuine consent, a public act of will that happens to take the form of silence. On any view of consent, silence or doing nothing can be actual consent in certain circumstances.[54] The classic example is agreeing to the minutes of a meeting by not speaking against them when it is possible and easy to do so. Tacit consent is importantly different from 'presumed consent' because, unlike tacit consent, presumed consent is not genuine consent. If den Hartogh is right that not opting out under ADR is tacit consent, ADR is an opt out scheme that satisfies a requirement of genuine consent.

However, even if in principle an opt out system such as ADR could satisfy a consent requirement, in practice it probably would not. Den Hartogh himself concedes that some people would not be reached by the forms and the publicity campaigns,[55] something highly likely in large multi-ethnic societies, especially those with illegal immigration. People who do not know an opt out system exists or how to opt out cannot be said to have tacitly consented when they fail to opt out. So we have to consider whether a system that in practice takes organs without some people's consent is unethical and here we can apply some earlier ideas.

Neither autonomy nor rights directly make the case for a consent requirement. Retrieving the organs of someone who did not consent could be ethically permissible if that person wanted or would have wanted retrieval. Consent can, however, be required for reasons apart from a direct consent requirement. A rule requiring consent can be the best way of protecting people from abuse, or the fairest way of allocating the burden of making wishes known. But I doubt that these reasons apply in the case of organ retrieval from the dead. Assuming they have a power of veto, families can help protect their relatives from abuse and, unlike other cases,

---

[51] Michele Goodwin, *Black Markets: The Supply and Demand of Body Parts* (Cambridge: Cambridge University Press, 2006), ch. 6, has numerous objections to presumed consent, but her target is a policy that, as she describes it, would permit taking organs without informing the family.

[52] Den Hartogh did not mention the internet or mobile phones, which could make opting out even easier, in the version of the report used here, although he tells me that he has updated the technology in a later version.

[53] Den Hartogh, *Farewell to Non-commitment*, p. 28.

[54] Wertheimer, *Consent to Sexual Relations*, pp. 152f.

[55] Den Hartogh, *Farewell to Non-commitment*, pp. 28, 57.

such as posthumous sperm retrieval, they have no conflict of interest. As for fairness, organs are of great benefit to other people, so it is hard to see why it is unfair to people who would prefer not to donate to ask them to take the minimal step of telling their families. Note how limited the conclusion is: I am arguing—in line with practice virtually everywhere—that people should not have to consent to become donors before their organs may be retrieved. I am not arguing that people should have their organs taken unless they have formally dissented.

Thus it could be ethically permissible to take organs without the deceased's consent. But when would it be? According to this chapter, it would not infringe upon people's claims over their bodies if their organs were taken in order to increase their 'expected utility' that is, after taking account of what they probably wanted and how much they wanted it. It would also be permissible to take organs from people whose wishes are not known, either because they had no wishes or because the evidence of what they were is mixed or non-existent. How, in practice, the information about the deceased's wishes should be gathered depends on various considerations, for instance about whether families know best. Quite possibly, the common practice of not insisting on individual consent but asking the family is the best that can be done to respect the moral claims of the deceased.

However, some opt in countries provide no formal means of opting out. In this respect, they do worse than opt out countries. People who are determined not to have their organs retrieved have no way to guarantee they would not be. They can tell their families, but their families could fail to pass the information on. If people really do have rights over their bodies after they die, as I have been arguing they do, these rights should be legally protected.[56] The ability to opt out formally would also help protect the dead from abuse and seems minimally required by fairness in allocating the burdens of making one's wishes known. Instituting a formal opt out mechanism could even increase supply. If people have not opted out when they could have done, that tells their families something different from their not opting out when they could not have done. Families may interpret silence when opt out is possible as acquiescence or, at least, not opposition; when opt out is impossible, they may now know what to think, and default to refusing retrieval.[57] Still, the main reason to institute a formal opt out is not to increase supply but to respect people's rights over their bodies.

REQUESTS TO THE FAMILY AND THE ETHICS OF FRAMING

I earlier mentioned the idea that the framing of requests to the family affects their willingness to donate. This idea is an example of a currently fashionable enthusiasm, in

---

[56] David Price writes, 'many presumed consent systems with (usually nationwide) opting-out (non-donor) registries seemingly provide a *more* reliable mechanism for ensuring *unwanted removal* does not occur than many express consent/opting-in systems.' 'From Cosmos and Damian to van Velzen: The Human Tissue Saga Continues' *Medical Law Review* 11 (2003), p.16 (emphasis in original).

[57] As den Hartogh believes they do, *Farewell to Non-commitment*, p. 25.

academic writings and policy circles, for steering people into socially desirable behaviour by taking advantage of their psychology. Rather than use coercion, the idea goes,
policy should rely on the deviations from economic rationality to which behavioural
economics and social psychology have drawn attention.[58] One deviation is being
swayed by defaults, that is, by what would happen unless one takes steps to avoid it,
and leaving it up to the family to raise objections is one version of the default idea.
Transplant organizations round the world have used other framing methods, such as
getting mothers of donors or specially trained requesters to ask, or even making
repeated requests. Suppose framing does affect families' decisions. I argued that it is
ethically permissible to take organs when it is not expected to be against the interests of
the deceased and when the family are not opposed. This view of what is permissible
may be thought to allow requests to be framed in such a way that families agree to
donate. But whether framing would be permissible depends on how it would affect the
quality of families' decisions.

Suppose the family have a request framed in such a way that they agree to donate,
but this method of framing causes them to overlook the evidence that their relative
would have wanted not to have organs taken. Or suppose the framing causes them
not to express their misgivings by, for example, making them think they are not
entitled to. The framing of the request would then have done its psychological
trick, but it would also have led to organs being taken wrongly. The effectiveness of
framing is a matter of psychology, not ethics, and the ethics of taking organs will
depend on whether the method of asking causes the family to make the right
decision, not whether it simply gets the organs.

How, then, should the family be asked? The answer depends on how the asking
affects the claims of potential recipients, the families of the dead, and the dead
themselves. To assess what the method does, we need evidence about how the
framing affects decisions which we can then evaluate against the standard of
permissibility. Unfortunately, we probably do not have the evidence we need.
Even though we know something about the effect of various methods of framing
on the family's agreement to donate, we know little about their effects on the
numbers of mistakes.

Let me nonetheless make a few remarks about evaluation in case some evidence
appears. Consider three criteria for evaluation: the number of organs retrieved, the
family's distress, and the number of takings by mistake, that is, contrary to the
deceased's actual or inferred wishes. Compare two methods of asking, method A
and method B. If method A leads to more organs, does not distress the family any
more, and makes no more mistakes than method B, A is better than B. We can
repeat the exercise for any comparison where some method is better on one
criterion than another and no worse (or better) on the other two.

---

[58] Thaler and Sunstein, *Nudge*. They apply their basic nudge idea to a range of topics, such as
savings and the choice of health insurance. They argue, in chapter 11, that nudging supports an opt out
organ donation scheme. But, as one may infer from my criticism of the opt out debate, this chapter is
one too many.

Suppose method A produced more organs but caused more distress to the family than method B, while making an equivalent number of mistakes about the claims of the dead. The family's distress, taken on its own, is outweighed by the needs of potential recipients (and their families). While the family's feelings can be important because they affect the organ supply or because the deceased would have cared about them, those reasons are taken care of by my stipulations that the supply goes up and the claims of the dead are unaffected. In this case, method A is better.

Some may object that the family has more of a claim than just not being distressed. Specifically, it could be objected that a method of framing manipulates the family, and manipulation is wrong. However, as chapter 5 argued, families do not have the status of consenters, but only the lesser status of people who ought not to be distressed. Unlike people who do have the status of consenters, the family has no claim to be free from all the manipulation that would undercut informed consent. Perhaps even then, some forms of manipulation would be wrong— lying, for instance—but the suggested ways of framing requests to the family fall a long way short of those. So in the evaluation, I considered only the family's distress.

The greatest difficulty in evaluating the methods comes when some method A would increase both the supply of organs and the number of mistaken takings when compared with some method B. A view that gives primacy to the claims of the dead would prefer B. My own view would depend on the numbers of organs and the numbers of mistakes; enough extra organs would outweigh a few extra mistakes, especially if people could have opted out and if their families' distress were unaffected. It would be premature to say more, in advance of chapter 7's comparison of the claims of potential recipients against the claims of the dead.

CONCLUSION

This chapter has discussed organ retrieval from the dead in the common cases where it is unclear or unknown what the now-dead person had wanted. The chapter defended a form of an opt out system. In summary, the argument was this: (1) The deceased's consent is neither directly nor indirectly required by their rights. (2) Insofar as it is the deceased's interests we are concerned with, their wishes should be decisive. (3) When their wishes are unknown, either they have no relevant interests or the best guess about their wishes should be followed. (4) There is no good reason based on a concern for the deceased to err on the side of not retrieving. In particular, arguments in the literature about bodily integrity and negative rights do not give such a reason. (5) But there is a pro tanto reason to retrieve in genuine cases of uncertainty: to meet the needs of potential recipients. (6) Hence it can be permissible to take organs in the absence of dead people's consent so long as there is no good reason to think they would have been opposed and so long as, to add a conclusion from chapter 5, their families have the power to veto retrieval.

It is time to take stock and put together the conclusions of this chapter and the preceding ones. The most striking conclusion is that there is no direct ethical requirement before taking organs to get the informed consent of either the dead person or the family. Here is a reminder of how we reached this conclusion. I argued that people have the right to give or withhold informed consent to organ retrieval after their deaths. The claim to personal sovereignty gives a power of veto over the use of their organs and it gives them the power to waive their veto. However, as this chapter has shown, there is no requirement to get their consent before taking their organs. Virtually no system requires consent from the dead anyway.

For different reasons, there is no direct requirement for consent from the family. This claim is in contrast to recent trends in legislation which do require the family's consent, as though the rights were bequeathed like the dead person's property. As chapter 5 showed, the family do not have a claim in its own right to give or withhold consent, but only the lesser claim to have their feelings taken into account. The exception is when the deceased have, as they rarely do, delegated to their families.

Throughout this chapter and the previous one, the needs of people for organs have appeared in a minor role. In the previous chapter, they appeared as a consideration in the consequentialist argument for the family veto and in this chapter only as a pro tanto reason. Should the need for organs be given greater weight? The next chapter is concerned with the claims of the dead over their bodies as against the needs of living people for organs. Why not conscript the organs of the dead?

7

Conscription

The topic of this chapter is the conscription of organs, primarily from the dead. Conscription is taking people's organs whatever their wishes or the wishes of their relatives. Conscription, it has to be said, does not appear to be a leading item on any actual policy agenda, but it is occasionally discussed seriously, at least in academic circles.[1] Conscription should be taken seriously. More can be said for it, ethically, than many think. Many people wait for new organs or miss out altogether, and so die or miss out on significant improvements in their quality of life. If failing to meet their needs is to be justified, something substantial must be on the other side.

Take the simplest and most powerful argument for conscription. Dead people are not using their organs any more, so why not conscript theirs and give them to the people who need them? Conscripting organs might not provide enough for everyone in need, but why not take what can be got? Improvements are still improvements even if they do not solve a problem completely. It is hard to deny that people with organ failure need the organs more than dead people do; hence the need for something substantial to oppose conscription. However, if people have a right to decide what happens to their organs after they die, that would be something substantial on the other side. In fact, I believe, and shall to some extent argue, that the central question about the ethics of conscription from the dead is whether it would wrongly fail to respect their rights. If the dead either do not have rights or their rights may be overridden, then the ethical obstacles to conscription, at least in principle, disappear.

Before getting on to the main arguments, some preliminaries. First, assume any conscription would be overt so as to avoid being sidetracked into the ethics of secrecy and lying. Second, some of the arguments in other chapters apply to conscription too. For instance, anti-market arguments that stress the value of altruistic donation as against sale should also stress the value of donation as against conscription, and would have the same force.[2] But I shall avoid repetition. Third, this chapter is concerned with the substantive merits of conscription. It has little popular or political support at the moment and, on plausible assumptions about

---

[1] For instance by John Harris, 'Law and Regulation of Retained Organs: The Ethical Issues' *Legal Studies* 22 (2002); Cécile Fabre, *Whose Body Is It Anyway? Justice and the Integrity of the Person* (Oxford: Clarendon Press, 2006); Eric Rakowski, *Equal Justice* (Oxford: Clarendon Press, 1991). This chapter will engage with their views.

[2] That is, very little, as I argue in chapters 9 and 10.

democracy and the political process, conscription should not be introduced now. But this point is about process, not about the substantive merits of conscription.

While conscription from dead people should be taken more seriously than it is, I shall nonetheless argue against it. I shall reject arguments for conscription based on justice, positive rights, the needs of the sick, and treating the supply of organs as a public good. The arguments for conscription are not good enough to justify infringing on a right to control what happens to one's body after death. Young children are, however, not covered by the rights argument. They do not have posthumous rights to control what happens to their bodies after they die. Whatever its other drawbacks, conscription of their organs cannot be objected to on the basis of the rights of the deceased.

Conscription from the living, which I shall briefly discuss first, should not be taken seriously. It would infringe on a right to bodily integrity, and its few defenders have said little to justify that.

CONSCRIPTION FROM THE LIVING

I suspect that conscription from the living is most prominent in textbook discussions of utilitarianism. Utilitarianism apparently implies that it would be not just permissible but obligatory to kill one innocent person in order to save five, a net four lives being a gain in aggregate utility. It furthermore appears obligatory to conscript kidneys and liver segments, the utility gap between no kidney and one being larger than the gap between one and two, and the liver segments perhaps making the difference between life and death for the recipients. But in the textbooks these examples are just intuition pumps, usually designed to cause trouble for utilitarians, not attempts at defensible policy. Utilitarians often respond by trying to show that they are not committed to taking organs and they do not disagree with the intuition that it would be repugnant to do so.[3]

Utilitarianism is not the only target for the conscripted-organs-intuition-pump. Egalitarians are held by some critics to be committed to taking organs from those with more and giving them to those with fewer.[4] Like many utilitarians, egalitarians who respond usually accept that the forced transfer of body parts would be a repugnant conclusion. They then spend their time trying to explain how egalitarianism could be developed to avoid that conclusion.[5] Eric Rakowski and Cécile

---

[3] For a utilitarian justification of rights against organ conscription, stressing adverse side-effects and considerations of human bias and fallibility, see R. M. Hare, *Moral Thinking* (Oxford: Clarendon Press, 1981), pp. 132–5. See also L. W. Sumner, *The Moral Foundation of Rights* (Oxford: Clarendon Press, 1987), ch. 6.

[4] The organ redistribution challenge to egalitarians can be found in Robert Nozick, *Anarchy, State, and Utopia* (Oxford: Basil Blackwell, 1974), p. 206 and Jan Narveson, 'On Dworkinian Equality' *Social Philosophy and Policy* 1 (1983), p. 16.

[5] See in particular G. A. Cohen's discussion of eye transplants and the spurious appeal of self-ownership in his *Self-Ownership, Freedom, and Equality* (Cambridge: Cambridge University Press, 1995), ch. 10.

Fabre are unusual. They have made an egalitarian case for conscription from the living.[6] It is their case that I shall outline and criticize in this section.

Rakowksi favours a theory of justice he calls 'equality of fortune', which says roughly that no one should have fewer resources or opportunities than anyone else through no fault of her own. Fabre claims that justice includes a principle of sufficiency that says people who have less than what they need for a minimally flourishing life have a claim right to surplus resources. Both Rakowski and Fabre see organs as candidates for distributive justice. In Rakowski's words, 'Human tissue is properly regarded as a resource, for it is something that a person needs to accomplish his ends, no different in this respect from the nutrients necessary to sustain life or the intelligence essential to prudent or productive action.'[7] In Fabre's account, a minimally flourishing life needs a healthy body, which for some people requires not only healthcare but also other people's blood, marrow, and organs. Hence body parts, like money, may be confiscated from those who have more than they need for a minimally flourishing life. In Rakowski's account, to have organ failure through no fault of one's own is to have less of a resource than people with healthy organs, which is unequal and makes a case for the forced redistribution of organs.

Rakowksi's actual conclusion about conscription is rather more complex than this simple argument suggests. He sets conditions for forced transfers, for instance that conscription would have to produce substantial benefits for recipients without imposing near-equivalent costs on those from whom the organs are taken. He thinks this condition probably would not be met because enough organs could be obtained from dead people (whose organs are to be conscripted), and from living donation and sale. Moreover, he believes that adults should be free to choose whether to be in an insurance scheme where organs are taken from those with more and given to those with fewer. He clearly thinks that rational people will join this scheme, but they do not have to (although it is not clear whether his is an opt in or opt out scheme). The element of force presumably comes in because, although voluntary, members whose unlucky number comes up and who are selected to provide the organs will not be able to refuse, so at that point the transfer is forced. Rakoswki's scheme does, furthermore, allow for conscription from and to children, who are not able to decide for themselves whether to be in the insurance scheme. And although Rakowski does not say it, conscription would presumably also be allowed for non-competent people apart from children and perhaps from adults to children too. Fabre goes further than Rakowski, at least in principle, by favouring compulsion rather than a voluntary insurance scheme for adult to adult transplantation. She thinks it would be unjust if the voluntary scheme leaves some sick adults without the resources they need for a minimally flourishing life, something Rakowski concedes is possible.[8]

The description of Rakowski's and Fabre's argument is just an outline. I shall question the premise that organs are proper objects of distributive justice when we

[6] Rakowski, *Equal Justice*, ch. 8; Fabre, *Whose Body Is It Anyway?* ch. 5.
[7] Rakowski, *Equal Justice*, p. 168.
[8] Fabre, *Whose Body Is It Anyway?* pp. 99–100.

get to conscription from the dead. Here I want to focus on the obvious objection to conscription from the living: it would violate the right to bodily integrity.

Given our strong intuitions that people have a right to bodily integrity, one would expect that anyone who proposed a policy inconsistent with it would try hard to undercut belief in that right. Rakowski, who says several times that arguments from the right to bodily integrity must indeed be confronted, never gives a detailed rejection. Fabre says that the view that control over one's own body could be valuable in its own right produces an impasse. All she can say is that, if both bodily integrity and a minimally flourishing life are independently valuable, it is not clear why bodily integrity should outweigh the needs of potential recipients for organs.[9] It is rather disappointing that Rakowski and Fabre do not offer a detailed and complete rebuttal of the intuition about bodily integrity. As Fabre herself stresses, the sense that the body is special is firmly rooted in our intuitions. Rakowski and Fabre really need to do more to undermine the intuitive view if people are not to take their conclusions about confiscation as a reduction to absurdity of their principles of justice.

Rakowski and Fabre do make some attempt to explain away the apparently conflicting appeal of a right to bodily integrity. Rakowski guesses that the intuition is based on squeamishness, that we would not want to be the ones who had to force people down and take their organs. This explanation seems most unlikely. The intuition is that forcibly taking people's organs is wrong whoever does it, and it is not displaced squeamishness about personal involvement in the taking. Rakowski also says our intuitions in favour of the right are based on a disposition that gives the wrong result in the organ transfer case.[10] It is in general good to be disposed to think cutting people up is wrong but those who think the forced transfer of organs is wrong have been led astray by this disposition. If Rakowski were right, the intuitions against forcible taking should be unstable, the kind of beliefs we might hold initially but would give up on reflection. However, the intuitions seem entirely stable. The belief may be wrong, but there is little reason to think it a disposition gone astray rather than a considered judgement.[11]

Fabre has a rather more plausible way of trying to debunk the intuitions about bodily integrity. She asks why bodily integrity is valuable. She sets aside the answer that bodily integrity is valuable in its own right. Instead, she concentrates on another answer, that bodily integrity is valuable as an all-purpose-means to having a minimally flourishing life, which she defines as an autonomous life. We can reinterpret the bodily integrity objection to conscription from the living as saying that people need their bodily integrity if their lives are to flourish above the minimum. Fabre then defends conscription by saying that people do not need control over the whole of their bodies to have a minimally flourishing life. Some

---

[9] Ibid., p. 110.

[10] Rakowski, *Equal Justice*, 187–8.

[11] Rakowksi also criticizes the well-known account of deontological constraints that Thomas Nagel gives in *The View From Nowhere* (New York: Oxford University Press, 1986), and he might intend this to be a criticism of a right to bodily integrity. However, Nagel's is just one way of understanding the constraints and there are many others.

people could have their body parts taken off them and still have flourishing lives. Moreover the people who get the new organs would no longer miss out on flourishing lives as they would if they continued to have organ failure.[12]

What is Fabre getting at by saying that people do not need control over the whole of their bodies to have a minimally flourishing life? To be clear, we are not talking about being unable to control a part of one's body in the sense that people with facial tics cannot control part of their bodies. We are talking of people whose bodies are to some extent under the control of others. How can it be true that people under the control of others are autonomous and so have minimally flourishing lives?

Perhaps Fabre has in mind some part–whole distinction: only a body part is under the control of others, not the whole body, and the 'self-rule' of autonomy is consistent with not ruling all of oneself. So for example, if because of conscription you have my kidney, I do not have control over my whole body; but I could still be autonomous. Whatever the merits of that idea, having part of one's body under the control of another does in fact require the loss of self-rule for a time. To be sure, once my kidney has gone to you, I may be autonomous; but for the duration of the compulsory kidney removal, all of me has to be there, under the control of someone else, so I am not autonomous then.

Perhaps Fabre thinks that being under the control of others at a particular time does not preclude an autonomous life, judged over a stretch of time. We could look back over the course of a life and judge it at least minimally flourishing even if bits were bad. That sounds plausible, but so what? Is the general principle that we may infringe on someone's bodily integrity, preventing her having a minimally flourishing life at a particular time, so long as we thereby serve some worthwhile goal and do not preclude a minimally flourishing life on the whole? Is it permissible for officials in China to enforce its one-child policy by physically forcing women to have late-term abortions? Victims of rape and torture may have minimally flourishing lives on the whole, especially if raped or tortured later in life. Could it then be permissible to rape or torture for the sake of some worthwhile goal so long as the victims have minimally flourishing lives on the whole? Fabre is anxious to deny that her view about confiscation of body parts commits her to permitting socially beneficial rape and torture.[13] Part of her point is that the psychological effects of rape are long-lasting; but what if they were not? Could rape be permissible then? Would rape or torture be permissible if the memories were removed? What if confiscating people's organs had long-term bad psychological effects on them? (In comparing confiscation with torture, Fabre makes claims about what confiscation of live body parts is usually like, as though we had some empirical data about this non-existent policy.[14]) Moreover, since confiscation would be public policy, people would know that they were vulnerable to being selected, and the fear they feel might blight their lives which, on Fabre's view, means that they would not have a minimally flourishing life.

---

[12] Fabre, *Whose Body Is It Anyway?* p. 110.
[13] Ibid., p. 111 and sec. 5.4.   [14] Ibid., p. 111.

Even if Fabre is right that intuitions about bodily integrity must be developed within her framework of a minimally flourishing life, she has not shown that the confiscation of someone's organs would be consistent with a minimally flourishing life. If bodily integrity has a value independent of serving a minimally flourishing life, as she defines such a life, she has not shown that bodily integrity is outweighed by the needs of the sick.

What is striking is that, in the end, both Rakowski and Fabre wobble on the question of whether organs may forcibly be removed. Rakowski concedes that even reasonable people who accept his overall theory might see forced removal as too great a sacrifice to impose on people, although he continues to think it permissible.[15] Fabre's wobbling occurs in the context of the risks of death and morbidity people may have imposed on them. She thinks that people should not have their prospects for a minimally flourishing life jeopardized. She does not tell us how much risk would be enough to exempt someone from confiscation and, perhaps for this reason, she does not tell us in the end whether she favours the forced removal of organs.[16] Rakowski's and Fabre's wobbling perhaps shows how hard it is to shake off the intuitive attachment to the inviolability of people's bodies. That said, Fabre does profess to favour forced blood transfusions and Rakowski writes, of attempts to evade conscription: 'But if the penalties for resistance and interference with the program were severe, there seems no reason to think that this difficulty could not be overcome.'[17]

As I said, conscription of organs from the living is not a serious policy. Conscription from the dead is, and it is to that we now turn.

CONSCRIPTION FROM THE DEAD

The rest of this chapter is concerned with conscription from the dead. I shall assume that conscription would work, in the sense of providing more organs. The assumption may be false, and conscription could backfire in some way and fail to provide more organs, but making the assumption allows us to focus on ethical questions about the claims of the deceased over their own bodies.

Let me say a bit more about the form conscription might take. Conscription could be uniform: all suitable organs would be taken whatever the objections of the deceased or their relatives. However, some of those who favour conscription would allow conscientious objection for people with deep religious, cultural, or spiritual objections, but not for those who oppose retrieval for trivial or foolish reasons, such as unjustified fears about the medical care of professed donors. Conscription with exemptions may well be unstable. It would be difficult to sort people so that all and only those who should be exempted are exempted. The government could use

---

[15] Rakowski, *Equal Justice*, p. 192.

[16] See Fabre, *Whose Body Is It Anyway?* pp. 116–17.

[17] Rakowski, *Equal Justice*, p. 194. This quotation, which would be chilling if there were the slightest chance of its being taken seriously as policy, at least shows that Rakowski should not be in charge of the public relations for his ideas.

conscientious objection tribunals of the sort that took place in wartime, but these have obvious costs and drawbacks. The government could simply ask people to declare whether they had conscientious objections. Such a policy risks collapsing into a system not much different from what many countries already have. Conscription with exemption would be vulnerable to bad publicity because people could opt out by claiming conscientious objections and, as chapter 5 explained, the risk of bad publicity is a strong reason for a family veto on retrieval. There may not be a practical alternative to uniform conscription other than asking the family for permission to take organs, and not taking them if the family dissent.

In assessing conscription, uniform or not, I begin with unfinished business from the previous section: Fabre's and Rakowski's idea that organs are objects of distributive justice. I reject this view. I then set out what I think is the most obvious and powerful argument for conscription: that the living need the organs more than the dead do. As against this argument, people have negative rights not to have their organs taken. I consider whether the people who need organs have positive rights to them and whether the negative rights can be overridden by their need. I show how the case for conscription is weakened if organs should be treated not as an emergency life-saving benefit but along the lines of allocating healthcare resources. I consider a public goods argument for conscription, and where it goes wrong. By this stage, I shall have tried to show that conscription would be unjustified. Finally, I argue that conscription from young children is not to be rejected as an infringement of their rights.

Confiscation and distributive justice

Rakowski's and Fabre's argument for conscription from the living relied on thinking of organs as resources to be distributed according to the same principles of justice that govern the distribution of material resources. I said that conscription from the living is wrong because it violates bodily integrity. Conscription from the dead, however, does not violate bodily integrity.[18] So if conscription from the dead is to be rejected, we have to confront their view of organs as resources.

'We do and should respect wills and honour the bequests of the dead; so we should follow the wishes of people about what happens to their bodies after death too.' This argument commonly occurs in discussion of the ethics of acquiring organs from the dead. But what if the argument were to be run the other way? 'Wills and bequests are indeed like people's wishes about what happens to their bodies after death; we should not respect wills and honour bequests, and we often do not, for instance when estates are taxed; so we should not respect wishes about bodies either.' This, in essence, is Fabre's argument for the conscription of organs from the dead.

Fabre writes,

> I aim to show that if one thinks that the poor's interest in leading a minimally flourishing life, and a fortiori in remaining alive, is important enough to confer on

---

[18] See chapter 4.

them a right to some of the material resources of the well off, by way of taxation and, in particular, by way of restrictions on bequests and inheritance, one must think that the very same interest is important enough to confer on the sick a right to the organs of the now-dead able-bodied.[19]

Broadly speaking, the argument is in two steps. Organs are like other resources and so they are proper objects of distributive justice. And the correct view of distributive justice calls for redistribution of organs after death, which amounts to conscription. I shall challenge both steps, beginning with the less fundamental second one.

Even if we accept the premise that organs are available for redistribution, it is not obvious that conscription would serve the goal of distributive justice. Arguably, confiscating organs would tend to transfer resources from the worse off to the better off. For instance, a large proportion of potential dead organ sources in the US are young homicide victims who will tend to have had worse lives than the recipients, not least because they died so young. The picture is made still more complicated when one takes account of the racial mix. For instance, in her criticism of presumed consent, which she takes to be the rough equivalent of conscription, Michele Goodwin argues that the policy would be relatively good for whites and relatively bad for African-Americans.[20]

Another problem for the justice approach to organs is to do with responsibility. Would it be fair to make people give, for instance, their kidneys to the irresponsible unhealthy? Fabre accepts that justice does not require supplying body parts to those responsible for their conditions.[21] But she asserts, with no evidence, that 'whether or not one has healthy organs is largely a matter of brute luck'.[22] Since a major cause of kidney failure is Type 2 Diabetes, and a probable major cause of that is swallowing too many calories and not taking enough exercise, why not think people are often responsible for their organ failure? A similar question can obviously be asked of alcoholics with liver failure and smokers with heart failure. Fabre points to difficulties and potential injustices in assessing responsibility, and judgements of individual responsibility are indeed tricky and often out of place in medicine. But even if we cannot or ought not to say in a given case whether a patient is responsible, we can say that the large-scale implementation of confiscation would produce injustices. Organs would be given to people with no claim of justice at the expense of the people whose bodies they came from. Why think that confiscation would be a net gain in justice?

I do not want to overstate the objection to conscription from within a justice approach to organs. Some of these may well be answerable. For instance, the point about the unfairness of transfers from African-Americans to white Americans is powerless against compulsory transfers from white Americans to African-Americans,

---

[19] Fabre, *Whose Body Is It Anyway?* p. 73. Fabre does not explain how one can be both able-bodied and dead.

[20] Michele Goodwin, *Black Markets: The Supply and Demand of Body Parts* (Cambridge: Cambridge University Press, 2006), ch. 6. See pp. 118–19 on the racial mix of people whose corneas were non-consensually taken in Los Angeles in the 1990s. African-Americans and, especially, Latinos were greatly over-represented.

[21] Fabre, *Whose Body Is It Anyway?* pp. 36–8, 74–5.   [22] Ibid., p. 77.

or from African-Americans to other African-Americans. Or perhaps the claim about justice could be restated so that transfers from worse to better off could be justified when the loss to the worse off is significantly smaller than the gains to the better off.[23] The fundamental problem is with seeing (non-legitimately acquired) organs as relevantly like other material resources, to be allocated according to distributive justice.

Organs clearly are a resource in some sense. They enable people to do things and can be swapped from person to person, which is why organ transplantation works. The question is whether the sense in which organs are resources makes them objects of distributive justice. Organs clearly are not ordinarily regarded as objects of distributive justice, and Fabre needs a good argument to overturn ordinary thinking. She takes it that those who favour transfers of material resources to the needy do so because they think people have welfare rights. One can then see Fabre's point. If you think it is simply the neediness of the badly off that justifies compelling the better off to hand over their spare material resources, should you not also think that neediness justifies compelling people to hand over their spare body parts? But one can justify coercive transfers of material resources in another way, which is to be found in the sizeable literature that criticizes libertarian arguments for private property.

Consider the criticism that libertarianism overlooks the difficulties with justifying individual appropriation of the external world.[24] When people turn something unowned into private property, they may deny others access. According to many writers, people who take resources out of the common stock owe compensation to everyone else. Coercive transfers are then justified not simply by the neediness of the recipients but by the injustice that would be done them if resources were appropriated without compensation. By contrast, people do not appropriate their own bodies, so no question of compensating others arises. There is then no obvious inconsistency in endorsing coercive taxation of material resources while rejecting coerced transfer of body parts or personal services.

In a later piece, Fabre points out that we depend on cooperative efforts for the continued growth and health of our bodies, and she thinks her point might open the door for saying that when our fellow-cooperators need our body parts, we ought to be made to transfer them.[25] Hers is the most slender of promissory notes, so I do not want to say more other than that it does not explain why, if we have benefited from the efforts of others (to whom we have contributed anyway) we owe our spare body parts and not, say, food and shelter, or the tax funds to pay for them.

Robert Nozick wrote: 'Things come into the world already attached to people having entitlements over them.'[26] I agree, when it comes to body parts. We have no reason to give up the intuitive view that organs are not objects of distributive

---

[23] Matthew Clayton suggested this application of 'weighted beneficence'.
[24] See e.g. Cohen, *Self-Ownership, Freedom, and Equality*, chs. 3 and 4; Judith Jarvis Thomson, *The Realm of Rights* (Cambridge, MA: Harvard University Press, 1990), ch. 13.
[25] Fabre, 'Reply to Wilkinson' *Res Publica* 14 (2008).
[26] Nozick, *Anarchy, State, and Utopia*, p. 160.

justice at the point of acquisition. This view does not say organs are never objects of distributive justice. They could be, *after* acquisition. In prevailing systems, organs from the dead are donated into a general pool, typically run by agents of the state. Rules of distributive justice are conventionally held to apply to allocation from this pool, which is why there is so much controversy about the relative weight that should be given to time spent on a waiting list, capacity to benefit, need, ethnicity, and urgency when deciding to whom to give organs. The point is that while organs can appropriately be the objects of distributive justice, they are not until they have been legitimately acquired.

Fabre herself limits her conscription policy in a way that seems to conflict with her view of organs as resources. She favours conscientious objection, albeit with rather stringent restrictions.[27] Justice, she claims, does not require people to blight their own lives and it would be unjust to blight someone else's. If fearing one's organs would be confiscated upon death would blight one's life, one should not have one's organs confiscated. The trouble with this argument is that it does not fit with Fabre's idea of organs as resources to be allocated fairly. If I hold on to some piece of property belonging to someone else, the property should be taken off me and given back to the owner. Suppose I have stolen the *Mona Lisa*, and would be distraught without it. The painting should nonetheless be taken from me and returned to its rightful owners, and the reason is nothing to do with how distraught they would be at not getting it back. If organs should really be regarded in the same way as material resources available for egalitarian redistribution, my attitude to my organs is irrelevant if they do not belong to me. By contrast, the claim that lives should not be blighted by conscription reflects the sense that organs are not like material property and are not available for egalitarian redistribution.

Organs may not be resources in the sense that Fabre needs, but she may be right that needy people have positive welfare rights. Positive rights, and how they fit with other people's negative rights of bodily control, are the subject of a later sub-section.

The needs of the sick and the rights of the dead

Take the following argument.

1. People who need transplants have a great interest in continuing to live or in large improvements in the quality of their lives.
2. People have a much lesser interest in what happens to them after their deaths.
3. We should follow a rule or act so that we fulfil the more important interests.

Therefore

4. If conscription of organs would better fulfil the more important interests, we ought to conscript organs.
5. Conscription would better fulfil the more important interests.

---

[27] Fabre, *Whose Body Is It Anyway?* pp. 89f.

Therefore

6. We ought to conscript organs.

Call this the 'greater need' argument.[28] It seems simple, straightforward, and powerful. But while it is indeed powerful, it raises matters that are complicated enough, and they are the focus of the rest of this chapter.

I want to begin with some initial comments on the greater need argument. Supporters of conscription often claim that the dead do not have interests.[29] Opponents often claim they do and think that if the dead do have interests, the argument is won. But the greater need argument makes no assumption about whether people have interests that survive their deaths, only that, if those interests exist, fulfilling them is less important than fulfilling the interests of potential recipients in getting organs.

Is it not obviously correct that more important interests are fulfilled if organs are taken at the expense of a loss of posthumous bodily control? Consider this thought experiment: suppose a plane were about to crash and the pilot could choose to crash either into the mortuary, where there are only people who are dead but who wanted to be buried intact, or into the main part of a hospital, where living people are (none of whom, as it happens, care about being buried intact). Obviously, the pilot should steer towards the mortuary even at the price of causing the interest of those now dead to go unfulfilled. The explanation seems to be that the interest in staying alive is greater than the posthumous interest.

The greater need argument is in consequentialist form in stating that more important interests should have priority. Consequentialism is a controversial view, but the way it is put here avoids certain objections. Consider the objection that, for consequentialism, a large enough total of lesser harms can outweigh a few large harms. The greater need argument, by contrast, says that more important interests should have priority. It need not, for instance, trade lives for headaches.

Some of the arguments against conscription themselves appear in consequentialist form. They point to the distress that conscription might cause the family or to the fear it would cause living people before they die or to the bad effects on the experience of dying in intensive care. These arguments are themselves vulnerable to the criticism that they trade off the greater interests of those who need organs for the sake of fulfilling lesser interests. As defenders of conscription argue, it is much more important to save a life than, say, to avoid distressing a family.[30] If we remain within the realm of consequentialist considerations, these criticisms of conscription look feeble.

---

[28] This argument is adapted from the writings of John Harris, who is probably the most prominent supporter of conscription. His fullest statement seems to be 'Law and Regulation of Retained Organs'. See also Harris's 'The Survival Lottery' *Philosophy* 50 (1975), and *The Value of Life* (London: Routledge & Kegan Paul, 1985), 118–23.

[29] Aaron Spital, 'Conscription of Cadaveric Organs for Transplantation: Neglected Again' *Kennedy Institute of Ethics Journal* 13 (2003), p. 171.

[30] Aaron Spital and James S. Taylor, 'In Defense of Routine Recovery of Cadaveric Organs: A Response to Walter Glannon' *Cambridge Quarterly of Healthcare Ethics* 17 (2008).

The claim so far is that the good that organ conscription would do for recipients is greater than the good it would do to the dead to have their posthumous wishes followed. Other things equal, it is better to do what would produce more net good. Because it is better, showing that the dead can have posthumous interests is not enough to rule out organ conscription. So much may be conceded to the greater need argument. But, as chapter 4 claimed, people have rights to control what happens to their bodies after they die, which is a powerful reason against conscription. Is the reason decisive against the greater need? Consider two arguments for thinking that the greater need wins out. One is that conscription of the dead involves a conflict of rights because potential recipients also have rights to the organs of the dead. The other is that conscription is a permissible infringement of rights because of the amount of good it would do.[31] These ideas are the subject of the next two sub-sections.

Positive rights

The main objection to the positive rights case for conscription from the dead is that it is also a case for conscription from the living.[32] Conscription from the living is wrong, so either the sick do not have a positive right to organs or else their positive rights do not outweigh the negative rights. Let me explain the objection more fully. It is not decisive but it is, I think, unanswered.

If the sick have a positive right to an organ from a dead person, who had a negative right against its being taken, there is a conflict of rights. The conflict needs to be resolved in some way. If negative rights should take priority over positive rights, the case for conscription is in trouble. But perhaps conflicts of rights should be resolved by minimizing harm to rightholders. The idea is that when deciding which rights to respect, priority should be given to the rightholder who would be more harmed if her right were not respected. Conscription could then be justified, assuming the living sick person would be more harmed by not receiving an organ than a dead person would be by having the organ taken. But suppose we apply the minimizing harm method to resolve conflicts of living people's rights. We are supposing a sick person has a positive right to an organ; for instance, someone with acute liver failure has a right to a piece of liver. But a living person has a right not to have a piece of her liver taken. Again, rights would conflict. On any sensible view of who can be expected to suffer most harm if the purported rights are not respected, it is the sick person. The sick person would definitely die without the liver, while the living person has only a small chance of death if the liver is taken. Consequently, if the sick person has a positive right and if conflicts are to be resolved by minimizing harms to rightholders, the living person's liver segment ought to be conscripted.

---

[31] Walter Glannon, 'Do the Sick have a Right to Cadaveric Organs?' *Journal of Medical Ethics* 29 (2003) vacillates between saying (1) the sick might have a positive right but it is outweighed by the negative right to refuse having one's organs taken and (2) because there is a negative right to refuse, the sick cannot have a positive right, not even one that is outweighed.

[32] This objection is derived from Thomson, *Realm of Rights*, pp. 160–3.

This is the wrong conclusion so—the objection goes—either the sick person does not have a positive right or else conflicts of rights should be resolved in some way other than minimizing harm. If you want to argue on the basis of positive rights for conscription from the dead but not the living, you have to find another way of resolving conflicts of rights that supports the one but not the other. It would be foolish to say this challenge could not be met, but I do not know of any serious attempts to do so.[33]

Overriding rights

If conscription from the dead does not involve a conflict of rights, what then of the idea that the rights of the dead may be overridden for the sake of the good it would do? Recall some of the ideas in chapter 2. Rights are moral claims—moral constraints on the behaviour of others—with considerable weight. But, since not all rights are absolute, at least some rights may be overridden for at least some benefits. When, then, may rights be overridden? We can approach this question with a general account of overriding rights. One plausible condition is that the total benefit from the infringement is larger than the loss to the rightholder.[34] It will thus be easier to justify overriding some rights rather than others because the loss to the rightholder will vary. Breaking into your car might be justified to get someone to hospital but breaking into *you* might not be. Other things equal, the more harm that would be suffered by the rightholder, the more good that would have to be done for the infringement to be justified. Another plausible condition is that, for overriding to be permissible, someone must gain at least as much as the rightholder loses. Thus a person's right against having her arm broken should not be overridden in order to prevent a large number of minor headaches even if preventing the headaches would produce a greater total benefit.

The benefits to recipients of getting an organ would typically be greater in aggregate and individually than the loss to dead people whose organs are conscripted. Conscription could thus meet some of the plausible general conditions for overriding rights. But is the extra good of more organs enough to justify infringing on the right? The answer depends on the amount of extra good that conscription would do and whether that amount of good warrants overriding the right of posthumous bodily control. The judgements involved are very difficult. I must concede, though, that although I am arguing against conscription, I cannot say that conscription could never be justified. Once it is said that the justifiability of conscription hinges upon the amount of good it would do, surely conscription could do enough good in some conceivable circumstances, even if not in the actual circumstances.

---

[33] Fabre's discussion of welfare rights is serious, but not an attempt to meet this challenge since she argues that positive rights could justify conscription from the living.

[34] This and other conditions are set out in Thomson, *Realm of Rights*, ch. 6 and Samantha Brennan, 'How is the Strength of a Right Determined?' *American Philosophical Quarterly* 32 (1995) and 'Thresholds for Rights' *The Southern Journal of Philosophy* 33 (1995).

Unfortunately, and rather unsatisfactorily, we do not have a good general account of how much good must be done to override rights justifiably.[35] In the case of conscripting organs, we have to turn to specific examples to see whether we think intuitively that people's rights over their bodies should be overridden. The near-complete absence of political pressure anywhere for organ conscription suggests it has little intuitive support, but perhaps other examples do support conscription.

Consider an example from Frances Kamm. She writes,

> Suppose five people are adrift in the sea after a shipwreck, and one of them dies of unavoidable natural causes. Are the other four justified, not merely excused on account of mental distress, if they save their own lives by taking the organs of the dead person when the deceased or family's wishes are not known? If they are too weak to take, may a third party who is in no need help them to do so? What if they or the third party know that the decedent or the family would be opposed to such taking? *If* all agents were justified in taking in all these circumstances, this would support the view that third parties may, in general, take organs no longer being used for the sake of those who would otherwise die.[36]

The shipwreck case is a powerful example. My initial intuition is that it is permissible for the agents to take even when the deceased and the deceased's families are known to object. But thinking it permissible to take in Kamm's shipwreck case does not require thinking conscription as a policy is permissible. Kamm's case is both underdescribed and disanalogous. She does not even say what the people on the raft do with the organs. Assuming they transplant them, she does not tell us how successful this would be, and how much longer the people would live with than without the organs. If the organ is a kidney, could they have dialysis instead? She does not tell us what resources they use, or what else these resources could have been used for. Could the resources have saved other people's lives, for instance through funding an expensive drug? In other words, Kamm does not tell us how much extra good would be done by taking the organs when compared with the alternatives. Nor does she tell us the history of the people on the raft. She tells us, in one version, that the deceased opposed retrieval, but not whether the deceased would have refused an organ if one of the others had died, nor whether any of the people on the raft had taken any opportunity to opt out of giving and receiving an organ.

Underdescribed shipwreck cases are poor guides to working out the value of more transplants when compared with overriding people's rights. But possibly if the shipwreck case were made more like organ transplantation, we would still think taking permissible, even from someone opposed. So I want to say more about weighing extra organs against respecting rights.

---

[35] Brennan, 'Thresholds for Rights', p. 146; Shelly Kagan, *Normative Ethics* (Boulder: Westview Press, 1998), pp. 311–12.

[36] Frances Kamm, *Morality, Mortality*, vol. 1 (New York: Oxford University Press, 1993), p. 215 (emphasis in original). Kamm does not make it clear whether she thinks this example shows taking in the face of opposition to be justified, but it appears by p. 218 that she does.

Trade offs and the benefits of organs

The force of the shipwreck case lies partly in its being an emergency. All sorts of niceties go by the board in emergencies. However, there is a well-known apparent split in social responses to risk. To take an example, societies might be willing to pay a lot to rescue trapped miners but not willing to pay anything like as much for safety precautions that would stop miners being trapped in the first place. Whether or not this split is incoherent, generalizing from our efforts in emergencies does not tell us much about what we should spend in the ordinary run of things (even though this ordinary run itself has people dying or suffering). Throughout the world, health systems struggle over what to do about expensive drugs or machinery, but no country spends all it could to save lives. At some point, in some way, the value of saving lives or improving their medical quality yields to other things people want. These things might be high-minded goods, like education, but they need not be. Outside healthcare, the value of prolonging life is traded off against other goods both by individuals, when they risk death by flying on their holidays for instance, and by societies, as when they build tunnels or set speed limits higher than the safest speed. For the sake of apparently trivial benefits, people run the risk of death. Nor is this merely a point about probability. It is certain that some people will die in a large-scale construction programme, but we do not on that account think the programme must be wrong.[37]

If we are willing to trade lives for what money can buy, we ought to be willing to trade lives for the sake of respecting rights of bodily control. We cannot say, then, that saving lives is so important it simply *must* have priority over rights. So how should we decide whether and when saving lives takes priority? People will differ in their answers and these differences will sometimes be based on different reasonable preferences. Some people may have a considered religious or cultural desire to be buried intact, and prefer intact burial even at the cost of a reduced supply of organs. Other people may not care what happens to their bodies after death and want more organs to be available for transplantation. This variation in preference need not be a sign of irrationality on anyone's part.

Assume, temporarily, that we are only considering reasonable preferences. An organ procurement policy would ideally provide for variety for two reasons. First, when people differ in how they value more organs as against the cost of donation, it would be fairer and perhaps produce more welfare if the policy gave different people what they would rather have. Second, the people who do not value more organs at the cost of their organs being retrieved have their preference protected by the right to refuse to donate. So consider a policy I shall call 'exempt and exclude'. People who preferred, say, intact burial to access to extra organs would be allowed intact burial so long as they forgo the access. They would then be better off than under conscription. Those who prefer the organs should get access at the price of giving up posthumous bodily control. In effect, access to organs would be like insurance

---

[37] For a recent discussion and qualified defence of cost-benefit analysis as applied to statistical lives, see Cass Sunstein, *Worst-case Scenarios* (Cambridge, MA: Harvard University Press, 2007), ch. 5.

and people who want access could get together with like-minded people. Those who did not want to pay the access price of giving up their right to veto retrieval would be excluded. Indeed, if people had well-worked out beliefs and reasons, there would be no need to moralize about those who have opted for exemption and exclusion. They merely would not want to participate in a cooperative scheme either as givers or takers. Exempt and exclude, on such assumptions, would be superior to conscription.

But exempt and exclude may not be feasible, if we are to believe a version of a public goods argument for conscription. John Harris says, in his defence of conscription, that organ supply should be regarded as a public good, participation in which should be mandatory.[38] Sometimes 'public good' just means 'good for a lot of people', and if this is all Harris means, then he is merely further describing his greater need argument. But in arguments influenced by economics, 'public goods' has a special meaning, which suggests a distinct argument. In the economic sense, a public good is one that is jointly supplied and non-excludable.[39] A jointly supplied good is one that, if supplied to anyone, goes to everyone. A non-excludable good is one from which it is not feasible to exclude non-contributors. Thus if a public good is supplied, even non-contributors will get it. For example, good sewerage reduces contagious disease and everyone benefits from less disease whether they have paid for the sewers or not.[40] By contrast, a live rugby match is not a public good, no matter how many people benefit from seeing it, because this good can be supplied only to those who pay for it. Public goods, in the economic sense, are the source of an incentives problem. If people would get the benefit whether they paid the cost or not, why pay the cost?

A public goods problem may justify coercion in two ways. One is if a public good would be undersupplied by voluntary contribution, where a good is undersupplied if people judge the cost of paying as less than the benefit to them of more of the good. The other is if people act unfairly by taking without contributing, and so may in all fairness be coerced into paying their share of the costs. So much for the public goods idea: how does it apply to organs?

Organs themselves are not a public good, since some people obviously are excluded from getting them: that is the problem with shortage. The supply does, however, have its public good aspects, since people have a chance of getting organs whether or not they are willing to supply them after death. Round the world, organs from the dead are typically distributed without regard to anyone's prior agreement to donate.[41] In the case of organ supply, why agree to have organs taken

---

[38] John Harris, 'Organ Procurement: Dead Interests, Living Needs' *Journal of Medical Ethics* 29 (2003).
[39] Virtually any economics text explains the ideas. One classic account is Mancur Olson, *The Logic of Collective Action* (Cambridge, MA: Harvard University Press, 1965).
[40] In 'Organ Procurement: Dead Interests, Living Needs', Harris gives jury service and compulsory autopsy as two examples of public goods with mandatory participation. I think jury service is a public good, but it is questionable whether the good of autopsy is primarily public. I will not pursue the question.
[41] Singapore is an exception. See Govert den Hartogh, *Farewell to Non-commitment: Decision Systems for Organ Donation from an Ethical Viewpoint* (The Hague: Centre for Ethics and Health, 2008), p. 50, n. 54.

if it makes no difference to eligibility to receive? People who receive organs but who would not contribute typically take organs that could have gone to others and so they are parasites.[42]

If the organ supply were a public good, then exempt and exclude would be infeasible because, by definition, it is not feasible to exclude from the good only those who would prefer not to pay their share. There would then be a case for uniform conscription to set against some people's rights over their bodies. However, the supply of organs is not a public good in the economic sense. It is technically feasible to exclude non-contributors from access to organs. Admittedly, it would be a bizarre policy if contributors were defined as only those who have actually contributed an organ, but it is not bizarre to have a rule making access to organs conditional on stating a willingness to donate. We have no reason to think exempt and exclude is infeasible in principle.

Exempt and exclude does, though, have potential drawbacks in practice.[43] It may exclude people who later change their minds. Not everyone who opposes the retrieval of their organs, let alone fails to favour it, does so for stable well-worked out reasons. This consideration leads some writers to prefer the current system of a pool open to all.

The three policies of conscription, exempt and exclude, and the current system each offer something different. In picking a policy for acquiring organs, we have to make trade offs. When we do, we should bear in mind the following: (1) people have rights not to have their organs taken; (2) some rightholders have well-worked out objections to donating, and it would be good to exempt them from donating and exclude them from receiving; (3) some would like to be eligible to receive without being liable to donate, which would be unfair; and (4) some people do not have well-worked out views or their views may change over time. The best policy will depend on how many people are in categories 2–4, and finding that out requires empirical evidence. Policy-makers should also bear in mind that (5) not all policies are stable, conscription with conscientious objection being a likely example, and (6) policies themselves may change preferences. Conscription, for instance, may make many more people dissent from organ retrieval, a dissent which is protected by a right.

Exempt and exclude may not be better in practice than the current system, but neither infringes on the right to veto retrieval and so both are superior in that respect to conscription. I believe that conscription could nonetheless be justified in some conceivable circumstances. The strongest case for conscription could be made in a society that largely supports conscription, where hardly anyone dissents for well-worked out stable reasons even after the introduction of conscription, where an exempt and exclude system would be infeasible for some reason, and where conscription would produce many more organs than the feasible alternatives. Then it may be said that the value of saving lives would be worth the cost of infringing on

---

[42] See David Gauthier's free rider/parasite distinction in his *Morals By Agreement* (Oxford: Clarendon Press, 1986), pp. 96–7.

[43] See chapter 9 for a discussion of giving priority to donors.

a few rights with little unfairness. As I said, when the ethical question of conscription comes down to overriding non-absolute rights, it must be possible that conscription could be justified. However, we have no reason to think that the society for which the strongest case could be made is anything like the societies we live in. We are thus in a situation where we know people have rights and we have been given no adequate reason to override them. In this situation, we should not override their rights. Conscription is therefore unjustified. There is, though, an exception to the rights argument, and that is conscription from young children.

CONSCRIPTION FROM YOUNG CHILDREN

The rights-based argument does not apply to young children (or anyone who never rose above the cognitive level of young children). They do not have the relevant rights because they do not have the relevant posthumous interests. All this section tries to show is the limit to the rights-based argument this chapter has given. I do not try to make a case for conscription as a policy, which would require considering other reasons for the common view that parents, or families more generally, should be allowed either to veto or consent to organs being taken from their dead children.[44] Policy would also need to take into account the supply and demand of children's organs. On the one hand, organs from children are in especially short supply since they tend not to die from the causes that make people suitable donors. On the other hand, families of dead children are much more willing to donate than families of dead adults, according to some evidence.[45]

People who believe that no one can have interests affected by events after death will find it obvious that dead children cannot. However, my claim that young children do not have such interests is based on a view about the sorts of interests that survive death and the conceptual abilities of young children. The kinds of interest that can survive a person's death are ones that presuppose a fairly high degree of intellectual ability and they will usually have to be ones that the person cared about. Living young children do not, for example, have interests in reputation or privacy for their own sake—that is, leaving aside any instrumental effects on other interests—because they do not understand the concepts and the concepts have to be understood to be had as interests. If young living children do not have these interests, it would be very surprising if young dead children did. I am not claiming that all interests have to be cared about or presuppose high reflective ability. Living young children have interests in their development or in being fed, even if they do not and cannot realize this. I am just making the claims about reflection and caring in the case of the interests that can plausibly be affected by

---

[44] For a fuller account, which considers arguments rooted in the claims of parents as well as children, see my 'Parental Consent and the Use of Dead Children's Bodies' *Kennedy Institute of Ethics Journal* 11 (2001). See also chapter 5 of this book, on parental bonds.

[45] John A. Morris, Jr, Todd R. Wilcox, and William H. Frist, 'Pediatric Organ Donation: The Paradox of Organ Shortage Despite the Remarkable Willingness of Families to Donate' *Pediatrics* 89 (1992), pp. 411–15.

posthumous events (and interests in development or being fed obviously do not fall in this class).

People who do not care probably do not, and those who cannot care cannot, have an interest in what happens to their bodies after death. Thus while adults and older children might have reasonably well-worked out views about what should happen to their bodies after death, and so might have an interest in their bodies not being used for medical purposes, younger children will not. Younger children will not have the interest in not being used because they have no conception of death that would be sufficiently well-worked out to ground an interest. There is universal agreement, at least in the universe of psychologists, that pre-school children do not understand death in the way that adults do. They do not understand that death is irreversible, for instance, or that it is inevitable.[46] Admittedly, it will be a matter of controversy at what age children tend to conceive of death accurately, so let me stipulate that I shall be talking of children who uncontroversially do not. Pre-school children, at least, do not have posthumous interests.

Because young children do not have posthumous interests, they do not have posthumous rights on an interest-based theory of rights. Young children have no rights at all on a choice-based theory.[47] Hence the conscription of young children's organs cannot be ruled out on the basis of their rights.

I want to consider finally the idea that children have a right based on dignity. It would surely be wrong, for instance, to display a child's remains in a circus. It could then be argued that conscription of children's organs would violate some duty of dignity. However, the dignity argument faces a problem. The circus display would be wrong whether or not the parents consent. But it is commonly thought that parents may donate the organs of their children. How could the dignity of a child depend on whether a parent consents? It cannot be because they are expressing the child's own view; the child could have had no view. If the dignity of the child really is in question, either all organ retrieval conflicts with dignity or else retrieval as such does not conflict at all.

Is it then inconsistent with the dignity of the children to take their organs for transplantation? One reason for thinking a circus display undignified is the trivial and unwholesome use to which the remains are put. Using the bodies of children to save lives or to reduce the effects of disease and disability is not trivial or unwholesome. So insofar as dignity depends on use, that use would not be contrary to dignity. It may be said that organ retrieval conflicts with children's dignity because it treats them solely as a means to an end. This seems to me to replace the obscurity of 'dignity' with the obscurity of 'treating solely as a means'. Be that as it may, it is not obvious that to use the remains of children is to treat them solely as a means and to fail to treat them as an end. Treating them solely as a means would be to treat the bodies as if they were mere things to be used or discarded in whatever way one

---

[46] V. Slaughter, R. Jaakkola, and S. Carey, 'Constructing a Coherent Theory: Children's Biological Understanding of Life and Death', in M. Siegal and C. Peterson (eds.), *Children's Understanding of Biology and Health* (Cambridge: Cambridge University Press, 1999), p. 73.
[47] See chapter 4.

chooses, with no more respect than one shows to scalpels or surgical gloves. This may be the way bodies are sometimes treated, but it need not be and considerable effort is often put into using bodies in a dignified way. Some might say that despite the effort, conscripting a child's organs would still treat them as a mere means. It would help if they were to develop their objection more fully.[48] And if they do, they must also show how the loss of dignity outweighs the putative gains in organs.

CONCLUSION

Organs should not be conscripted from the dead, leaving aside dead young children, because of the rights people have over their bodies. Still less should organs be conscripted from the living. The living have rights of bodily integrity that clearly conflict with organ conscription. The occasional writer willing to defend conscription from the living has done nothing like enough to undercut the strong intuition that living people are not to be cut up for the benefit of others. Conscription from the dead conflicts with a right of personal sovereignty—not the same as bodily integrity—and that right, especially in the case of the dead, is sufficiently less stringent than bodily integrity to make conscription worth discussing at length. But I have argued that, even when set against the alleged positive rights or genuine need of the sick, the right wins out and conscription is unjustified.

Up to this point in the book, we have largely focused on organ retrieval from the dead. The next chapter focuses on the living, exploring the implications of our rights over our bodies in the context of living donor organ transplantation.

---

[48] One may think that one avoids using solely as a means only if one gets the consent of those one uses. There are problems for that view in addition to those I have mentioned in the context of young children. Kant, at least, did not take the principle that way. For discussion, see Cohen, *Self-Ownership, Freedom, and Equality*, pp. 238–42.

8

Living Donor Organ Transplantation

Although the earliest successful organ transplants had been between living relatives, living donation was initially thought of as a stopgap, awaiting the time when transplantation using dead donors would work well. But now transplants from dead donors do work well; the problem is not enough dead donors. Whether or not the unanticipated need for living donors' organs caused the change, the laws and regulations of several countries have become more permissive about who can be a living donor, no longer making it difficult or impossible for non-relatives to donate. Having begun with identical twins, organs have been taken from genetic relatives, then spouses, then friends, and then strangers. Complicated pairing arrangements have been devised so that people whose organs are unsuitable for their relatives can swap organs with strangers in the same position. Organs are taken from donors who would have been rejected a few years ago.[1] The upshot is that living donors now supply about half the kidneys in some countries, including the US, and a third in the UK. In 2009, the US had over 6,000 living donors and, in a comparable year, the UK had over 900 living kidney donors.[2] According to an estimate for 2006, 27,000 living donor kidney transplants occur worldwide each year and constitute 39 per cent of all kidney transplants.[3] And still the pressure is on to find more.[4] As one editorial put it, 'Alternative sources of donors, especially live donors, must be sought in order to address the unremediable disparity between the number of available cadaveric organs and the number of potential recipients.'[5]

Let us scan some of the facts about living donor organ transplantation, beginning with the kidney, the organ most commonly taken from living donors. Kidneys are in particularly short supply, given the high demand for them, and kidneys from living donors are usually better for recipients than kidneys from dead donors.

---

[1] Some centres will now take organs from living donors who would previously have been rejected because of their age and/or hypertension. See Stephen Textor and Sandra Taler, 'Expanding Criteria for Living Kidney Donors: What are the Limits?' *Transplantation Reviews* 22 (2008).

[2] For the US numbers, see the Organ Procurement and Transplantation Network's website, <optn. transplant.hrsa.gov> (last accessed August 2010); for the UK numbers, which are for 1/4/08—31/03/09, see <www.uktransplant.org.uk> (last accessed August 2010).

[3] Lucy Horvat et al., 'Global Trends in the Rates of Living Kidney Donation' *Kidney International* 75 (2009), p. 1090.

[4] For a recent survey of trends in law and policy, see David Price, *Human Tissue in Transplantation and Research: A Model Legal and Ethical Donation Framework* (Cambridge: Cambridge University Press, 2009), ch. 7.

[5] A. J. Langone and J. H. Helderman, 'Disparity Between Solid-Organ Supply and Demand' *New England Journal of Medicine* 349 (2003), p. 705.

Kidney retrieval is reasonably safe for a healthy donor. The risk of mortality during surgery is generally estimated as less than 1 in 3,000[6] and '[s]urvival and the risk of ESRD [end stage renal disease] in carefully screened kidney donors appear to be similar to those in the general population'.[7] Since the late 1980s, living donors have also been used to acquire livers. The liver, unlike the kidney, is capable of regenerating in the donor. Liver donation is nonetheless riskier than kidney donation, with an estimated mortality risk of 0.2–0.5 per cent for donation from adult to adult, and 0.06–0.18 per cent for donation from adult to child.[8] Although it is riskier to donate a piece of liver than a kidney, the recipients of livers often stand to gain more than recipients of kidneys because people with acute liver failure have no equivalent of kidney dialysis to keep them alive. On a small scale, there have also been live donations of segments of the lung and, on a smaller scale still, the pancreas and the small intestine. Living people have even donated hearts, although not with the fatal consequences one might expect: donations have occurred in domino fashion, when patients who receive heart–lung transplants donate their original hearts.[9]

Transplanting organs from living people raises many ethical questions. One set of questions, which I can here only mention, is about the boundaries of the living. Deceased donor organs are overwhelmingly taken from people declared whole-brain dead, but some writers say that whole-brain death is not genuinely death.[10] Anencephalics, who are born with most of their brains missing but with their organs often intact, are considered alive both in law and according to prevailing medical views, yet considered dead, or at least not alive, on some conceptions of death.[11] Some non-heart-beating deceased donors have organs removed following withdrawal of life support, but it is not clear for how long their hearts must stop for them to be really dead.[12] In this chapter, however, I set aside the problem of the boundaries of life and consider only the uncontroversially living.

The chapter starts with the implications for living donation of duties to do no harm and to respect autonomy. These duties are frequently assigned to doctors in writings on medical ethics. On the face of it, the duties would conflict in the case of living donation because taking organs from healthy people appears to harm them and yet they could wish to donate. On a closer look, the duty to do no harm would

---

[6] See e.g. Arthur Matas et al., 'Morbidity and Mortality After Living Kidney Donation, 1999–2001: Survey of United States Transplant Centers' *American Journal of Transplantation* 3 (2003).

[7] H. Ibrahim et al., 'Long-Term Consequences of Kidney Donation' *The New England Journal of Medicine* 360 (2009), p. 459.

[8] ASERNIP-S (Australian Safety and Efficacy Register of New Interventional Procedures–Surgical) 'Live Donor Liver Transplantation—Adult Outcomes: A Systematic Review' (2004). The risks of donating organs may be higher for 'expanded criteria' donors, such as those with hypertension.

[9] For references and further discussion of the facts of living donor transplantation, see David Price, *Legal and Ethical Aspects of Organ Transplantation* (Cambridge: Cambridge University Press, 2000), pp. 217–29.

[10] Peter Singer, *Rethinking Life and Death* (Melbourne: The Text Publishing Company, 1994), chs. 2 and 3; Jeff McMahan, *The Ethics of Killing* (New York: Oxford University Press, 2002), pp. 423–43.

[11] Singer, *Rethinking Life and Death*, ch. 3.

[12] Robert Veatch, *Transplantation Ethics* (Washington, DC: Georgetown University Press, 2000), ch. 13.

not rule out all living donation, while respecting autonomy does not require acceding to all requests to donate. The duties will often not conflict in practice. A later section then argues that when well-being and autonomy do conflict, people should be permitted to sacrifice their well-being to some degree. We should, however, bear in mind that the transplant team would have to help them make the sacrifice, and team members have their own interests which ought to be considered. Even so, on a wide range of sensible views about harm, autonomy, and transplant teams' discretion, living donation is morally permissible.

It is of course widely accepted that living donation is morally permissible, as the figures for living donation suggest. Getting clear on why it is permissible, though, turns out to have major implications. In a later chapter, I show how many of the arguments for living donation are also arguments for permitting sale. Here, I point out that, if we take the arguments for living donation seriously, current screening practices may not be permissive enough. I also argue that, contrary to trends in practice, competent children should be allowed to donate, subject to the same caveats as apply to adults, and that, when donation is in their interests, organs may be taken from non-competent people too.

WELL-BEING AND THE DUTY TO DO NO HARM

The duty not to harm patients, or non-maleficence, is to be found in codes of medical ethics from the oldest times to now. The duty appears to prohibit surgeons from removing the organs of healthy people and transplanting them into others. Unlike standard surgery, organ removal for transplantation is not done for the therapeutic benefit of the patient. The removal of an organ puts the donor at risk from the operation, from post-operative infection, and, in the case of non-regenerative organs, from the drawbacks of losing one. If physical harms were the only relevant harms, the duty not to do harm would prohibit transplants from live donors.

We shall later ask whether living donation should be ruled out if it would harm donors, but let us first assess attempts to justify it by broadening medical harm to include what are usually called 'psychosocial' aspects. The attempts point out, for example, that most parents would suffer greatly if their children die, and still more so if they are prevented from saving their children by donating their organs. In addition to avoiding grief, donating an organ can benefit donors by preventing the death of a companion or reducing the burden of caring for a sick relative. At a lecture I once gave on transplantation, a woman in the audience told us she had donated an organ to her husband, who was sitting next to her. As I recall, she said, 'I did it for selfish reasons. I didn't want to lose my playmate.' If we consider the psychosocial as well as the physical, a living person may not be harmed overall by donation because the psychosocial benefits would outweigh the physical risks.

From a philosophical point of view, widening the conception of harm to include the psychosocial does not go far enough. On a fairly standard view of harm, a harm is a setback to an interest, and most philosophical views of well-being allow for vicarious interests, that is, interests in the well-being of others. Thus a loving parent has a vicarious interest in the welfare of her child. If the child is harmed, the harm to the child is also a harm to the parent. The harm to the parent is not limited to mental suffering, although a parent whose child is harmed usually would suffer mentally. The parent would be harmed even if she did not know what had happened to the child.[13] So if a child dies for want of an organ, the parent is harmed vicariously over and above the harmful mental suffering.

Now the view of harm has been broadened, we can say in the abstract that people's overall interests could be more, less, or just as well met if they donate organs. Judging overall interests is often hard in actual cases, and some may be tempted to avoid the difficulties. They may say that having an organ taken is bad for one's health and doctors should not do what is bad for their patients' health. But as an argument against living donation, this will not do. Health is more than the grossly physical. Feeling depressed at the loss of a relative is not only a falling short in health but also causally likely to lead to other bad effects on health. Donating an organ could thus be better for one's health than not donating.

In any case, why consider only the effects on health? Health is important as a component of well-being, understood as life going well. Exactly how important health is depends on how we understand health and well-being, but, on any sensible view of either, people trade off health against other goods. They risk injury and even death through sport, or flying, or driving, and taking the risks need not be irrational because health is only part of a worthwhile life. If we ask how important health is and when some part of it is worth trading off, surely no single answer applies to everyone. The importance of some health improvement depends on individual details. But if we accept that health is not just physical, that it is subject to trade offs with other goods, and that the trade offs vary from person to person, living donation could be good for some donors even if not for others. Only if a donor's overall interests are set back by donation should we say that the donor has been harmed.

Assessing whether donation is for or against the donor's overall interests requires a complicated judgement. In the first place, some judgement must be made of each of the relevant elements—the size and nature of the physical and psychosocial effects, and the importance of the vicarious interest in the recipient's well-being, together with the probabilities of these effects occurring. Then some overall judgement must be made that trades off the elements when they compete with each other, as they will when donation is against people's physical interests but in their other interests.

Some of what a judgement needs is empirical evidence. For instance, empirical evidence is needed of the nature, size, and predictability of the physical risks of having an organ removed. Evidence is also needed of the likely effects on the recipient since, other things equal, prolonging a recipient's life for a few weeks is less in a donor's interest than prolonging the recipient's life indefinitely at high quality.

---

[13] See the discussion of interests in chapter 3 of this book.

We should also take into account evidence about how donors subsequently feel about their donation so as to see, for instance, whether they are prone to depression (although donors seem largely glad to have donated).[14]

Comparing the various effects to form some overall judgement of the effects on potential donors' well-being is not empirical and may not be easy. How is anyone to decide whether staying in hospital for a week, having to take three weeks off work, and risking a 1/600 chance of death is worth it for pleasure of retaining the company of an uncle or acquiring praise for being a donor? The transplant team might be authorities on the physical risks to the donor and perhaps the likely psychological effects, but they are not authorities on how important these effects are to the well-being of the donor, and how they compare with the potential benefits. Transplant teams that include psychiatrists or social workers might have a better sense of the non-physical harms and benefits than teams of only medical and surgical staff, but the question remains of how expert they can be on such personal matters.

No doubt many potential donors would not consider donating only in terms of their own various interests. They would also consider the benefits to potential recipients without translating them into vicarious benefits for themselves. They may think it should be up to them whether to sacrifice their own interests to help recipients, a view that seems to conflict with doctors' duty to do no harm. However, even if potential willing donors should not have their interests sacrificed, the complexity of judging overall interests and the limits of outsiders' insight gives a reason to let people decide for themselves whether to donate. While people are fallible judges of their own interests, one would hope that, with a proper informed consent procedure, not many people would make mistakes. I do not mean this to be a rhetorical question, but why would free informed competent people consider donation and then consent *by mistake*?

We can come to the following conclusion. The duty to do no harm only rules out taking organs from people who would be harmed overall. Donating an organ need not be against the donor's overall interests, so the duty need not rule out living donation. Indeed, given the difficulties of making an overall assessment of the well-being of donors, it will be hard to show in many cases that people would be harmed overall if they donated.

I have been discussing the duty to do no harm, a rule that some see as an outmoded relic of medicine's paternalistic days.[15] They believe neither doctors nor the law should decide whether an operation is too risky; potential donors

---

[14] See the evidence reported in Price, *Human Tissue in Transplantation and Research*, p. 167. Retrospective interviews with donors are not perfect: donors may look back with excessively rosy views and the interviews do not tell us how those who refused subsequently felt. Some reports suggest that donors are more likely than the general population to commit suicide but, if true, there are numerous possible explanations besides any ill effects of donating. For instance, related donors will often have lived with the recipients, and it can be very hard to live with people who have organ failure.

[15] Veatch, *Transplantation Ethics*, p. 202. However, not every justification for the 'do no harm' rule is paternalistic. Protecting the reputation of the medical profession, whether or not a good reason, is not paternalistic.

themselves should decide. The unlimited freedom to donate may seem to follow from chapter 2's view of personal sovereignty. Let us see.

LIVING DONATION AND PERSONAL SOVEREIGNTY

This section is about the requirements of personal sovereignty and the next will be about its importance compared with well-being. Conventionally, respect for a competent person's personal sovereignty is held to require free informed consent before donation may proceed. Consent is required because people have a right not to have their organs taken and, at least in the case of living competent people, only their consent lifts the barrier to taking their organs.[16] The consent must be in some sense free so not, for instance, obtained as the result of physical threats. The consent must be informed; people must know what they are consenting to. And the potential donor's consent is valid only if the person is competent to give it, which means the person must have some capacity to understand the options and a set of values coherent enough for her to decide between them.[17]

Some aspects of informed consent in living donation are sufficiently uncontroversial that I need mention them only briefly. For instance, I doubt anyone would deny that, when consent is required, it must be informed, so that potential donors must be told and told truthfully of the harms, benefits, and their probabilities. Nor will there be much argument about at least some aspects of the usual physical and psychosocial evaluation and information process. For example, people are screened to see how likely they are to be able to cope with donation or to see whether they understand that, in the case of anonymous donation, they will not subsequently be involved in the life of the recipient.[18] If the purpose is to make sure people know where they stand, and perhaps protect recipients from unwanted involvement with a donor, the screening seems fair enough. There are also interesting questions, which I do not have the room to discuss, about the best ways to inform people and establish what they understand. For example, it may well be a mistake to check that potential donors have deliberated carefully in the light of all the facts because people may pay attention only to what matters to them and yet still give consent that expresses their personal sovereignty.[19]

Rather more controversial have been the questions of whether organs should be taken from people who are desperate to donate to save a relative, or who are pressured by their families, or have what I shall call 'suspect' motivations. The typical advice is to screen for excessive sense of duty, undue influence, unconscious internal neurotic influences, abnormal emotional involvement, or excessive social

---

[16] Chapter 6 argued that consent was not required by personal sovereignty in the case of the dead.

[17] Allen Buchanan and Dan Brock, *Deciding for Others* (Cambridge: Cambridge University Press, 1990), pp. 23–5.

[18] Sheila Jowsey and Terry Schneekloth, 'Psychosocial Factors in Living Organ Donation: Clinical and Ethical Challenges' *Transplantation Reviews* 22 (2008).

[19] See Jonathan Baron, *Against Bioethics* (Cambridge, MA: MIT Press, 2006), section 6.7 and p. 124.

pressure. Since these factors are matters of degree, we need to know how much of them would make agreement invalid, a question often left unanswered in the literature. We clearly cannot say that just any sense of duty or influence by others would make agreement invalid. To think through the problems, let us consider some general points about valid and invalid consent.

The first general point is about voluntariness. The usual way to raise questions about the validity of a decision to donate is to ask whether it was voluntary. The assumption is that if a decision is not voluntary, it is contrary to a person's personal sovereignty. But 'voluntariness' is a difficult and elusive concept, and this assumption can be, and perhaps has been, misleading. In ordinary usage, the word 'voluntary' has a descriptive meaning. If I make an intruder leave my house by threatening him with a gun, we would not ordinarily say that he left voluntarily. But nor would we say that his autonomy was infringed upon, even though he left involuntarily. Personal sovereignty is, as we saw in chapter 2, a matter of acting within legitimate boundaries, and the intruder is within my legitimate boundaries and outside his when he comes into my house. Not all involuntary decisions, in the descriptive sense of 'voluntary', will be contrary to personal sovereignty.[20]

In many cases involving transplantation, the distinction between voluntariness and personal sovereignty will not matter. We have rights over our bodies and if we act involuntarily, that is, against our wills, it will usually be because of threats or lies that infringe upon our rights. Involuntary decisions would usually be contrary to personal sovereignty. Arguably, however, involuntary agreements to donate would not always be contrary to personal sovereignty, as I shall later show in the context of social pressure.

The second general point is about standards for valid agreement, which vary according to how much information, clarity of thought, firmness of will, and absence of pressure they require. How demanding those standards should be changes with context. For example, standards for upholding a contract differ from the standard for moral praise or blame.[21] No doubt, for something as serious as the removal of an organ, the standards should be high. A standard for valid consent should not, however, be so demanding as to require perfect voluntariness, that is, the complete absence in any degree of factors that, at extremes, make choices invalid.[22]

Third, the factors that can compromise validity are sometimes divided into those internal and those external to the person choosing. Examples of internal factors certainly include being too immature to understand what organ retrieval is and why it is being considered, and may include agreeing to donate out of a powerful psychological urge to adopt a sick role or agreeing to sell because one is blinded by the prospect of money. Examples of external factors certainly include brutal

---

[20] Robert Nozick would reach a contrasting conclusion. He says: 'Other people's actions place limits on one's available opportunities. Whether this makes one's resulting action non-voluntary depends on whether these others had the right to act as they did.' See Nozick, *Anarchy, State, and Utopia* (Oxford: Basil Blackwell, 1974), p. 262. G. A. Cohen replies that Nozick's view has 'the absurd upshot that if a criminal's imprisonment is morally justified, he is then not forced to be in prison'. See Cohen, *History, Labour, and Freedom* (Oxford: Clarendon Press, 1988), p. 256.

[21] Joel Feinberg, *Harm to Self* (New York: Oxford University Press, 1986), p. 123.

[22] Ibid., pp. 113–17.

threats, for instance if a woman's relatives threaten to kill her unless she donates or sells an organ, and may include lesser social pressure. Parents' desperation to save their child, which is sometimes thought to make their donation of suspect validity, could be classified as internal, external, or both. I discuss the example of parental desperation in the next sub-section, which is about suspect motivations.

Suspect motivations

Sometimes people want to donate organs because they want to be heroes, or to attract sympathy and attention in the sick role, or to please their cult leaders (as some suspect in the case of the Jesus Christians). People with these motivations need not be delusional and their reasons need not be the outcome of voices in their heads. But if they choose to donate on the basis of these motivations, and they are not delusional, are they choosing non-voluntarily? They may fail psychosocial assessments, and perhaps they should. But why? Questions of voluntariness and motivation are difficult ones in philosophy and psychology and I shall not be able to give a full answer—I have neither the space nor the answer. I can, however, say a few things, beginning with an instructive mistake.

In earlier days of living donation, it was sometimes asked whether parents could freely refuse to donate to their children.[23] Parents themselves sometimes feel as if they have no choice. Nonetheless, the idea that their agreement to donate does not express their personal sovereignty is, and was, a mistake; and it would have been an even bigger mistake to stop them donating, since, whether or not their agreement did express their personal sovereignty, stopping them would make things worse for the parents as well as for the child.

Why would anyone have thought parents were unfree? Three separate explanations suggest themselves. Parents are supposed to be unable to think clearly, to have no reasonable alternative to donating, and to have a sense of duty or love that is in some way suspect. None of these shows parents to be unfree.

The idea of an inability to think with clarity refers to some cognitive failure, such as not understanding the implications of donation, as opposed to the supposed motivational failing of not caring enough about them. But there is no reason to think parents are cognitively unable. Parents may decide quickly and may not appear to pay attention to all the information but, even if so, they may simply know what they really care about.[24] The idea that the choice situation makes the decision

[23] Robert Crouch and Carl Elliot quote the bioethicists Arthur Caplan and George Annas as raising this question. (Annas is quoted as saying: 'The parents basically can't say no.') Crouch and Elliot, 'Moral Agency and the Family: The Case of Living Related Organ Transplantation' *Cambridge Quarterly of Healthcare Ethics* 8 (1999), p. 276. But the quotations appear to be soundbites and may not represent considered opinions.

[24] The early evidence that donors did not grasp the implications was based on a dubious assumption about how people would reason when acting voluntarily. See Carl Fellner and John Marshall, 'Kidney Donors: The Myth of Informed Consent' *American Journal of Psychiatry* 126 (1970). Fellner and Marshall provide evidence of how people did decide and criticize the then-existing guidelines, which required 'a reasoned, intellectual decision, not an emotional decision' (p.1245). See also the discussion in Price, *Legal and Ethical Aspects of Transplantation*, pp. 285–7.

unfree, by leaving parents with no reasonable alternative, is a mistake I shall discuss in a sub-section on desperation. As for the supposed motivational failing, it is absurd, once brought out and inspected, to see anything suspect in wanting to save the life of one's child. Both love and duty are entirely normal, sensible, and desirable motivations, not pathological, and it is hardly an overreaction to care so much about one's child that one would run a small risk to one's life and health for the sake of the benefits a transplant would bring to him or her.

It was always a foolish error to doubt the possibility of valid parental decisions to donate. If we ask why it was an error, we may come to wonder whether current views of invalidity are also in error. If we assume potential donors are not subjected to threats, understand the implications, and do not have delusional beliefs, that is, if we focus purely on the question of their motivations, what makes acting on some motivations suspect?

A motivation could be suspect, from the point of view of personal sovereignty, because of its origin (a procedural criterion) or because of what it is (a substantive criterion). On the procedural side, if people want to do something because they have been brainwashed or otherwise manipulated, what they want to do does not express their personal sovereignty. It is not easy, however, to find a good general account of the causes of a person's motivations that would make them express personal sovereignty.[25] In working out the procedural criteria, we should avoid the error of thinking that motivations must be chosen to be autonomous. If we return to the case of parents, they usually love their children but they cannot help loving their children and did not choose to love their children; yet to regard their unchosen love as contrary to their personal sovereignty would be moral idiocy.[26] Moreover, requiring motivations to be chosen is incoherent. Even if we could make sense of the idea of choosing some of our tastes, say cultivating a taste for art, we would have to cultivate them for the sake of some reason, and that reason would itself be based on some other motivation, such as to fit in with a certain crowd.[27] As a matter of logic, not all one's motivations could be chosen, so it cannot be a general requirement of voluntary choice that the motivation for the choice was itself chosen voluntarily.

What, then, of apparently pathological motives, such as the desire for a sick role or to please one's cult leader? Are these objectionable on substantive grounds—that is, that they are motives that could not be the basis for a personally sovereign choice no matter how they came about? Of course, the presence of a particular motivation may raise suspicions about *why* someone has it. If someone wants to please a cult leader, it could be asked whether the person was brainwashed. But what if the procedure really is unproblematic? Perhaps a choice caused by a truly unintelligible motivation, such as for a saucer of mud (for no further reason), would be an invalid choice however the motivation came about. In general, though, a substantive

[25] Richard Arneson, 'Autonomy and Preference Formation', in Jules Coleman and Allen Buchanan (eds.), *In Harm's Way* (Cambridge: Cambridge University Press, 1994).
[26] See also Crouch and Elliot, 'Moral Agency and the Family', pp. 276–8.
[27] See also Ronald Dworkin, *Sovereign Virtue* (Cambridge, MA: Harvard University Press, 2000), p. 52.

criterion will be controversial. Personal sovereignty does not tell us what sort of life to lead; it aims to ensure that the lives we lead are our own. No one can sensibly think the test of reasonable motivations is having the same motivations as the tester. If we favour a liberal approach to personal sovereignty, is it justified to regard acting on 'pathological motivations' as invalid? Unfortunately, as I said as the start, I do not have the space to answer this question, but only to raise it.

Social pressure

Social pressure is a catch-all term that includes persuasive argument, the weight of expectation, the implicit or explicit threat of ostracism, and perhaps even the threat of violence. If we ask when social pressure makes an agreement to donate invalid, some cases will be easy. A credible threat of violence makes agreement invalid, for instance. Other cases will be harder to assess. The extent to which social pressure undercuts the validity of donation is not just a matter of the effectiveness of pressure in getting someone to agree; it is also a matter of the nature and source of the pressure.[28]

Different forms of social pressure may be equally effective at determining a decision and yet some may not infringe on personal sovereignty while others do. Someone may be just as motivated to avoid blame within the family as they would be by a threat of violence. But while potential donors have a right not to be threatened with violence as well as a right not to become the objects of violence, they do not have a right to other people's good opinions or to other people's company. Suppose someone agrees to donate to avoid criticism or ostracism, but also suppose people have a right to express their views and choose their associates. The agreement to donate may not be voluntary, in the descriptive sense, mentioned earlier, that an intruder's leaving a room at gunpoint is not voluntary. Yet, even if not voluntary in the descriptive sense, agreeing to donate to avoid ostracism or public shame *may* be valid agreement nonetheless, being a response to pressure others had a right to exert.

I have emphasized the 'may' in the conclusion to the previous paragraph because I believe we do not have a clear and correct view of when social pressure undercuts personal sovereignty or, more generally, restricts freedom in a way that should ideally be prevented. A libertarian may say that people have a right to withhold their good opinions and company and so, if someone could retain these only by donating, that person's donation is a voluntary act within the space left by others' legitimate actions.[29] The libertarian view may not be correct. People may have a right not to employ someone or buy his goods, and yet a boycott of a person because of his religious or political views may be more effective than criminal penalties in blocking his religious or political freedom, freedom which should also

---

[28] Note that family members can pressurize each other into not donating. Fellner and Marshall write: 'In one family, the father successfully dissuaded his two sons from even coming for initial blood tests, his wife from participating beyond the halfway point, and ended up as the triumphant donor himself.' 'Kidney Donors: The Myth of Informed Consent', p. 1248.

[29] Compare Nozick in n. 20.

be protected by a right.[30] The practicalities of large societies often make it possible to avoid having to answer the moral and conceptual questions of what types and how much social pressure would make decisions invalid. In a society with many employers or buyers, whether and when boycotts are legitimate exercises of power or illegitimate pressure usually need not be decided because boycotts are not very powerful. In the case of living donation, however, donors cannot shop around for different families to approve of them, so the moral and conceptual questions are not irrelevant. But nor can they be fully answered here.

The question of when social pressure makes agreement invalid bears on the practice of telling 'white lies'. Doctors often help reluctant potential donors get round social pressure by declaring them medically unsuitable and giving them untrue excuses, such as anatomical unsuitability, to tell those exerting pressure. One reason for white lies is the sense that people who agree to donate because of social pressure do so involuntarily. However, Govert den Hartogh criticizes this common justification of telling white lies.[31] He believes that agreeing to donate to avoid a breach in relations would still be voluntary. People often have to make decisions which can invoke undesired reactions from others. If they decide a certain way so as to avoid the unwelcome reactions, their decisions need not be involuntary and third parties need not help them out by supplying them with white lies. We could add that some unwelcome reactions would be justified. Recall the hypothetical case in chapter 2 of the man who refused to donate to his son. Why should he be protected from the blame he deserves?

Note that den Hartogh was primarily criticizing one argument for white lies. He does not want to exclude white lies on all occasions, since they could protect the potential donor from aggressive or disproportionate reactions that do undercut voluntariness. I would add that white lies may be permissible for reasons besides respecting personal sovereignty. For instance, doctors may tell white lies so that they are not in the position of operating on the unwilling; or the donor may have been unfairly selected by the family, and the doctor may not want to be a party to exploitation. We can, however, say that not all social pressure makes agreement to donate invalid, even though we do not have a good general account of when it does.

Coercion and desperation

Writers in medical ethics often use 'coercion' to stand in for any factor, internal or external, that they think would make a donation invalid. Writers in political theory, philosophy, and law usually restrict coercion to external factors, and not just any

[30] Mill's *On Liberty* stresses the harmful effects of social pressure to conform. Unfortunately, *On Liberty* is of little help in working out when pressure makes agreement invalid because its focus was not on voluntary actions but on the harmful effects, at a social level, of conformity in thought and actions. Indeed, Mill thought that people may avoid others whose lifestyle they disapproved of. See *On Liberty* (Harmondsworth: Penguin English Library, 1982), ch. 4, par. 5.
[31] Govert den Hartogh, 'When Are Living Donations Voluntary Enough?' in W. Weimar et al. (eds.), *Organ Transplantation: Ethical, Legal and Psychosocial Aspects* (Lengerich: Pabst Science Publishers, 2008).

external factors at that. I shall consider coercion only in its restricted sense (the other factors that medical ethicists call 'coercive' have been considered earlier in this chapter). Even with the restricted sense, difficult questions remain. Does coercion require a coercer, that is, some intentional agent to do the coercing? If so, must coercers threaten if what they are doing is to count as coercion, or could their offers also be coercive? Or is coercion a matter of having a poor choice situation, so that a choice counts as coerced when one has no reasonable alternative, whether or not anyone makes it the case that one has no reasonable alternative? Fortunately, we can go over coercion quite quickly. While coercion is quite a difficult concept to analyse and its normative importance is sometimes unclear, the basic moves, as they apply in the context of organ transplantation, are well known.[32]

On any view of coercion, some cases of agreement to donate are coerced and invalid. For instance, credible threats of violence are coercive and agreeing to donate because of such a threat would make the agreement invalid. The coercion may be genuine but hidden from all but the coercer and coerced, and the team responsible for the donor's consent process should try to uncover it and find a way to block donation, such as by telling 'white lies'. However, while hidden coercion may be hard to discover, it is not hard to conceptualize as coercion. Other cases are less conceptually clear.

The question for this sub-section is whether being desperate because of a poor choice situation is itself enough to make an agreement invalid. Let us reconsider parents. Some people want to donate an organ to their child. They are desperate to prevent their child dying or suffering the ill effects of dialysis. Their consent to organ retrieval occurs in a situation where they have no reasonable alternative. But would their consent be coerced, invalid, or both?

Desperation alone does not make a choice both coerced and invalid, as the following example shows. Suppose someone needs life-saving surgery, say the removal of an appendix before it bursts. Suppose, even, that the person's appendix will burst because of deliberate poisoning by an enemy, not simply because of natural bad luck. Most people whose appendices are about to burst would not only agree to the operation but be desperate for it. If the appendix bursts, peritonitis sets in and is often fatal, whereas the operation to remove it is simple and relatively risk-free. A person who consents to the operation, we can suppose, has no reasonable alternative. But the consent has its usual moral force. Consent waives the person's rights of bodily integrity and personal sovereignty. Consider what would follow if the consent were invalid because of desperation. Invalid consent would not waive the rights so the rights would remain intact, in which case the surgeon who removed the appendix would violate those rights. Third parties would be permitted

---

[32] Alan Wertheimer, *Coercion* (Princeton: Princeton University Press, 1987), is a very good book-length discussion. In the context of organ transplantation, much of the sophisticated discussion of coercion is about organ sales rather than donation but, as I shall argue in chapter 10, the same points apply. Wertheimer doubts whether organ sales need be coercive at pp. 67–8. On coercion applied to organ retrieval, see e.g. Stephen Wilkinson, *Bodies for Sale: Ethics and Exploitation in the Human Body Trade* (London: Routledge, 2003), ch. 6 and much of James S. Taylor, *Stakes and Kidneys* (Aldershot: Ashgate, 2005).

to prevent the removal if they can, as they may if the removal were against the person's wishes. These conclusions are absurd, just as it would be absurd to describe a surgeon who says 'have the operation or you will die' as coercing the person who has no reasonable alternative.

We may want to say, about the life-saving operation, that the person consenting is not coerced at all, and so the consent is not made invalid because coerced. That way, we can say that coercion always undercuts validity, and because the consent is valid, it must not have been coerced. Or we may want to say that the choice situation is coercive because it is so bad, but since the consent is valid, we would then have to give up the link between coercion and validity.[33] Either way, the point is that the person's consent is valid despite being given in a situation where she had no reasonable alternative and where she is desperate.

If someone said, 'have the operation or I will make it the case that you die from peritonitis', the consent to the operation would be both coerced and invalid. But when the surgeon says, 'have the operation or you will die from peritonitis', warning of a fact the surgeon has not brought about, the consent to the operation would be neither coerced nor invalid. The options in both cases are the same: the operation or death. But how the options come about makes the difference to whether the consent is coerced and invalid.

The obvious application to donation is to say that, simply because parents are desperate to save their children, it does not mean their consent would be invalid. In fact, the point is so obvious that it is worth asking how anyone could think otherwise. I suspect they have something like this in mind: the potential donors are unfree because all their alternatives are so bad, so their consent is unfree. Or they may think that the value of personal sovereignty requires a choice from an array of reasonable options, which in this case the parents do not have. Or they may think it unfair that parents choose from such a bad set of options, so the consent is given in unfair circumstances. However, while desperate parents may be unfree and their choices may not be ones they would make in a position of full autonomy, the parents are not in a position of a free choice or full autonomy. Their situation may be unfair, but if no one or nothing will get them out of it, then—just as with the poisoned patient who needs the appendectomy—it makes no difference to the validity of their consent what they would do if they were in a better situation.

I close this section with some conclusions about personal sovereignty and living donation. Most obviously, living donation can express the donor's personal sovereignty. However, not all agreements to donate would be autonomous. Conceptual difficulties arise in distinguishing agreements which are autonomous from those which are not. While some cases are easy, such as agreements caused by threats of violence or the absence of proper information, others are not easy. I have argued that agreements can be valid even when they are the result of supposedly suspect motivations, social pressure, or desperation.

---

[33] This is Joel Feinberg's view. See Feinberg, *Harm to Self*, pp. 245–8.

What follows if agreements are invalid? We should avoid the mistake of assuming that, when a person's choice is not voluntary, he should not get what he chose. Perhaps what he chose non-voluntarily is in his interests, a point I take up in the section on children and incompetents. But the tricky cases occur when personal sovereignty appears to conflict with well-being.

PERSONAL SOVEREIGNTY VERSUS WELL-BEING

How far should respect for personal sovereignty go? If kidneys may be taken, if livers may be taken, are there any limits? May a second kidney be taken from a person who has already donated one? May a parent, who will thereby die, donate her heart to save her child? Or anyone's child? What if people voluntarily choose to act in a way that would be worse for them? In other words, what if their personal sovereignty conflicts with their well-being?

Before trying to answer the questions, bear in mind that clear cases of conflict may be hard to find. The lesson from the section on well-being was that, while physical health is part of well-being, it is not all of it, and people may be no worse off for donating an organ. To the extent people want what is in their interests, have the correct beliefs about what will be in their interests, and then act on those beliefs, what they choose would make them better off *and* express their personal sovereignty. The same point works the other way. If people want what is in their interests but they are making gross mistakes or they are coerced, then what they choose may well be bad for them and fail to express their personal sovereignty. Again, well-being and personal sovereignty would not be in conflict.

As a further preliminary to discussing personal sovereignty versus well-being, note that personal sovereignty does not require acceding to all the choices of potential donors. Interventions with their choices may be justified to check whether they are voluntary, as for instance with forcibly preventing a man walking across an unsafe bridge on the grounds that he probably does not know it is unsafe and would not want to walk across it if he did.[34] Nor does personal sovereignty clearly justify donation even when all parties say they are willing, because of difficulties in ensuring proper consent.[35] If we consider the question of donating hearts, or other organs necessary for life, one might defend limits on what organ removal can be consented to as a protection for personal sovereignty. That way, some people would not be bamboozled or pushed into doing something very harmful that they do not really want to do. (Compare the abuse argument against voluntary euthanasia: that some people will be killed even though they would not really want to be.)

Still, suppose for the sake of argument that we can tell that a person's choice is valid but would be bad for him or her. Broadly speaking, there are three options when well-being conflicts with personal sovereignty. Well-being could have absolute priority over personal sovereignty, personal sovereignty could have absolute priority over

---

[34] Mill, *On Liberty*, ch. 5, par. 5; Feinberg, *Harm to Self*, pp. 124–5.
[35] Price, *Legal and Ethical Aspects of Transplantation*, ch. 7.

well-being, or—and this is an option with a large number of variants—some way could be found to trade off well-being against personal sovereignty.

Well-being should not have absolute priority over personal sovereignty. What people should be allowed to do is not settled by the effects of their actions on their well-being. People want to run their own lives and make their own mistakes, at least to some degree in some ways. It is disrespectful to adults—and perhaps younger mature people—to treat them like children. At least to some extent, everyone accepts that people should be allowed to act in a way that does not maximize their well-being. After all, no one favours forcing people not to watch movies they will later regard as a waste of their time, or to choose from a menu the meal they would most enjoy.

The view that personal sovereignty should have absolute priority over well-being holds that, in principle, people should be allowed to act on their voluntary choices within their personal sphere whatever the cost to their well-being. Call this the 'liberal' view. It says that voluntary sacrifice and unreasonable choices must be allowed.[36] The liberal view can be reduced to what some, but not all, writers take to be absurdity. The view seems to imply that a man would be allowed to donate a second kidney to a second son, and have to live on dialysis. It seems to imply that people should be allowed to donate their hearts even though they would consequently die. The liberal view even seems to imply that voluntary slavery should be permitted.

Whether allowing voluntary slavery or heart donation actually follows from the liberal position is unclear because, as I said earlier, prohibiting them may be a way of protecting the personal sovereignty of people who are coerced or deluded.[37] Nonetheless, some object at the level of principle to the liberal view. They think it gives too much weight to voluntary choice. But if we consider the main ways in which the liberal view could be restricted, we shall see that they are irrelevant to mainstream living donation. Both the original and modified liberal views would permit people to donate organs against their self-interest.

The liberal view would in principle allow people to ride motorbikes without wearing helmets or to donate (or sell) their hearts. Many liberal democracies, however, make riders wear helmets and forbid the removal of organs necessary for life, or anything approaching that level of risk, even when all parties consent.[38] Perhaps the liberal democracies constrain voluntary choice only for the practical reasons of the liberal view, to protect the coerced or deluded, rather than because of a rejection in principle of voluntary choice. But their restrictions suggest some ways to modify the liberal view which would give substantial weight to voluntary choice and allow people on occasion to act against their own interests, without going so far as the liberal view.

One modification is to restrict the scope of choice to important matters in people's ways of life.[39] So people should be allowed to follow their religions, say what they think politically, and refuse medical treatment rather than suffer the

[36] John Harris, *Clones, Genes, and Immortality* (Oxford: Oxford University Press, 1998), p. 137.
[37] Feinberg, *Harm to Self*, pp. 79–81.
[38] Price, *Legal and Ethical Aspects of Transplantation*, pp. 243f.
[39] Feinberg considers the modification in *Harm to Self*, pp. 54–5.

indignity of bodily invasion. But the wearing of helmets or seatbelts is not at the core of most people's lives so, when the evidence shows the harm of not wearing helmets or seatbelts, the state may restrict choice. Whatever the merits of this modification, it has little application to the topic at hand. People who are considering donating an organ are considering something that is surely a matter of importance in their lives. Donation is not like wearing a seatbelt, which people absent-mindedly forget to do.

A second modification is to stop people acting on voluntary decisions that would be catastrophic for their welfare. Donating organs needed to live would probably be such an example (although not necessarily, since parents who donate to save a child may correctly see their consequent shorter lives as not much worse than a life without having saved their child). Again, the modification does not apply to the living donation of organs that are not vital to life. As we saw, giving up one's organ may be better for someone, other than in respect of physical health, or at least not much worse.

The liberal view interferes only to establish voluntariness but otherwise lets people act on their decisions. The liberal view would therefore permit living donation. The modified liberal view lets people act on their voluntary decisions except on either relatively trivial matters or when they will make very big mistakes. Neither typically applies in the case of the retrieval of kidneys or livers (or blood or bone marrow), so the modified liberal view would also permit the live donation of these organs. Except in the fringe cases of the donation of organs necessary for life, which the liberal view might or might not permit, we do not have to choose between the liberal and modified liberal views. Both permit living donation.

THE ROLE OF THE TRANSPLANT TEAM

Up to this point, the donor's well-being and personal sovereignty have been the focus of the chapter. I have been asking whether and when living donation ought to be allowed given what organ retrieval does to people. The members of the transplant team have their autonomy too, though, and it would be unreasonable to insist, against a team's wishes, that they perform a risky operation on a healthy person, however willing that person is. Even if potential recipients and donors have a right to consent, they do not have a right to insist on donation. Arguably, and resembling the compromise over abortion that exists in some countries, a transplant team might have a right to refuse but a duty to refer a person to another transplant team, if any, who would be willing to perform.

It is likely that teams should be left with considerable discretion in proceeding with transplantation. However, from the perspective of a transplant team, having the discretion does not tell them how to exercise it. If the potential donor and recipient are keen and competent, would it be wrong for the transplant team to refuse, even if it had the discretion to decide either way? The answer might well depend on why the team refuses and, in particular, on whether it is motivated by reasons that are not its affair. Classifying potential donors as crazy, as transplant doctors freely did in the earlier years of transplantation, is an objectionable exercise of power, even if it does not violate negative rights of personal sovereignty.[40]

Consider three arguments for refusing to perform the operation when the potential donor and recipient consent validly. One is that to go ahead in some cases would bring transplantation into disrepute and reduce the number of organs from other sources. (Imagine a case of risky donation where the donor dies, thus putting others off becoming living donors.) This reason is no insult to the autonomy of potential donors. Another reason for refusal is that the transplant team do not want to be causally responsible for killing or severely harming a healthy donor in the event that the operation goes wrong. This reason is understandable and also, I think, no insult to the autonomy of potential donors, since it is a reason based on how the team expect to feel rather than on a judgement of the interests of the donor. A third reason a transplant team might refuse is because they think potential donors should not run such risks because of the bad effects on them or their family.[41] Arguably, this reason would insult the potential donors' autonomy, even if not contrary to their negative rights of personal sovereignty. These risks should be their affair, and so should the decisions about their duties to others.[42]

CHILDREN AS ORGAN DONORS

The rest of this chapter considers the retrieval of organs from living people who are not competent or whose competence is questionable. I begin with children. Children have had organs removed for transplant, albeit rarely. In the United States, between 1987 and 2000, kidneys were taken for transplant from people under 18 in at least 60 cases. A handful of other cases have been reported round the world.[43] Live children have not yet been used as a source of organs in the UK. Margaret Brazier writes, 'Would an English court be prepared to sanction a kidney donation, or transplant of a liver segment from a child? It seems unlikely. In any case renal transplant surgeons in this country appear of their own volition to have ruled out kidney donations by minors.'[44]

---

[40] Larissa MacFarquhar, 'The Kindest Cut' *The New Yorker*, 27 July 2009.

[41] C. Elliott, 'Doing Harm: Living Organ Donors, Clinical Research and *The Tenth Man' Journal of Medical Ethics* 21 (1995).

[42] S. Shiffrin, 'Paternalism, Unconscionability Doctrine, and Accommodation' *Philosophy and Public Affairs* 29 (2000).

[43] The figures are from the United Network for Organ Sharing (UNOS) and cited in L. Ross, J. Thistlethwaite Jr., and the Committee on Bioethics, 'Minors as Living Solid-Organ Donors' *Pediatrics* 122 (2008), p. 454. The figure of 60 kidneys from children compares with approximately 40,000 live kidney donations in the same period.

[44] Margaret Brazier, *Medicine, Patients and the Law* (3rd edn.) (London: Penguin Books, 2003), p. 423 (endnote suppressed). However, the text on the rest of the page makes it unclear whether, by 'child', she means only children who are not competent or whether she also means competent children. For a discussion of the inconclusive state of British law, see Price, *Legal and Ethical Aspects of Transplantation*, ch. 8. I have been told by people involved in transplantation in New Zealand that children would not be used as donors there.

In the next two sub-sections, I argue for a more permissive approach than the one taken by many in transplantation. I shall claim that competent children should be treated the same as adults when it comes to living donation and that, at least in some cases, it would be ethically permissible to take organs for transplant from incompetent children. However, although I argue that it can be ethically permissible to take organs from children, whether organs should be taken depends on the possibility of distinguishing well enough in practice between permissible and impermissible cases. I say little about procedures to prevent abuse, concentrating instead on clearing away bad arguments against organ donation by children.

Competent children

Let us first ask about the competence of children. According to a standard view, children at or above a certain age (16, in many jurisdictions) are presumed to be competent to decide on their own treatment, this presumption being rebuttable by evidence of incompetence. Children below this age are not presumed to be competent or incompetent, but they may decide for themselves whether to have medical treatment if judged sufficiently mature in the particular cases they face. Such children are sometimes called 'mature minors' or, in jurisdictions influenced by English cases, 'Gillick competent' children.[45] The idea is that some children younger than the presumed age of maturity will be able to understand the facts, grasp the implications, and give voluntary consent. While the standard view was devised for therapeutic decision-making, the underlying idea applies equally to non-therapeutic organ retrieval. The age for deciding on donation should perhaps differ from the age for medical decision-making, but being below a certain age should not on its own rule out a child's deciding. What matters are the capacities of the child, which are only contingently associated with age.

I do not have much to say here about how to tell whether a child is competent. I only want to make two observations. One is that it seems unfair to hold children to a higher standard of competence than adults, so competence assessments for children should not make them demonstrate understanding to an extent many adults, regarded as competent, would be incapable of reaching. The other is that children whose close relatives need an organ may have an unusually good grasp of what is involved in organ donation. Children do have a good grasp of serious disease in other cases to which they have been exposed.[46]

Assuming we can tell that a child is competent, the next question is how much competence matters. In cases of adults, competence in decision-making is

---

[45] See Brazier, *Medicine, Patients and the Law*, pp. 361–71 for an explanation of the ideas and a description of the Gillick case. Brazier believes later judicial decisions show that respect for Gillick competence does not accurately characterize English law.

[46] P. Alderson, K. Sutcliffe, and K. Curtis, 'Children's Competence to Consent to Medical Treatment' *Hastings Center Report* 36 (2006).

sometimes taken to entail that they ought to make the decision.[47] But as we saw
earlier in the chapter, even competent adults could have some decisions taken out
of their hands, such as the decision to donate a heart. In the case of children, many
would go further in limiting the force of a child's competent decision. Thus
Buchanan and Brock claim that children, unlike adults, may have their decisions
limited by parental rights.[48] Ross would permit forced *removal* of bone marrow
from a competent child who dissents because she thinks the child could benefit in
the long run from being a donor.[49] I do not think these are good arguments for
treating competent children differently from competent adults. Both the parental
rights and long-term interests arguments seem arbitrary if applied only below a
chronological age since they could equally apply to adult children, such as 19-year-
olds who live with their parents. At some point, which may not be a chronological
point, children's medical decisions are their own and parental rights must yield
however much parents are still contributing to their children's welfare and even if
the children are making decisions that are less than ideal from the point of view of
either their long-term autonomy or the interests of the family.

Of course, children may be more vulnerable to pressure or less aware of their
long-term interests than adults, and assessments of consent should take account of
both. But unless we think the assessments are no good, in which case we should
look for better ways of assessing, why treat a competent child differently from a
competent adult? Doctors perhaps should refuse to take organs from a competent
child if it would put a family's interests at risk, but the ground for their refusal—
third party interests—applies to adults as well as children. Competent adults also
may not get what they want because of third party interests too; for instance,
perhaps doctors could properly refuse to take organs from someone who wanted to
donate to a stranger and thus neglect his parental responsibilities.[50] Perhaps doctors
should have to refuse to take organs in cases of excessive sacrifice too, so if a
competent child wants to make an excessive sacrifice, her organs should not be
taken. Again, though, the ground applies to adults as well as children. In conclusion, I do not see a good reason for treating competent children who want to donate
any differently from competent adults who want to donate.

I have discussed competent children who wish to donate. As for competent
children who refuse to donate, their organs should not be taken. I have seen no one
who disagrees, except a few writers who think organs from the living should be
conscripted anyway.

---

[47] Buchanan and Brock, in *Deciding for Others*, generally take competence to have this entailment
but they are not consistent in their usage, and sometimes allow that competent people should not get
what they want because of third party interests.

[48] Buchanan and Brock, *Deciding for Others*, pp. 235–7.

[49] L. F. Ross, *Children, Families, and Health Care Decision Making* (Oxford: Clarendon Press,
1998), p. 118. In the preceding section of her book, she said that kidney retrieval from competent
children should be permitted if they consent and not if they do not, and she stresses the freedom we
grant to the competent to make sacrifices. I cannot understand how Ross can hymn children's
autonomy in one section and denigrate it on the following page.

[50] But perhaps, as the previous section pointed out, family responsibilities are not the affair of the
transplant team.

Incompetent children

Let us turn now to children who are not competent and briefly list the relevant considerations. Some of these children will be able to express their views—assent or dissent—and others, such as very young children, will not; having organs taken could be against a child's interests in some cases but perhaps in a child's interest in others; parents and guardians could either consent or dissent; potential recipients could stand to gain a great deal from a transplant or not much (if, for instance, a transplant provided only a few extra weeks of life); and the family's interests could be affected for better or worse by a transplant. The various considerations are not fully separate from each other. To take one example, an argument that a donor child needs her sibling would apply with diminished force if a transplant would save her sibling for only a short time. To take another example, parental consent will generally be based on an assessment of the interests of the family, which are anyway not separate from the interests of its constituent members.[51]

I shall focus on the interests of children, which can, I shall argue, justify taking their organs in some cases. Children, like adults, have a variety of interests that can pull in conflicting ways. On the one hand, children's physical interests are almost always against organ retrieval. If, on the other hand, we look beyond the narrowly physical, children can have interests in donating, for instance so as not to suffer grief from a sibling's death or perhaps to feel they have done some good. They can also have psychological interests against donating, for instance if they are terrified of hospitals. Some children, like some adults, will have vicarious interests in the welfare of potential recipients, that is, interests in the others' well-being separable from any psychological benefits they might get by donating.[52] Children typically differ from adults in being more dependent on their families, so that changes to the well-being of the family may causally affect their welfare (think of parents who would split up after the death of their child or become too depressed to look after their remaining children as well as before). Children also have developmental interests beyond those that adults normally have, and some writers believe them relevant to donation if, for instance, donation teaches the virtues of altruism.

Some writers deny that children's interests are major factors in deciding whether taking their organs is permissible. However, their reason is usually a false inference from rejecting one interpretation of a Best Interest standard for decision-making.[53] The Best Interest standard, as critics often interpret it, states that parents should decide, and be required to decide, in the best interests of the child, and the standard takes the interests of the child to be purely self-regarding (and thus not include the

---

[51] Some believe the family can have interests over and above the separate interests of its members, a belief that Buchanan and Brock think a 'dangerous reification' (Buchanan and Brock, *Deciding for Others* p. 236). I think they mean not only that the idea of family interests invites abuse ('dangerous') but is false ('reification').

[52] That children can have vicarious interests is argued by Lynn Jansen, 'Child Organ Donation, Family Autonomy, and Intimate Attachments' *Cambridge Quarterly of Healthcare Ethics* 13 (2004), pp. 138–40.

[53] Ross draws this false inference at *Children, Families, and Health Care Decision Making*, p. 126 n. 5.

vicarious interests mentioned above).[54] As against this standard, critics say it is too demanding, in failing to take account of the legitimate interests of parents; that it cannot be put into practice when parents have more than one child whose interests conflict; and that its conception of interests is too narrow. These criticisms of the Best Interest standard may be sound. The mistake is to conclude from them that the interests of children are not major factors in determining whether their organs may be taken.

Take the criticism that a Best Interest standard considers only self-regarding interests; the Best Interest standard could simply be extended to include other-regarding interests.[55] Take the criticism that decisions could or should not be made in the *best* interests of a child; that leaves open whether a child's interests could be taken into account in some other way, for instance under a rule that permitted retrieval only when not against the child's interests. In fact, any number of rules besides a Best Interest standard could refer to and require an assessment of a child's interests. In short, to refute a Best Interest standard is not to show the irrelevance of children's interests.

Children's interests seem obviously important to the permissibility of taking their organs and, in the absence of any good argument to the contrary, I shall assume they are. Could it be in a child's interests, or at least not against them, for the child's organs to be removed for transplanting?[56] Some writers imply that it never could. Fleck writes: 'the benefits that are supposed to be the substance of the best interests of the donor child appear speculative and contrived for the most part.'[57] And Ross considers judgements that donation would be in a child's overall interests to be 'speculative at best'.[58] These writers seem to be sceptical about whether children really do have psychological, vicarious, or other non-physical interests in donation. They also seem doubtful about whether it is possible to weigh up physical interests against non-physical interests and decide correctly that donation is in a child's overall interests.

To take these doubts in order, why believe that children have no non-physical interests or, less strongly, that we can never get good enough evidence about the likely psychological or other non-physical effects of having organs taken for transplantation? I have seen no reason given, and it is worth remembering that live donation by adults is often accompanied by extensive psychosocial assessments that look out precisely for these other interests. As for the difficulties of making an overall judgement, these judgements are not always impossible. Some judgements will be obvious. Still, comparing physical interests with other interests can be difficult, so perhaps Fleck

---

[54] Buchanan and Brock, in their leading book *Deciding for Others*, p. 133 are often cited as endorsing a Best Interest standard that ignores other-regarding interests. They do, although not because they deny children have other-regarding interests but because they think that, if children do have the interests, a substituted judgement could be made instead.

[55] Jansen argues that a Best Interest standard should be extended beyond self-regarding interests to include 'intimate attachments'. Jansen, 'Child Organ Donation, Family Autonomy, and Intimate Attachments', p. 139.

[56] I leave open whether the rule for children should be to take their organs only when taking would not harm them or, more strongly, only when taking would benefit them.

[57] Leonard Fleck, 'Children and Organ Donation: Some Cautionary Remarks' *Cambridge Quarterly of Healthcare Ethics* 13 (2004), p. 162.

[58] Ross, *Children, Families, and Health Care Decision Making*, p. 126 n. 5.

and Ross are right to say that *some* such judgements are 'speculative'. But we should not look for more precision than the subject admits. We should not look for precise assessments of how much a child stands to gain or lose by being a donor because what is being assessed—well-being across several dimensions—is not precise. The problem is not an epistemic one, not a problem of getting the right information or making predictions. The elements of well-being are either incommensurable or only roughly comparable and the harms and benefits being judged will be imprecise, and intrinsically imprecise at that. The imprecision of well-being is not something to be ignored in the search for precision. Judging a child's interests entirely on supposedly precise estimates of physical risk, while ignoring the less easy to measure non-physical interests, would be precisely wrong rather than vaguely right.

Because children's interests are broader than the narrowly physical, organ retrieval could be in their overall interests. But some may argue that, faced with uncertainty about overall interests, we should give priority to protecting a child's basic needs. If a child's basic needs involved only physical interests and if giving priority to basic needs meant not risking them at all, then organ retrieval from children would be wrong.[59] Why, though, should we regard children's physical interests as more basic, in any morally relevant sense, than their psychological interests and why should we rule out any marginal risk to physical interests? Are psychiatrists always acting wrongly when they prescribe medication for children's mental disorders that has a small chance of physical side-effects? Do parents act wrongly if they take their children on holiday, but slightly increase the chance of their having an accident while travelling? It is wholly implausible to allow no trade offs between physical and other interests or to ban all increases in risk to physical interests. Consequently, the extra risk to the children's physical interests if they donate could be offset by the gains to their psychological or other interests. Taking an organ is not, of course, a minor risk, which is why it has to be carefully weighed, and perhaps, once weighed, it should not be allowed. But the weighing should not be ruled out by the indefensible absolute of 'no risk to basic physical needs'.

Assuming it could be in a child's interests to have an organ taken for transplanting, the question arises of how far its being in their interests justifies the taking. As I said earlier, there are considerations besides the child's interests, such as whether parents consent, the interests of the wider family, and the interests of potential recipients. I cannot attempt a full discussion here, which would require analysing and weighing these factors when they point towards opposing actions. But we should be able to decide what to do when they all point in the same direction.[60] If it is in someone's interests to receive an organ, if it is in a child's interest to supply the

---

[59] Ross argues against organ retrieval from non-competent children on the grounds that the fulfilment of their basic needs should be at 'no risk of sacrifice' (ibid., p. 116). But she has a wider view of basic needs besides the narrowly physical (see pp. 5, 16 n.10) and she is willing to tolerate extra risk to children's physical interests when it comes to taking bone marrow, so her 'no risk to basic needs' argument against organ retrieval is incompatible with her other views.

[60] Some early US court decisions approved of organ retrieval from minors when all the factors supported it, although the minors in those cases were of an age regarded as adult now. See Ross, ibid., pp. 111–12.

organ, if it is in the family's interest that the transplant proceed, and if the parents consent, taking the child's organ for transplant is morally permissible in principle.

It is a further step to conclude that children should have their organs taken in practice. To allow organs to be taken would require adequate procedures to guard against mistakes and abuse. Some writers argue that each case should be decided in courts. Others argue for donor advocates within a transplant team. I have seen no reason to think procedures could never be adequate, so I conclude that organ donation by children should not be legally prohibited or automatically blocked by transplant teams.

INCOMPETENT DONORS

Children are not the only people who can be incompetent. So too are some people who are intellectually disabled or mentally ill. Consider two major arguments that try to justify some living donor transplantation from incompetents. As with children, one allows donation from the incompetent when it would not harm them; the other claims that the incompetent have obligations to donate. I endorse the first argument; the second is seriously flawed.

As we have seen, the idea of harm should be taken in a sense broader than just the physical and, once it is, it becomes an open question whether performing the operation would be in or against the overall interests of the donor. Two American court cases illustrate this reasoning. In one, a Kentucky court ordered a kidney donation from Jerry Strunk, a 27-year-old man said to have a mental age of six, into his brother, Tommy. The brothers were very close to each other, and the court held that the donation was in the interests of Jerry. In the second case, a Wisconsin court declined to order a transplant of a kidney from Richard Pescinski, a catatonic schizophrenic who had been institutionalized for many years, into his sister. Richard Pescinski had no concern for anyone, and so not for his sister, and the court was given no evidence that it would be in his interests to have a kidney transplanted.[61] The argument for retrieval when it does not harm the incompetent person requires good grounds for thinking that the person really would benefit in some way from the donation so as to compensate for the physical harm.

The argument from harm taken broadly is somewhat controversial, although mainly on the grounds of potential for abuse rather than that it is incorrect.[62] Some writers, however, argue for other justifications. Robert Veatch draws a parallel between organ retrieval from living incompetent people and their use in research. He claims that it is permissible to use the incompetent in research on certain conditions, notably that risk is no greater than some minimum, on the grounds that

---

[61] Ronald Munson, *Raising the Dead* (New York: Oxford University Press, 2002), ch. 6.
[62] To set against the risk of abuse, consider Jeffrey Spike's point: 'But for mentally handicapped individuals . . . to be denied the right to donate an organ to a loved one may feel like another measure of their failure to be normal.' See Spike, 'Cultural Diversity and Patients with Reduced Capacity: The Use of Ethics Consultation to Advocate for Mentally Handicapped Persons in Living Organ Donation' *Theoretical Medicine* 22 (2001), p. 523.

the incompetent have moral obligations to the wider community. He accepts that organ removal is significantly more risky than any research that should be permitted on the incompetent, but argues that extra risk may be justified within families. This is because the bonds between donor—or 'donor'—and family are stronger than those between research subject and community at large, and that more may be expected of the incompetent in the family sphere. However, on Veatch's view, there is a limit to what risk may be imposed on the incompetent and, given their current risk profiles, the limit is reached with the kidney and exceeded by lung lobe and liver transplantation.[63] A supplementary argument can be found in the case of Pescinski, where a minority opinion held that doing the decent thing by his sister is probably what Pescinski would have wanted had he been competent.[64] This opinion is an attempt to connect the idea of moral obligation to the idea of substituted judgement, familiar in deciding for the incompetent. There are many problems with these views, some of which I shall now mention.

First, the conclusion of the obligation argument may only be that taking non-competent people's organs is permissible so long as they do not dissent. Or it may be that their organs may be taken even if they do dissent. However, even if the non-competent people had the moral obligation that Veatch claims they have, it is a further question whether they may be forced to give up their organs so as to fulfil those obligations. Not all our moral obligations may be enforced against us, not least because we have rights against some enforcing.

Second, any argument that relies on the alleged moral obligations of incompetent people is, at best, likely to apply only to certain subsets of the incompetent. Consider the argument about the bonds of family. This argument is likely to work only where there are indeed tight bonds, and so would not work in a case like Pescinski's.

The argument from moral obligation faces more fundamental objections. It is conventionally held that, to be a subject of a moral obligation, one must be an agent, that is, able to understand the obligation and perform it. We do not think, for instance, that it makes any sense to attribute a moral failing to a male trout for neglecting its offspring, because trout clearly do not have the necessary conceptual apparatus to understand an obligation to nurture one's young. Certain typically incompetent people, such as 12-year-olds, clearly can have the capacity for agency, but others, such as all one-year-olds, do not. For this reason, organ retrieval from people below some intellectual and moral capacity could not be justified by citing an obligation they could not have. The point about agency also shows why it makes no sense to claim that people like Richard Pescinski would have wanted to donate. He had never had the capacity for those kinds of judgement.[65]

The lack of agency shows up the argument from moral obligation as an odd one. The language switches from the active—that the incompetent should donate—to the passive—the organs of the incompetent may be removed. There is a parallel in

---

[63] Veatch, *Transplantation Ethics*, pp. 196–8.
[64] Munson, *Raising the Dead*, p. 136.
[65] Buchanan and Brock, *Deciding for Others*, p. 115.

Bertie Wooster's description of a man over whom a bucket is emptied: 'In one second, without any previous training or upbringing, he had become the wettest man in Worcestershire.'[66] Training and upbringing are relevant for doing something, but irrelevant to being made the wettest; agency and obligation are relevant to doing (including permitting) something, but irrelevant to removing the organs of those incapable of agency. Perhaps a different argument should be made: the very lack of agency that precluded Richard Pescinski, say, from having obligations also precluded him from having a full set of rights, and, in particular, no right against the removal of his organs. I only mention this line of argument, rather than endorse it. I note that it fits better with the practice the argument from moral obligation purported to justify, namely, doing things to incompetent people rather than having them do things.

CONCLUSION

As I said at the beginning of this chapter, the laws and regulations of many countries have become more permissive about who can be a living donor and the number of living donors has greatly increased. The use of minors and other incompetent or marginally competent people has been an exception because their organs are never taken in some countries and only rarely in others. Generally, this chapter supports and would extend the permissive trend. In principle, it is permissible to take organs from competent children who consent and from non-competent people who would probably not be harmed by donation. Moreover, the categories of invalid consent should not include people with unusual motivations, or who experience just any social pressure, or who are simply desperate. That said, people can be genuinely coerced into agreeing to donate, and a consent system should take care to screen them out.

Allowing living donation is not very controversial at the policy level. However, many of the same arguments will crop up again in the chapter on the sale of organs and they will there have more radical implications. But before we discuss sale, I turn to a more controversial aspect of living donation, which also arises for donation after death: whether and when transplant services should accept offers of organs when the offers have strings attached.

[66] P. G. Wodehouse, *Life with Jeeves* (Harmondsworth: Penguin, 1981), p. 501.

9

Impartiality, Acquisition, and Allocation

The ethical problems of transplantation are not only about acquiring organs but also about allocating them. Historically, the field of transplantation has shown great concern for the just allocation of organs. Organs may not be bought or sold, in part to prevent greater access by the rich, and they are not allocated according to any criteria of desert or merit. While details vary, organs tend to be allocated according to a mix of capacity to benefit, severity of condition, urgency, and time spent waiting. Living donation has, however, been an important exception because the donors have been able to stipulate that their relatives receive the organs.

Allocation and acquisition are not separate. The rules governing allocation can affect the number of organs acquired. A system may have to choose whether, for instance, to accept organs offered with conditions or to refuse them so as to allocate the organs it does have strictly according to need. This chapter is about the ethical problems that arise when acquisition interacts with allocation. In particular, the chapter is about getting impartiality in the right place. It has rightly been thought that organs should be allocated in an impartially defensible way, but it has wrongly been thought that allocating in an impartially defensible way requires allocating on the basis of impartial principles such as fairness or meeting the greatest need.

Impartiality may be abstract, but we need some abstraction to think through real cases. While allowing live donation within families is not very controversial, accepting conditions from other donors is. Some people waiting for organs have taken to advertising on billboards or the internet, or asking in their churches for living unrelated donors.[1] Sometimes strangers want to donate only to a named celebrity, or to children, or to co-religionists. Sometimes potential donors attach racist conditions.[2] In a recent British case, a dying woman wanted to donate her organs after her death to her mother and, because the donation could not be made while she was alive, her request was denied.[3] Should some or all of these conditions be accepted? What I shall call 'conditional allocation' need not be due only to

[1] C. Robertson, 'Desperate Patients Solicit Volunteers' *The Journal of Law, Medicine, and Ethics* 33 (2005).

[2] For a 1998 British case and the resulting furore, see my 'What's Not Wrong With Conditional Organ Donation?' *Journal of Medical Ethics* 29 (2003) or my 'Racist Organ Donors and Saving Lives' *Bioethics* 21 (2007). For some US cases, see Robert Veatch, *Transplantation Ethics* (Washington, DC: Georgetown University Press, 2000), ch. 25. Neither the US nor the UK will accept donations with racist conditions or, in the UK, any conditions at all (bar living donation to family and friends).

[3] 'Dying Woman's Last Wish to Donate Kidney to her Mother Denied by Rules' *The Times*, 12 April 2008.

conditions set by the donor.[4] Organs could also be allocated either exclusively or under some priority system to potential recipients who have themselves agreed to donate (a version of the system I called 'exempt and exclude' in chapter 7). Would a priority scheme violate sound principles of allocation?

The first section describes and criticizes traditional views about acquisition and allocation in transplantation. I argue that traditional views misunderstand the ideas of gift and altruism and overrate their value. They should play little role in determining either acquisition or allocation. I then turn to partiality in allocation and distinguish between donations that are based on valuable relationships, such as donations to family members, and donations that are not, such as donations to celebrities. The subsequent few sections will discuss conditional allocation based on bad motives, such as racist donations. I argue that even bad conditions ought to be accepted, if the result would be more organs for some and no worse access for anyone else. I defend this view against the objections that conditional allocation would be unjust. Finally, I discuss giving priority to donors in receiving organs, which I argue has advantages in principle but drawbacks in practice.

DONATION AND IMPARTIALITY—TRANSPLANTATION'S SELF-IMAGE

On the acquisition side, the field of transplantation has historically been dominated by the idea of the gift as well as the ideas of generosity and altruism that are often taken to be synonymous with donation.[5] So powerful is the idea of donation that the term 'donors' is often used to describe anyone from whom organs are taken, including young children or sellers, whether or not they did anything that could be construed as giving. Many writers believe donation is so special that it can be used to rule out conditional allocation, priority for donors, and organ sales,[6] although they do not usually set out their reasons in any detail.[7] By contrast, I believe the idea of donation has little relevance to determining what system for allocation or acquisition there should be.

The ideas of gift, altruism, and generosity are commonly run together, but careful writers distinguish them.[8] Gifts are given for all sorts of reasons which may have nothing to do with a concern for the welfare of the recipient. Gifts can be given out of spite or to humiliate the recipient[9] although, in traditional societies

---

[4] A common term for accepting donor stipulations is 'directed donation', but 'conditional allocation' is better, since the controversy is not primarily over the donor's attaching a condition to an offer but over the transplant service's accepting it and allocating according to the condition.

[5] Veatch, *Transplantation Ethics*, chs.1, 9. Very many official donation websites use the language of the gift of life, generosity, and altruism.

[6] Chapter 10 considers organ sales at length and criticizes arguments based on altruism against permitting sales.

[7] Govert den Hartogh, *Farewell to Non-commitment: Decision Systems for Organ Donation from an Ethical Viewpoint* (The Hague: Centre for Ethics and Health, 2008), p. 35.

[8] The ideas in the next three paragraphs draw on den Hartogh's excellent account, ibid., pp. 36–7.

[9] See 'Christmas Giftmanship' in Stephen Potter, *The Complete Upmanship* (London: Rupert Hart-Davis Ltd., 1970). My thanks to James Taylor for the tip-off.

organized on the basis of gifts, they are the basis of mutual benefit and reciprocity. Altruism, in its normal sense, refers roughly to a non-self-interested concern for the interests of others. A commonly cited example is blood donation, where people give their blood with no prospect of personal return and the blood goes to whoever needs it. However, a wide variety of other-regarding motives can be described as altruistic, such as a special concern for the deaf, or the poor, or children, or animals. Altruism is not limited to disinterested general benevolence or wanting to meet the greatest needs.

The connection between giving and altruism is contingent. Some gifts could be altruistic in the sense of disinterested general benevolence, but giving out of spite is not altruistic and neither is giving for the sake of immediate return. However, the concept of altruism is sufficiently elastic that contribution to a mutually beneficial scheme may be considered altruistic in some sense, so long as it is not motivated by the prospect of immediate return.

Given the variety of motives for gifts, we can surely conclude that a gift in itself has no special value. This conclusion is all the stronger when we realize that gifts need not be voluntary. In societies organized on the basis of a gift relationship, people are expected to give and not giving would be subject to sanctions. Some writers argue that even receiving a gift can restrict the recipient's freedom. In the case of organ transplantation, they say, recipients of organs from dead people cannot reciprocate the gift and become subject to moral pressure, for instance to comply with medical instructions to preserve their new organs.[10] In sum, whatever is appealing in the idea of donation must come from the connection with altruism, not gift.

Organs taken for transplant are often referred to as 'amazing gifts' from deceased donors or their families,[11] and their 'generosity' warmly praised. Given that individuals and families can veto retrieval under current rules, it may be politic to call donation generous, but whether the description is accurate is another matter. As den Hartogh points out, we should not confuse the importance of the gift to the recipient with its value to the giver. Many people do not care what happens to their organs after they die. If they do not veto the taking of their organs, their altruism is 'similar to the altruism shown by a motorist seeing a fellow driver whose car has run out of petrol standing at the roadside and taking him to the nearest petrol station, which he has to pass anyway. It is rather excessive to praise this to the skies, and a true altruist will be the first one to feel a trifle embarrassed by such praise'.[12]

Den Hartogh's point may not apply to all donors. Some may be strongly inclined not to donate, say for religious reasons, but nonetheless donate for the sake of the potential recipient. They could be more accurately described as generous than those

---

[10] L. Siminoff and K. Chillag, 'The Fallacy of the "Gift of Life"' *Hastings Center Report* 29 (1999). I am unpersuaded, though, by their argument. An organ is rare and precious and whoever gets one has done so at the expense of someone else. Recipients could be pressurized into not wasting their new organ whether or not it is conceived of as a gift.

[11] Organ Donation Taskforce, *The Potential Impact of an Opt Out System for Organ Donation in the UK* (London: Department of Health, 2008), p. 2.

[12] Den Hartogh, *Farewell to Non-commitment*, p. 39.

who fit either den Hartogh's description or those who die never having given serious thought to organ donation at all. Nonetheless, people who do not care much about their remains or do not think about donation surely make up the bulk of those from whom organs are taken and, if so, describing them as generous or amazing gift-givers would typically miss the mark.[13]

Are families who donate more suitably described as 'generous' than the dead relatives from whom organs are taken? The answer turns not just on what they were thinking when they agreed to donate but also whether the organs of someone else are theirs to be generous with. Chapter 5's view of the role of the family casts doubt on whether families are being generous. According to that chapter, families do not have the right to decide based on their own interests. Families should decide only because the deceased transferred authority to them, or because letting families decide is the best way to give the deceased what they wanted, or because overriding the family would have bad publicity. Only when the deceased transferred authority could families be described as generous if they donate because only then would they be exercising their own claim. If they agree to donate because the deceased wanted to, any praise for generosity should accrue to the deceased. And whatever the families' motive for agreeing in the case where they are neither authorized by the deceased nor acting on the deceased's behalf, they could not properly be called generous when they fail to exercise a veto they have been given merely to avoid bad publicity. To conclude, while some donors and some families may deserve to be called generous, to describe the actually existing system of donation as based on generosity and amazing gifts is sentimental hyperbole.

On the allocation side, transplantation has, as I said, been greatly concerned to allocate organs according to some impartial principle or principles. While impartiality can be justified in several ways, it is sometimes supposed to be justified by the importance of altruistic acquisition. An official British Panel, in arguing against the acceptance of racist conditions, said: 'to attach any condition to a donation is unacceptable, because it offends against the fundamental principle that organs are donated altruistically and should go to patients in greatest need.'[14] Regrettably, the Panel's reasoning is obscure. Altruistic donation and allocation according to greatest need are quite distinct ideas. How do they together form one fundamental principle? The Panel did not say.[15]

[13] I am speculating somewhat, based on evidence about public ignorance of organ donation, the relatively few people who take active steps to donate, and a guess that a subset of them would both care about their remains and end up having their organs taken. 'Despite the importance of the subject, little is known about the characteristics of potential organ donors. Previous research on the subject is mostly either theoretical, or empirical with nonrandom, small, geographically limited, or convenience samples.' N. Mocan and E. Tekin, 'The Determinants of the Willingness to Donate an Organ Among Young Adults: Evidence from the United States and the European Union' *Social Science and Medicine* 65 (2007), p. 2528.
[14] Department of Health, *An Investigation into Conditional Organ Donation* (London: Department of Health, 2000), p. 25.
[15] For more detailed criticism of the Panel's moral reasoning, see my 'What's Not Wrong with Conditional Organ Donation?' For a criticism of their legal claims, see A. Cronin and J. Douglas, 'Directed and Conditional Deceased Donor Organ Donations: Laws and Misconceptions' *Medical Law Review* 18 (2010).

How could the motive of the donor be relevant to allocation? The answer cannot be that a registration system should *require* altruism. The system cannot possibly check people's motives and does not try to at all in the case of dead donors. If someone wants to donate an organ, the system does not ask whether his reason is selfless concern for others or to spite his family. The most that can be said is that a system should promote altruistic giving, perhaps by refusing to tempt people into non-altruistic agreements to organ retrieval. It might be said, for instance, that the system should not offer money or allow people to vent their racist hatred.

Even then, the altruism argument against conditional allocation has limitations. A desire for altruistic giving does not rule out all conditions because people can, as I said, be altruistic even when their altruism does not take the form of satisfying the greatest need. People might want to attach different conditions, such as offering their organs to a child, or a co-religionist, or a group that usually has less access to organs (such as African-Americans in the US, or Maori in New Zealand).[16] These conditions would be less objectionable than ones based on hatred or contempt and it is consistent to accept some conditions but not others. Condemning people who want to donate to a child, say, for their lack of altruism is as unattractively rigoristic as condemning someone who sponsors a child in a poor country, sponsoring being less efficient and perhaps less just than putting money into a general pool.

Consider a final problem with the altruism argument. Valuing altruistic giving can come at the expense of meeting the greater need. Suppose that accepting donors' conditions or giving priority to declared donors would increase the supply of organs even as altruistic giving declined. It is not incoherent to prefer fewer organs given for the right reasons to more organs given for the wrong reasons, but this preference for altruistic giving is itself counter-altruistic. People in need, by hypothesis, would do worse as a result of the altruistic giving and altruistic people would prefer more organs to more altruism.

When stripped of its hyperbole and careless formulation, the traditional idea of donation is an inaccurate picture of the moral value of giving. Giving need not be altruistic. Even when giving is altruistic, its value is overstated, since neither the deceased nor the family typically deserve the high praise given for donating. What value there is in altruistic giving has little relevance to acquisition, since a system for acquiring organs cannot check motives, or to allocation, since there is no good reason why a system should prefer altruistically given organs to more organs.

PARTIALITY AND IMPARTIALITY

I now turn to allocation and consider disagreements about the relative importance of acquiring more organs, meeting the greatest needs, and following fair procedures.

---

[16] Wayne Arnason sympathizes with a form of conditional allocation of kidneys where potential black donors are encouraged to donate by being told that the organs they donate are more likely to go to blacks, and the UNOS criteria for allocation are changed so that this is indeed so. See W. Arnason, 'Directed Donation: The Relevance of Race' *Hastings Center Report* 21 (1991).

These disagreements can all be thought of as being about the correct impartial principles that the organ transplantation system should follow. However, there is a prior question about the scope of impartiality, and some writers believe, drawing their cue from living donor organ transplantation between family members, that more weight should be given to partiality than it currently is.[17] This section explains how partiality in allocation can be impartially defensible when the partiality is morally legitimate.

Let me say first why the question of impartiality arises at all in organ allocation. Transplantation is not just a private matter. The supply and allocation of organs are typically organized by state or quasi-state agencies which, in many healthcare systems, also fund the hospitals and staff who are involved in donation and transplantation. Some writers believe that the role of the state means transplantation should be carried out on the basis of certain impartial principles. They conclude that the state should not accept conditional offers of organs if allocating according to those conditions would breach impartial principles. This conclusion, they believe, would rule out accepting racist offers or offers to donate to celebrities or to strangers met over the internet.[18]

I believe the move from 'the state plays a role' to 'allocation must be on impartial principles' is a mistake, most clearly shown by living donation between family and friends. Even critics of conditional allocation accept or do not object to the involvement of the state's agents in allocating living donors' organs to friends or relatives who would not receive them under an impartial system. But why not? Principles of justice do not say 'to each according to the luck of being a celebrity' but they also do not say 'to each according to the luck of having family and friends able and willing to donate'.

Clearly, in many cases of living donation to family and friends, the organs would not be made available unless they were guaranteed to be transplanted into the designated recipient. The incentive to donate provides a reason to deviate from an impartial principle which could apply equally to accepting conditional offers to celebrities, co-religionists, or members of specific races. Accepting those offers for the sake of more organs may appear to be a, perhaps justified, concession to undesirable motives. But in the case of donation between family and friends, surely we would not see deviating from impartial principles as a mere incentive. Rather, the partiality involved is entirely legitimate and valuable enough, from an impartial point of view, for it to be in no way morally questionable for the state's agents to help it along, as they do in living donation, with psychosocial assessments of potential donors, performing the operations, supplying the anti-rejection medication to the recipient, and so forth.

---

[17] M. T. Hilhorst, '"Living Apart Together": Moral Frictions between Two Coexisting Organ Transplantation Schemes' *Journal of Medical Ethics* 34 (2008).

[18] E.-H. Kluge, 'Designated Donation: Private Choice in Social Context' *Hastings Center Report* 19 (1989); American Society of Transplant Surgeons, 'Statement on Directed Donation and Solicitation of Organs', 23 October 2006, available at www.asts.org (last accessed 5 November 2009).

In endorsing the state's role in helping family and friends donate to each other, we need not thereby give up a commitment to impartiality.[19] At a high level of abstraction, impartiality and partiality need not conflict. Only a fanatic believes parents ought to love all children equally rather than their own especially. An impartial theory can allow people to give special weight to their morally valuable close attachments. The conclusion is that the impartialy defensible value of love and friendship justifies deviating from impartial principles of allocation.

If living donation between family and friends is a paradigm of entirely legitimate partiality, what of other cases? One obvious parallel is donation after death between family and friends. As far as the supposed breach of impartiality goes, what is the difference between donation by living or dead relatives? Dead people's organs are normally allocated by the state or its agents while living people's organs are not, but that distinction is multiply irrelevant. As I said, in many countries the healthcare system that carries out transplantation from both living and dead donors is paid for and organized by the state, so the state's role is not confined to donation after death. In any event, if we value the relationship in living donation, why is it not also valuable in donation after death? The rules were surely wrong when they denied the dying woman's last wish to donate a kidney to her mother.[20]

If we leave aside donation to family and friends, what if someone wants to donate to a fellow church-member, or to someone who has solicited over the internet, or to a celebrity? Would accepting those conditions be a justified response to legitimate partiality? What if someone wants to donate to a member of a group, such as children, or a co-religionist, or a fellow-national? Den Hartogh writes, 'We cannot assume a special duty of care on the basis of a "relationship" with someone who does not even know we exist. A special relationship cannot be merely imaginary.'[21] From this claim, we could infer that donation to a celebrity or a stranger could not be the legitimate partiality of people who are close, of which we approve and even appreciate.[22] I think den Hartogh overstates his claim, since one could assume a special duty of care, or some other mark of a special relationship, with someone who does not know one exists. A natural parent of an adopted child could assume such a duty even if the child did not know the parent existed. But den Hartogh's major point remains. We can value donation between family and friends as the expression of a valuable relationship, but not every conditional offer expresses such a valuable relationship. Donation to a celebrity *qua* celebrity would not. There are then boundary questions. Could donation to a fellow church member express some special tie? Could donation to a co-national (as opposed to a racist donation)?

I shall have to leave these questions aside, but I want to remind us of the point of asking them. We are asking about the value of the relationship that donation

---

[19] Whether an impartial view of ethics can give adequate weight to partiality and how it should do so are two large questions I cannot go into. See e.g. Brian Barry, *Justice as Impartiality* (Oxford: Clarendon Press, 1995) and Thomas Nagel, *Equality and Partiality* (Oxford: Clarendon Press, 1991).

[20] 'Dying Woman's Last Wish' *The Times*.

[21] Den Hartogh, *Farewell to Non-commitment*, pp. 86–7. Den Hartogh is writing of the conditions under which living donation is permissible rather than organ retrieval from the dead.

[22] Ibid., p. 87.

expresses and whether the value gives an impartial system a good reason to depart from the allocation rules it would otherwise apply. We are not asking about making concessions to undesirable motives. The distinction may or may not matter in practice. For the sake of more organs, accepting conditional offers could be justified regardless of the value of the relationship expressed. But possibly not all conditional offers would, if accepted, produce more organs, in which case it could matter whether the offers express legitimate partiality.

IMPARTIAL PRINCIPLES AND LEVELLING DOWN

Let us now consider conditions that should not be respected out of consideration for legitimate partiality. Racist conditions are perhaps the clearest example since nothing can be said for the motive, an expression of hatred, fear, or contempt. Nonetheless, I shall argue over the next few sections that conditional allocation could be justified even if on the basis of racist offers, so long as the effects on the supply of organs and their distribution meets certain conditions. I argue that the allocation of organs need not be based on an impartial principle, that conditional allocation may not be contrary to formal justice and could be justified even if it were, and that conditional allocation could be fairer than the alternative or, at least, better. This section provides some foundations for my arguments by presenting the distinction between impartial principles and impartially defensible methods, the injustice argument against conditional allocation, and the idea of levelling down.

Since organs should be allocated in an impartially defensible way, it may seem to follow that organs should be allocated according to impartial principles. However, impartial principles should be distinguished from impartially defensible methods of allocation. An impartial principle is a principle with impartiality built in to its content. 'Allocate organs to those in greatest need' is an impartial principle; 'allocate organs to your friends' is not. An impartially defensible method is one that can be defended from an impartial perspective. We had an example in the previous section, where the partial motive of family love could be impartially defended. In deciding on the ethics of conditional allocation, we should avoid the fallacy of assuming that only impartial principles of allocation are impartially defensible.

Consider an impartial principle of allocating according to greatest need, which might be thought to rule out conditional allocations.[23] Allocating according to greatest need may not in fact lead to the greatest needs being met. Suppose that following the principle causes needs to be less well met than they would be by some indirect method. If we care about meeting needs, the indirect method should be chosen. This point is no mere piece of hair-splitting; it is fundamental in other fields, notably economics. The most famous defence of a market allocation of goods appeals to its superiority to any direct method, such as state allocation. That is why the vital need for food is largely met through the market. People sell food to people

---

[23] The British Panel argued against conditional allocation as violating a principle of allocating according to need. They committed the fallacy I am describing. See n.14.

with money rather than allocate their food according to need and, from the point of view of meeting needs, the outcome is better, at least outside emergencies. Although this reason for the market allocation seems clearly correct, it need not be accepted to make the point that wanting needs to be met is only contingently connected to a principle of allocating according to needs.

The distinction between an impartial principle and an impartially defensible method shows that conditional allocation is not to be rejected just because the allocation is not based on an impartial principle. The outcomes matter and not, or not only, the principles of allocation. We should bear this distinction in mind as we consider the major argument against conditional allocation, which is that it is unjust.

The injustice argument says that when an organ is allocated conditionally, it bypasses the queue in the general pool. The queue is ordered justly and for some people to bypass it simply because they are lucky enough or famous enough to attract a donor is unjust.[24] Conditional allocation is still more unjust if it expresses the donor's discrimination.

To make the obvious reply to the injustice argument, what if accepting a condition would make extra organs available without reducing anyone's access to organs? Is there a conflict of values between justice and meeting needs for organs and, if so, how should we understand the conflict and decide what to do? The transplantation literature usually takes a simplistic approach to these questions by framing the ethical problems of allocation as utilitarianism versus justice. However, apart from the question-begging assumption that utilitarianism does not offer an adequate theory of justice, it is a harmful simplification to assume that what justice requires is clear and that the problem is only of how much weight it should have. What justice requires in the case of conditional allocation is, I shall argue, by no means obvious.

In order to test various views of justice, I shall assume for this and the next two sections that the alternative to conditional allocation would be 'levelling down'—making some worse off with no gain for others. On this assumption, if one wants to say that conditional allocation is unjust and thus all-things-considered wrong, one would have to show both that justice requires levelling down and that this justice overrides meeting people's needs for organs. Can we find an argument for levelling down? Quite a bit has been written in political philosophy on the topic, usually in discussions of egalitarian justice, but few writers want to level down in practice.[25] Some writers, who oppose egalitarianism, have argued that it is an error to value directly the relation of equality between people. They say that equality is not good in itself because it is not intrinsically good for anyone.[26] Egalitarians have usually replied by arguing that what is of moral importance need not be limited to what

[24] Kluge, 'Designated Donation'.
[25] See, for example, Derek Parfit, 'Equality or Priority?' in M. Clayton and A. Williams (eds.), *The Ideal of Equality* (Basingstoke: Macmillan, 2000); Larry Temkin, *Inequality* (Oxford: Clarendon Press, 1993), ch. 9; John Broome, *Weighing Goods* (Oxford: Basil Blackwell, 1991), ch. 9.
[26] Joseph Raz, *The Morality of Freedom* (Oxford: Clarendon Press, 1986), ch. 9; Harry Frankfurt, *The Importance of What We Care About* (Cambridge: Cambridge University Press, 1988), ch. 11.

would be good or bad for people. But they have been less concerned to show that equality is of moral importance and still less have they argued that its importance would be great enough to justify levelling down.[27] Egalitarians in political philosophy have not generally gone beyond claiming that equality makes levelling down in *one way better*, as opposed to being *all-things-considered better*, than an unequal world where some are better off and none worse off.

My purpose here is not to convince by the sheer number of people against levelling down, but to point out that those who prefer levelling down to conditional allocation have a job on their hands. It is rather disappointing, then, that they have said so little in defence of their view. In one of the few major philosophical discussions devoted to the topic, Robert Veatch rejects conditional allocation on the basis of what he calls 'true egalitarianism', which seems to be a view about fairness.[28] He realizes his view requires the claim that fairness is more important than beneficence, understood to require meeting needs for organs, but he does not defend that claim. Instead he takes the rejection of conditional allocation as a datum and works back to a criticism of Rawlsian maximin justice. But whatever the answer to the question of whether conditional allocation should be rejected, it is certainly not a datum or, in Rawlsian jargon, a considered moral judgement. There is simply too little consensus and too much to be said on both sides to make it that.

I shall reply to the fragmentary arguments given for preferring to level down rather than allocate conditionally. One criticism of conditional allocation says it would violate the principle of formal justice that requires like cases to be treated alike.[29] Formal justice is the subject of the next section. Another criticism says conditional allocation would be unfair, and fairness is the subject of the subsequent section.

FORMAL JUSTICE

Notoriously, treating like cases alike leaves open what should count as a like case but, if the principle is ever clear, it is surely so in circumstances where one gives an organ to one person and not a similarly placed other simply on grounds of race. Allocating on the basis of some or perhaps all conditions appears to violate formal justice. Nonetheless, I aim to cast doubt on the scope of the formal justice objection to make it at least unclear whether the objection applies to conditional allocation. I shall also comment on the weight of the objection, in the light of the earlier remarks about levelling down.

First, then, the doubts about the scope. Who is supposed to have duties of formal justice? There seem to be three relevant people or groups: recipients, donors, and

---

[27] Temkin, *Inequality*, p. 282.

[28] Veatch, *Transplantation Ethics*, ch. 25.

[29] This is not the place to make grand claims in moral and political philosophy, so let me say that one way to think of formal justice is as a subset of justice, itself a subset of morality. For one account, see John Rawls, *A Theory of Justice* (rev. edn.) (Oxford: Oxford University Press 1999), sec. 10.

the transplant team and wider framework of procurement and allocation they are embedded in. If we take these in order, we can first ask: Is it unjust and consequently wrong for someone who needs an organ but is not top of the queue to accept one from a living person? Some high-minded writers think so,[30] although it seems hard to see why, given that, by hypothesis, no one else in the general pool loses. Should someone stranded on a rock as the waters rise refuse the offer of a boat ride when someone else, who cannot now be rescued anyway, was not offered a ride?

One might say that the donor is acting unjustly, but even that is unclear. Donors may act wrongly, but I doubt whether they act contrary to principles of formal justice because I doubt whether formal justice applies to them in their role as donor. People need not treat like cases alike when disposing of their property in their wills. Similarly, if they wanted to direct their organs to their relatives, we would not think they acted contrary to formal justice. Our thought is not based on the desirability of family love; we certainly would think it contrary to formal justice if a judge or professor gave especial preference in sentencing or marking papers to someone they loved. The point is that how donors dispose of their organs is not a matter for formal justice.

What, though, of the public transplant services—should they not follow principles of formal justice in allocating organs? They should for organs that have been donated without conditions so, unlike in the case of the donor, principles of formal justice do apply to them. But it is unclear that formal justice applies when organs have been donated with conditions. The organs are not then freely available for allocation. To be sure, it might be said that the transplant service should turn them down on the grounds that, if they were to accept them, they would violate formal justice. But why should we believe that? The state's actions do not conflict with principles of formal justice when it upholds, through enforcing property rights, an allocation of private property not based on those principles. To take a second example, many people do not think public universities violate principles of formal justice when they administer privately donated scholarships for students from, say, a particular city or religion, although they would violate them if they were to use public funds in this way.[31] The conclusion is that formal justice, however important, may not be compromised by conditional allocation.

I am less confident of the conclusion about the scope of formal justice than I am in concluding that its weight is not enough to justify levelling down in cases involving access to organs. Where formal justice is held to be of great importance, it is rarely tested by considering situations in which it would be very bad for some and good for no one. The exception is in punishment, where giving similar punishments might indeed be bad for someone and good for no one else. But punishment is a special case where, if levelling down is justified, it is on the grounds

---

[30] E.g. Kluge, 'Designated Donation'.
[31] These examples show that Kluge is making a false inference when he says that organs must be allocated in accordance with justice and equality because organ donation occurs in a social context. The conclusion might be correct, but the argument has missing premises. See ibid.

that offenders deserve to be punished.[32] In cases such as access to organs, where, we can assume, no one deserves to be badly off, the challenge for those who would reject conditional allocation as formally unjust is to think up parallel cases where we are inclined to uphold formal justice at comparable expense for the innocent and with gain to none.

While conditional allocation has not been shown to be ruled out by formal justice, there is clearly more to justice than formal principles. In the next section, I consider an idea of fairness in a more substantial sense to try to show that conditional allocation should not be rejected because it is unfair.

MEETING NEEDS AND FAIRNESS

An obvious objection to conditional allocation is that it is unfair. Whether the objection is any good depends on what fairness requires and its weight. In this section, I aim to show that fairness is not the basis of a good objection to conditional allocation by comparing conditional allocation with the current practice of transplanting organs despite their scarcity.

Organs are scarce and not all who need them get them, and yet organs are generally transplanted when available. One might think that transplanting organs when they are scarce is unfair because some people receive a benefit while others, with equally strong claims, do not. But I assume no one would want to ban transplants on the ground that not everyone who needs an organ can get it. If one thinks current practice is unfair but should nonetheless be permitted, then presumably one must think meeting needs beats fairness. One could not then argue against conditional allocation on the grounds that fairness always beats meeting needs.

Alternatively, one might have a different view of fairness. One might believe that fairness requires organ transplants, for two plausible reasons. Suppose fairness is taken comparatively: whether one is treated unfairly depends on how one is treated relative to others. Because people who need organs are worse off than the vast mass of people with healthy organs, it would be unfair to those who need organs not to give them when available so that they can be closer in health to the healthy. A second, non-comparative, interpretation of fairness might say: people who need transplants have claims of needs. It is unfair not to satisfy their claims when one could do so without thereby failing to satisfy anyone else's claims. Both seem like good fairness reasons for the current practice of transplantation. Both reasons also support permitting conditional allocation, assuming it would worsen no one's access to organs. If conditional allocation were rejected in favour of levelling down, potential recipients who could have received the conditionally donated organ would be treated unfairly both comparatively and non-comparatively.

---

[32] See the saints and sinners example in Temkin, *Inequality*, pp. 273–6.

The conclusion at this stage can be put as a dilemma: either transplantation is unfair, in which case meeting needs beats unfairness and fairness does not justify banning conditional allocation; or transplantation is required by fairness, in which case conditional allocation is at least not obviously unfair and is still required by meeting needs. What now of the position that transplantation in conditions of scarcity is neither fair nor unfair but, if it is going to happen, it has to be done fairly? It could then be said that conditional allocation is unfair while transplantation need not be.

One argument might be that when two people have equal claims on one organ, a fair procedure, such as random choice, should be used to choose between them. Whoever wins gets the organ, so it is not wasted, and the loser has not been treated unfairly. But denying someone an organ because of, say, a racist condition would be unfair. Hence one can justify transplantation in conditions of scarcity without justifying conditional allocation. The trouble with this argument is that it envisages a situation where meeting needs and fairness do not conflict. It is not a case of levelling down because the organ is not wasted. To make it a test case of levelling down, suppose, for some reason, the results of the fair procedure cannot be acted on. Perhaps the winner under the fair procedure has just had dinner and cannot be safely operated on now, when the organ must be used. Surely the organ should not be wasted in that case, even though not allocated in accordance with the fair procedure. By extension, respect for a fair procedure would not justify wasting a conditionally donated organ.

Another argument might be that the excess demand for organs can be managed fairly by having a fair queue. With a fair queue, transplantation under conditions of scarcity is not unfair, whereas conditional allocation would be unfair because it would permit some to jump the queue. But the reasons for thinking that queue-jumping is unfair do not clearly tell against conditional allocation. Suppose queues are fair when based on a fixed rule which does not admit of discretion or bias; in other words, the fairness involved is the fairness of following a fixed procedure. Fairness in this sense need not condemn conditional allocation since it could be made a fixed rule that conditionally donated organs will be accepted. Suppose substantive criteria of fairness should determine the way in which the queue is organized. For instance, a queue might be organized on the basis of time waited, and queue-jumping would then be unfair. The trouble with this argument, for those who are not radicals about queues, is that it would condemn as unfair the transplantation queuing methods in most countries. In general, the criteria for their queues are a mix of fairness, severity, urgency, capacity to benefit, and time waited. Some of these criteria give weight to the needs of potential recipients, which would justify taking a conditionally donated organ when the alternative is no organ. The final placings may trade off fairness against other criteria, such as meeting needs, or use a view of fairness that includes meeting needs, but either way the criteria that justify existing queues do not clearly condemn conditional allocation.[33]

---

[33] Some critics of HLA-matching for kidneys in the US, which has the by-product of making it harder for African-Americans to receive cadaveric kidneys for transplant, object on the mixed grounds that (1) HLA-matching is not as efficient as it is made out to be and (2) equity is not given enough weight. See Arnason, 'Directed Donation' and Robert Gaston et al., 'Racial Equity in Renal

One argument remains to show that fairness could not defeat all conditional allocation. What would be unfair if conditional donations were accepted and the organs used only when they went to the people who would have received them had the donation been unconditional? Who then would be treated unfairly? Everyone receives what she would have done had the donation been unconditional, and not by accident: accepting the conditional donation was itself conditional on no one being unfairly passed over. Of course, the organs would be wasted when potential recipients of a conditional donation would not be the same as if the donation were unconditional, a waste I have argued against here. But how could those who think the waste is justified by fairness continue to think so in the limited cases where conditional allocation does not cause anyone to be treated unfairly?

I do not, however, want to say that conditional allocation would be perfectly just. An allocation that discriminates on morally arbitrary grounds, especially when the result of unjust motives, is less just, other things equal, than one which does not. But, on the assumption that to reject conditional allocation would level down, other things are not equal. Accepting the condition would be all-things-considered better and perhaps more just (although not perfectly just) than turning down the offer of an organ. Conditional allocation would be a justified concession to the unjustified motives of a person who is free not to offer an organ.

THE EFFECTS OF CONDITIONAL ALLOCATION AND THEIR EVALUATION

I have been assuming that the alternative to allocation would be levelling down, reducing access to organs for some and increasing it for no one. The assumption was made to test certain views of justice, and it may be false. A policy of conditional allocation may make it harder for some groups to get access to organs; it may even reduce the overall number of donations. It is not hard to imagine how bad effects might occur. Perhaps people who would have donated unconditionally instead would attach conditions, skewing access to organs. Perhaps people who would have donated instead would refuse to donate at all out of disgust at the policy of conditional allocation. On the other hand, it is not hard to imagine how conditional allocation might have better effects than no conditional allocation. Perhaps people who would not have donated otherwise would donate if they could attach conditions, which could even benefit those discriminated against, since a conditional donation could shrink the pool of competitors for other organs. Perhaps people would think that, if organs are turned down because they come with conditions, organs could not be very scarce, so they withhold their own.

Transplantation: The Disparate Impact of HLA-based Allocation', in A. Caplan and D. Coelho (eds.), *The Ethics of Organ Transplants* (Amherst, NY: Prometheus Books, 1998). Whatever the merits of the criticism of US practice, even these critics believe that efficiency, in the sense of getting more years of benefit, should be a major consideration in allocation.

Importantly, we are only speculating about the effects of conditional allocation. In the actual British case of racist donation that caused so much fuss, someone would have died without the liver and her life was very likely to be saved by receiving it, and indeed was saved, as matters turned out.[34] In such a case, with only speculation on the other side, we may well think it best to try to save the person. In the actual case, saving the person required accepting the racist offer.

Working out what would happen under various policies of conditional allocation requires empirical investigation. We should need to know, or estimate probabilistically, how many organs would be obtained and how they would be allocated, that is, whether to the less needy or those waiting a shorter time. We also need to think about the effects at the time of the conditional offer and over a longer run period. Without a proper investigation, speculation about the wider effects of conditional allocation provides no reasons for or against it.[35] It could be better or it could be worse than the alternatives.

Still, without pre-empting the results of any such investigation, note that the effects are likely to be different in different times and places and the effects on wider patterns of donation may well be negligible, especially if the policy is not widely known. It is also worth mentioning that some of the effects might be altered by various modifications of policy. One suggestion—there might be others—is to use the pool of unconditional donations as a float to prevent unequal access. Thus if a racist refuses to donate to blacks, his offer would be accepted but the next organ from the pool of unconditionally donated organs would go to a black.[36]

Even if we knew the effects on organ supply of a policy of conditional allocation, we would also need some way to evaluate them. For our purposes, it is enough to consider the three theories of justice mentioned earlier in the book: utilitarianism, priority to the worst off, and egalitarianism.[37] If the effects were to reduce access for everyone, then conditional allocation would be a mistake on any view.[38] If the effects were to increase access for some without reducing anyone else's access, then both utilitarianism and priority to the worst off would recommend it and what an

---

[34] Department of Health, *An Investigation into Conditional Organ Donation.*

[35] But for an attempt to go beyond speculation, see Aaron Spital, 'Should People who Donate a Kidney to a Stranger be Permitted to Choose their Recipients? Views of the United States Public' *Transplantation* 76 (2003). Spital argues that his results, based on telephone interviews with the general public, suggest that conditional allocation should not be permitted in the case of kidneys donated by living non-relatives in the US, with the exception of conditional donations to children.

[36] Paul Brown suggested this to me.

[37] Is there a fourth theory, based on rights? People's rights over their bodies do not give them the power to decide, on the basis of whatever reasons they like, who should get their organs. They do not because they have no right that their offer of an organ be accepted so it would not infringe on their rights if the transplant service turned down their offers. See the parallel argument about the family veto in chapter 5.

[38] There are considerations besides access to organs. Jonathan Wolff draws attention to the importance of symbolic value in his partial defence of levelling down. See his 'Levelling Down', in Keith Dowding, James Hughes, and Helen Margetts (eds.), *Challenges to Democracy: The PSA Yearbook 2000* (Basingstoke: Palgrave Macmillan, 2001). I respond to his idea and others in 'Racist Organ Donors and Saving Lives'.

egalitarian view would say is not, as I argued in the previous section, at all obvious.[39] There are many other possibilities.

To bring out some more of what a full evaluation would need, compare two situations that might arise from accepting conditional donations. Suppose there are two groups, whites and blacks, and let the numbers refer to organs available for each group. Compare two possible outcomes of conditional allocation against a baseline of refusing conditional donations.

> No conditional allocation: Whites 90 organs, Blacks 15 organs
>
> Outcome 1: Whites 100 organs, Blacks 10 organs
>
> Outcome 2: Whites 94 organs, Blacks 15 organs.

How conditional allocation should be evaluated in the light of these two distributions depends upon the importance of saving the greatest number of lives, preserving or promoting access for groups, and not worsening the position of individuals. To explain, a principle of meeting needs would recommend conditional allocation if the result were Outcome 2 or even if the result were Outcome 1, that is, where blacks do worse than in the baseline, because conditional allocation would meet more people's roughly equally important needs. A principle that showed concern for access for groups would oppose Outcome 1 but should have no objection to Outcome 2, since no group has worse access than in the baseline of no conditional allocation.[40]

Outcome 2 still leaves it open that, if conditional allocation were adopted, individual members of a group would do worse. The policy might change the timing of donations causing some to miss out even though others from their group subsequently got organs they would not otherwise have had. It might be enough to say to people who lose out when others from their group gain that a policy of meeting needs without reducing the access of any group is prospectively in everyone's interests, and consequently justified.

These sketchy remarks about evaluation obviously do little justice to difficult topics in moral and political philosophy: whether the greater number should be saved, whether group inequality is morally significant over and above individual inequality, and under what conditions sacrifices can legitimately be imposed on some. A critic could certainly try to develop further arguments against conditional allocation as a policy. But let me repeat the claim that conditional offers of organs should be accepted if doing so would increase access for some without reducing anyone else's access to organs. Conditional allocation may even be justified when it

---

[39] Thus the British Panel do not give themselves a hard enough time when they assume supporters of conditional allocation must believe that the increase in the supply of organs is the overriding principle. See *An Investigation into Conditional Organ Donation*, par. 6.5. One does not have to say that to permit conditional allocation.

[40] O-type blood group people on the organ waiting list are an example of a badly off group because they already have to wait longer than other people for organs. The Dutch Health Ministry rejected a living donor list exchange system that would have had some people getting first priority to a dead donor's organ if they could get a living person to donate an organ to someone else. Their reason was that O-type people would be disadvantaged. Den Hartogh, *Farewell to Non-commitment*, p. 83.

would reduce some people's access, depending on how many extra organs become available and who gets them. As for the effects of conditional allocation, they are a matter for empirical investigation and, until there has been one, speculative appeals to the wider effects do not make a case for or against conditional allocation.

PRIORITY FOR DONORS

This section considers the proposal to give priority in receiving organs to people who have declared their willingness to donate after they die. Priority schemes usually aim to increase the supply of organs, by giving a motive to people to donate, and to make the allocation fairer, by giving priority to people who are willing to contribute organs. One proposal would give bonus points to declared donors who need an organ. The bonus points would be added to the points they get for fulfilling criteria such as the urgency of their condition, its severity, and the degree of match in an available organ. Nadel and Nadel suggest awarding two bonus points, which they compare with the four points already awarded to people who have been living kidney donors and with the range of 10–25 points that potential recipients need to be given a transplant.[41] Obviously, the extent to which donors are given priority depends on the relative number of points they are awarded. Other proposals would exclude from transplants people who have declared their unwillingness to donate, or put them at the bottom of the list, so that a barely adequately matched organ would go to a declared donor even if it were perfectly matched to a non-donor. I shall leave the details of priority schemes aside and focus on whether they would be fairer and increase supply. Priority schemes may well be fairer but I doubt whether they would increase the supply of organs. First, though, I shall defend priority schemes against what we might think of as 'traditionalist' objections.

Priority schemes would depart from the self-image of transplantation in both their motivation and allocation. If people are motivated to donate by the prospect of priority in receiving organs, they would be donating partly out of self-interest, whereas the supposedly ideal motivation is disinterested altruism of the kind thought to motivate donation to blood banks. If people receive priority in the allocation of organs because they have agreed to donate, then the criteria for allocation are not just the medical criteria of urgency, need, and so on. Does it matter that a priority scheme would not be based on blood-bank type altruism and would add a non-medical criterion for allocation?

Supporters of priority schemes claim that priority is altruism of a sort, namely 'reciprocal altruism', where people give but expect others to give too.[42] If what we are supposed to value in altruistic donation is the 'gift relationship' then bear in

[41] Mark Nadel and Carolina Nadel, 'Using Reciprocity to Motivate Organ Donations' *Yale Journal of Health Policy, Law and Ethics* 5 (2005), p. 314.

[42] Ibid., p. 320; David Steinberg, 'An "Opting In" Paradigm for Kidney Transplantation' *American Journal of Bioethics* 4 (2004), p. 6.

mind that reciprocal altruism actually characterizes 'gift relationships' better than disinterested benevolence to the world at large. As I said earlier, gifts are typically expected to be reciprocated and the expectations are often backed up by sanctions. In any case, it does not matter whether the meaning of altruism can be stretched to include virtually anything besides cruelty and cash transactions. Altruism is not important enough as a motive to play much role in choosing transplant allocation and acquisition systems. We may set aside the objection that a priority scheme is not altruistic.

A further traditionalist objection points out that a priority scheme would add a non-medical criterion. But what would be wrong with that? Non-medical criteria are already used when existing systems give some priority to people who have waited longer for an organ or who live in the same region as donors. These criteria cannot be defended as proxies for the medical criteria of need and urgency, and the reasons given for them are the non-medical ones of fairness, for time spent waiting, and encouraging donation, for priority to locals. The objection to giving priority to declared donors may be based on a fear that the next step would be allocating on the basis of social worth; but giving priority to those willing to contribute has nothing to do with judging people's social worth.[43] In fact, one of the advantages of a priority scheme would be that people who do not want to donate or receive organs could do so with no adverse judgements on their morality because they would simply be choosing not to take part in a kind of insurance scheme. There would be no need to praise donors or criticize non-donors.

Let us turn to the questions of whether priority for donors would be fair and would increase the number of organs. The questions are related because, insofar as fairness is a property of outcomes, fairness could not be judged without knowing the outcomes of priority schemes. (If priority schemes for some reason caused fewer organs to be available, the outcome would arguably be unfair to the badly off people who miss out.) Nonetheless, I shall treat fairness and outcomes separately.

Priority for donors has an advantage from the point of view of fairness. It is a basic view of fairness that people act unfairly when they take but do not give when they could have given. Thus it is unfair not to give priority to declared donors over those who would choose not to donate.

As some critics point out, a priority scheme would reduce access to organs for people who refuse to contribute for profound personal reasons, such as their religious beliefs. But conscientious non-contributors seem the easiest exclusion to justify. If people refuse for religious reasons, then their reduced access to organs is simply a cost of their religious beliefs. People who want expensive churches for religious reasons should not be able to shift the costs to non-believers. In the case of organs, the argument is even stronger. How can those who think it wrong to give organs expect other people to give their organs to them?[44]

[43] Nadel and Nadel, 'Using Reciprocity to Motivate Organ Donations', p. 321; Den Hartogh, *Farewell to Non-commitment*, p. 53.
[44] Den Hartogh, *Farewell to Non-commitment*, p. 53.

People act unfairly if they take without contributing when they choose not to contribute. However, not all failures to contribute are unfair. A priority scheme must deal with people unable to contribute, such as children or people with HIV, and people who do not find out about a priority scheme, such as those on the margins of society.

Supporters of priority schemes try to find ways to include those unable to contribute. For example, sometimes they suggest that people with HIV could contribute in some other way, such as agreeing to donate their organs for research, or they suggest simply including those unable to contribute.[45] The risk to a priority scheme of including people who have not declared their willingness to donate is the incentive to cheat, and enough cheating would cause a scheme to fail. However, being a young child or having HIV are hard to fake, so admitting them may have little effect on the viability of a scheme.

What if some people need a transplant but have never heard of the scheme or have changed their minds and would now like to join? They were able to contribute but did not consciously refuse to do so. One's attitude to the unfairness of excluding those who did not sign up but claim they wish they had done may depend on why they did not. There is a difference between not signing up because one is homeless and did not know and not signing up because one did not get round to it.

Suppose we have worked out who, ideally, should be included and excluded from a priority scheme. The challenge is to devise a priority scheme that would not unravel. Not having heard of a scheme or changing one's mind are easier to fake than being a young child or having HIV. Suppose, in the face of the fraud problem, that a priority scheme would unravel unless it excluded people who would ideally be included. Could one object that such exclusions would make a priority scheme unfair? One could argue that those excluded have not contributed and so, in fairness to those who have, should not receive priority. Or one could accept that the exclusions are not ideal, but argue that a priority scheme is still fairer on balance than the alternatives because it is unfair not to give priority to people who are willing to contribute. While not *obvious* that a priority scheme would be fairer than the current scheme, it could be fairer.

As I said earlier, a full assessment of fairness depends on the effects of a priority scheme on the organ supply. Some, although not all, of its defenders think a priority scheme could greatly increase the supply. I have my doubts. The claim that a priority scheme would increase donations hinges upon its making people more likely to agree to donate and finding some way to prevent their families vetoing retrieval. According to Nadel and Nadel, people would be more likely to donate because, at the moment, many are only slightly opposed to or neutral about donation and the extra chance of receiving an organ under a priority scheme would be enough reason for them to donate.[46] Perhaps Nadel and Nadel are

[45] Nadel and Nadel, 'Using Reciprocity to Motivate Organ Donations', pp. 315–16. In some poorer countries and the United States, some way would also need to be found to reward declared donors who do not have the money to receive a transplant.
[46] See ibid., pp. 317–18 for these and other speculative reasons.

right, although they do not provide any evidence. But perhaps people do not like thinking about their deaths, or do not invest much effort in finding out about transplantation, and would not be swayed by the extra chance of getting an organ in the unlikely event that they need it. We can only speculate in advance of empirical testing of some kind (which Nadel and Nadel sensibly recommend).[47]

If a priority scheme is to motivate people with the prospect of a greater chance of getting organs, it needs to overcome the problem of the family veto. Some supporters believe that the family should be legally prevented from vetoing the wishes of someone who agreed to donate as part of a priority scheme.[48] I agree that there is no objection in principle to preventing the family from vetoing a clear agreement to donate. However, for the reasons given in chapter 5, overriding the family is likely to come at too high a price in bad effects on the supply of organs. Realistically, a priority scheme would have to work with the family's power of veto.

Would families be any less likely than they are now to veto the retrieval of organs from a relative who has agreed to donate under the priority scheme? Perhaps families would be less likely to veto because they could be told that the relative had agreed for the sake of a greater chance at getting organs, and so, unlike now, a veto would renege on the deceased's promise.[49] But perhaps some families would be more likely to veto, cynically thinking they can veto at no cost now to the deceased or themselves. Or perhaps some families would not be motivated by the increased chance of an organ the deceased had had in life given that, as would very often be the case, the deceased had not in fact received an organ while alive. Or perhaps some families do not think in a calculating way at all but would be unable to bring themselves to agree, whatever was said about a priority scheme. If we ask why families veto retrieval now, sometimes they veto because they do not know what the deceased wanted, or because they think the deceased had changed their minds since agreeing to donate, or because of some revulsion against organ retrieval, all of which could still apply under a priority scheme. As with the individual motive to donate, we can only speculate about how a priority scheme would affect the family's decision.

I cannot conceal my doubts about whether a priority scheme would increase the supply of organs. However, the ethical objections to a priority scheme, to do with the loss of disinterested altruism, the use of non-medical criteria, and the unfairness of exclusions, are all unpersuasive and, at the level of principle, a priority scheme may well be fairer than the current system.

CONCLUSION

This chapter has been sharply critical of many traditional ethical views in transplantation. Altruism and gift are poorly understood and misapplied to existing

---

[47] Nadel and Nadel, 'Using Reciprocity to Motivate Organ Donations', p. 319.
[48] Steinberg, 'An "Opting In" Paradigm for Kidney Transplantation', p. 11, n. 5. Nadel and Nadel do not recommend overriding the family.
[49] This is Nadel and Nadel's view in 'Using Reciprocity to Motivate Organ Donations', p. 318.

practice. The prevailing views of justice are crude and incomplete in the context of conditional allocation, and generally end up with the wrong conclusions. However, the extent to which practice should change is another matter. I have argued that conditional allocation should not be ruled out absolutely (as it is in the UK) but left it open that the current refusal to accept conditions could be justified if the effects on the organ supply turn out a certain way. I have argued that a priority scheme for donors may be fairer than the current system, but we do not have a good reason to think it would increase the supply of organs, and we cannot assess its fairness definitively without knowing its outcomes. Perhaps, then, the status quo is better than the alternatives, although perhaps not. However, the status quo should probably be changed in one respect: its opposition to organ sales. Sales are the subject of the next chapter.

10

Organs and Money

One measure that may relieve the shortage of organs is to permit their sale. While full-blown markets are not legally permitted anywhere, some countries permit methods and levels of compensation that come quite close, and sale appears to have passed from the unmentionable to the mentioned-but-largely-dismissed-by-authorities stage. How we should assess permitting sale depends on what would happen to the supply of organs, to the people who would sell them, and to social relations more broadly. Some of the considerations are factual, to do with estimates of willingness to supply or the effectiveness of regulation. Others involve applying certain difficult concepts, such as autonomy, coercion, exploitation, and altruism.

However, we first need a clearer sense of what we are discussing. Throughout the chapter, I shall be discussing whether sales should be legally allowed rather than the ethical questions raised by black market sales, such as how doctors should treat patients who have illegally acquired organs. The initial section lays out some of the systemic options for permitting and discouraging sale. The subsequent section asks how permitting sale might affect the supply of organs from both the living and the dead. I then discuss a specific problem with the purchase of organs from the dead before turning to evaluating the effects on living sellers. I consider whether we have a right to sell our organs and whether and how it would matter if selling makes sellers worse off than not selling. I also consider the view that permitting sale would cause exploitation and injustice. I next turn to the objection that sale undercuts altruism and wrongly commodifies people, or parts of people. I then attempt to reach final conclusions about the sale from the living. On the whole, I believe that prohibiting sale infringes upon people's rights over their bodies and, in some circumstances—which may well be the actual ones—sale should be allowed. But I concede there are certain circumstances when sale may be legally discouraged.

MONEY AND ORGANS: SOME OPTIONS

When it comes to exchanging money for organs, the choice is a good deal broader than between absolute prohibition and a free market with private buyers and sellers. The aim of this section is not to recommend, but only to give, in a neutral form, some of the options.

First, note that permitting sale does not mean sale would occur. To permit sale would be to abstain from coercing people into not buying and selling. But people may be free to buy or sell without exercising their freedom. As we shall see, a certain kind of market in organs from the dead simply may not form because the gains for buyers and sellers would be too small.

If money exchange were allowed, the state could regulate prices. It could insist on a minimum price, perhaps to prevent exploitation of sellers. It could insist on a maximum price, perhaps to prevent exploitation of buyers, or to prevent sellers being tempted in some way by an irresistible offer. Or the state could set a fixed price. The state could also regulate the conditions in which people contract to give up organs, for instance requiring psychological evaluations or independent advice for potential sellers, or requiring a certain level of post-operative care. Or, instead of regulating, the state could leave pay and conditions to be set by a market. Prices could then track supply and demand, and potential sellers and buyers could agree on the conditions of sale. Possibly the market equilibrium price and conditions would be very similar to what the state would require anyway.

The state could regulate who is allowed to buy organs. It could make itself the sole purchaser by prohibiting private purchase. Or it could buy organs in an open market to provide free to certain recipients while allowing people to buy their organs privately in the same market. Note that a market need not mean that those most in need would have to pay for the organs, and state provision of organs would not require the state to be the sole purchaser of organs. Just as with housing, where state provision coincides with private sale and purchase, how and to whom organs are supplied are not determined by how they were acquired.

A further question is whether money exchange should be restricted within borders. A rich country could permit a market within its borders while forbidding cross-border trades. Or it could permit trades only between co-nationals.[1] The likely rationale for restricting trade across borders would be to prevent abuses of vulnerable people, who may be poor, unable to speak the language, not understand what they are getting involved in, and ineligible for the social welfare protection provided in rich countries. Or countries could permit a trade across borders, reasoning that it is the poor of other countries who would benefit the most, or that their own citizens would be unlikely to supply organs in large numbers.

In the case of organ retrieval from the dead, people could be paid while alive for their organs after they die (a futures market), or their next-of-kin, or others with some entitlement, could be paid at the time of deciding on retrieval (a current or spot market). Those who favour a free market tend not to go into details about what form buying and selling should take. The absence of detail is not a failure of imagination on their part; rather they think one of the virtues of the market is to find the most efficient ways of matching buyers and sellers. Consequently, they favour freedom rather than prescribing institutional forms.[2]

---

[1] According to Alireza Bagheri, non-Iranians are not allowed organs from living unrelated Iranians. See his 'Compensated Kidney Donation: An Ethical Review of the Iranian Model' *Kennedy Institute of Ethics Journal* 16 (2006), pp. 272, 275.

[2] David L. Kaserman and A. H. Barnett, *The U.S. Organ Procurement System: A Prescription for Reform* (Washington, DC: AEI Press, 2002), pp. 122–3.

Just as there are numerous ways to organize sales, there are numerous ways to try to discourage them. Several countries make it a criminal offence to buy or sell organs.[3] That is to say, not only is there no right to sell one's organ, there is a legally enforceable duty not to sell which is backed up by the threat of criminal punishment. Alternatively, it could be made an offence to buy an organ but not sell one (as it is an offence to buy but not sell sex in Sweden). Or contracts to sell could be made unenforceable. Or the money could be confiscated. Or doctors could refuse to carry out transplantation, or be required to refuse by their professional bodies.

With so many options, we should take care when arguing about sales. People who argue against permitting monetary exchange should think about whether their arguments apply to all exchange or only to certain ways in which exchange might, but need not, take place. People who argue for permitting exchange should think about whether their arguments support exchange in any conditions, or only under certain conditions. And in all the arguments, we should be clear whether what is in question is money for organs from the dead, the living, or both.

SALES AND SUPPLY

The primary reason for considering the sale of organs is to get more of them, yet it is an open question whether sale would increase supply. We cannot glibly assume the standard supply and demand curves of economics texts. *A priori*, permitting sale could cause supply to go up, down, or stay the same. *A priori*, the quality of organs could also go up, down, or stay the same. This section briefly reviews the theory and empirical evidence of what might happen to quality and quantity if sales were permitted.[4]

It is sometimes feared that, if organs were bought and sold, their quality would be low. The usual reason offered for fearing the effects on quality is based on an analogy with the conclusions Richard Titmuss drew about paid blood donation in the 1960s.[5] He claimed that the quality of paid blood in the US was lower than the quality of donated blood in the UK. He explained the lower quality by saying that the sellers had a financial incentive not to disclose their infections and the buyers (who were not the end users) had an incentive not to be picky about the quality of the blood. By extension, it is sometimes claimed that the people who accept the offer of money

---

[3] Mark Cherry has a long list of legislation in various jurisdictions that restricts the sale of organs. See his *Kidney for Sale By Owner* (Washington, DC: Georgetown University Press, 2005), pp. 163–8. In England in 2007, a man named Daniel Tuck was given a 12-month suspended sentence for putting his kidney up for auction. He was subsequently found hanged. See 'Kidney Sale Man Found Dead' *Birmingham Mail*, 25 September 2007.

[4] I leave aside financial cost as a possible drawback of sale. If permitting sale would improve the quality and quantity of organs supplied, the state may well find the extra costs worth paying. See chapter 1 on the cost-effectiveness of transplantation. I also leave aside any costs to a public health system of looking after sellers who become sick. Such costs may also be worth paying or could be transferred to buyers by making them buy insurance.

[5] Richard M. Titmuss, *The Gift Relationship* (Harmondsworth: Pelican Books, 1970). Titmuss's book predated the major problems in the 1980s with HIV-infected blood that had been donated altruistically.

for their, or their dead relatives', organs would have an incentive not to disclose infections or other causes of low quality. The critics of sales also point to evidence of the poor quality of organs donated in the black market. As against these claims about poor quality, it has been argued that advances in screening for quality since Titmuss wrote make it possible to tell whether organs are of poor quality. Unlike in a black market, and unlike with the legal blood suppliers in Titmuss's time (who had been freed from legal liability for unsafe blood), the threat of liability and the high value of organs compared with blood would give buyers the incentive to screen organs for quality.[6] Moreover, criticizing the quality of bought organs is rather ironic since the organs used now are often hardly in pristine condition.[7] Compared with current quality, there does not seem much reason to fear a serious drop in the quality of organs if sale is permitted. Indeed, if sale led to a net increase in supply, transplanters could afford to be more choosy about which organs they took (as appears to have happened in Iran, which has had graft survival rates comparable to those in the United States).[8]

As for quantity, the question is whether permitting sale would lead to a net increase in the supply of organs. We cannot assume that, because organs currently have a price of $0, anything above $0 would lead to more organs. While permitting sale may lead to some people becoming sources of organs who otherwise would not, it may also cause other people, who would have donated, to refuse. If organs may be bought, fewer people may become live donors to family members because people who need an organ would not want to put their own family members at risk or may not want to have to feel the necessary gratitude. To take another possibility, if sale were permitted, some people may not want to donate their, or their relatives' organs after death, for instance because the donation would have a price rather than being the 'priceless gift of life', or because they are offended by the offer of money, or because transferring organs acquires a stigma as something people do for money.

It is certainly possible that permitting sale would reduce supply from some groups. What matters is the net effect. If supply went down from some groups but increased from others by a more than compensating number, then permitting sale would achieve the aim of increasing supply. So we should ask what the evidence shows or, at least, suggests.

If we consider the effects of money on supply, standard economics tell us that supply increases with price. But recent developments in behavioural economics and psychology cast doubt on whether supply always increases with price. To take only one example, there is evidence that paying people in a way visible to others makes them less willing to help charities compared with not paying them (or with paying them privately).[9] Critics of markets cite numerous other examples from

---

[6] Richard Epstein, *Mortal Peril* (Cambridge, MA: Perseus Publishing, 1999), p. 257; James S. Taylor, *Stakes and Kidneys* (Aldershot: Ashgate, 2005), pp. 177–81.

[7] Gretchen Reynolds, 'Will Any Organ Do?' *The New York Times Magazine*, 10 July 2005. Reynolds's article starts by describing the deaths of four people from rabies in Dallas after receiving infected organs. Poorer quality organs are acquired under the euphemism of 'extended criteria'.

[8] Taylor, *Stakes and Kidneys*, p. 180.

[9] Dan Ariely, Anat Bracha, and Stephan Meier, 'Doing Good or Doing Well? Image Motivation and Monetary Incentives in Behaving Prosocially' *American Economic Review* 99 (2009).

the recent economics literature.[10] More directly related to transplantation, evidence from Iran and Kuwait shows that the number of living related donors falls when it becomes possible to buy organs.[11] And, as evidence that people are less likely to donate to their relatives when organs become available from another source, the priority given to kidney transplant candidates under 35 in the US has caused a drop in living donations.[12]

The evidence, while hardly conclusive, shows it is more than a bare possibility that net supply could fall if money were offered. Here is some evidence on the other side, about payment to living suppliers. While Iran did, as mentioned, see a fall in the number of living related donors after introducing compensation in 1988, the fall was greatly exceeded by the number of new organs available. Indeed, fresh demand and the backlog represented by its waiting list had been met by 1999. Iran's scheme has certain specific features, such as permitting only co-nationals to engage in the organ transaction and in permitting only state-set compensation rates (although these may have been added to by illicit extra payments), and Iran itself may be importantly different from other countries, so one could not generalize with total confidence to other schemes and other countries. Still, in the one place it has been legally tried on a large scale, generous compensation increased the overall supply of organs.[13]

As for payment for organs from the dead, we have some theoretical reason to predict a net increase in supply. Demand is great and probably inelastic, meaning that if necessary a high price would be paid for an organ, and many organs currently are not supplied that could be, which suggests that some price would call forth a greater net supply and still be worth paying.[14] There is not much empirical evidence to show whether enough extra people would be willing to supply organs and, if so, at what price. In one study, Kaserman and Barnett surveyed 392 students at a US university and, on the basis of their results, estimated an equilibrium price of US$1,000 (in 1997 prices) as enough to meet annual demand for organs.[15]

None of the evidence that payment would increase net supply is compelling, but it is rather stronger than the evidence against. The open-minded should draw the following conclusion. The existing supply is inadequate and there is reason to think that payment would increase supply, although there is some risk of some decline. If our aim is to increase the supply of organs, and we bracket moral concerns about the monetary method, then offering payment would be worth trying on some

---

[10] S. M. Rothman and D. J. Rothman, 'The Hidden Cost of Organ Sale' *American Journal of Transplantation* 6 (2006), pp. 1524–6.

[11] Taylor, *Stakes and Kidneys*, cites evidence at p. 175.

[12] 'Pediatric Transplantation: Common Themes', in *2007 OPTN/SRTR Annual Report: Transplant Data 1997–2006*, ch. 3.

[13] The perhaps-rosy interpretation of the Iranian experience has been challenged by J. Zargooshi, 'Iran's Commercial Renal Transplantation Program: Results and Complications', a paper presented at the European Platform Conference, Rotterdam, April 2007.

[14] Kaserman and Barnett, *The U.S. Organ Procurement System*, pp. 81–2.

[15] Ibid., p. 114. The authors are well aware of the limitations of their survey, for instance in surveying undergraduates rather than the general population, and looking at what people say rather than do.

experimental basis, perhaps after more social science research to try to establish what people would do if they were offered money.

That was the conclusion given the sole aim of increasing supply. What about the morality of the method?

BUYING ORGANS FROM THE DEAD

Let us consider buying organs from the dead. Broadly speaking, organs could be bought from the dead in a futures market, where living people sell the right to their organs after they die, or a current or spot market, where money for the organs of the dead is given to the living people who are in a position to consent to retrieval. There are grounds for doubting that, even if it were permitted, a futures market would form. As previous chapters have explained, most people's organs cannot be retrieved after they die and, when they can, their families would and probably should have a veto on their being taken. It would not be economic to pay a large sum to everyone in advance, given that most people's organs could not be used and the family would be able to block retrieval from relatives who had been paid. Paying people in advance may produce so few extra organs that the price would be below the administrative and other transaction costs, which means no market would form.[16] But offering to pay next-of-kin, or the deceased's designated heirs, may produce a current market.

Just as with sale by the living, buying organs taken from dead people in a futures or current market is objected to as coercive, exploitative, wrongly commodifying, and so forth. These objections have more force in the case of the living than the dead, since the dead would not be physically harmed by retrieval, so I shall set out and assess the objections when we come to the living. This section is concerned with a problem that arises specifically for current markets from the dead: the paid decision-makers are not the people whose organs are sold.[17] If families were to be paid to donate their relatives' organs, would the families be tempted to infringe on their relatives' rights? Suppose someone opposes the retrieval of her organs but her family, who would not have donated them, sell them despite her opposition. In that case, the money would be an incentive to infringe on this person's rights over her body.

The problem of retrieval from those opposed can be partially avoided if people are able to veto formally the retrieval of their organs, which, as chapter 6 argues, they should be able to do anyway. The problem could be entirely avoided if money were offered to relatives only when the deceased had consented in advance to the

---

[16] David H. Howard, 'Producing Organ Donors' *Journal of Economic Perspectives* 21 (2007), p. 30; Epstein, *Mortal Peril*, p. 252.

[17] Payment need not be directly monetary. Paying funeral expenses is sometimes suggested instead, which may be more effective in persuading some families than outright payment, since it may have less stigma. Payment to families raises practical problems, for instance, in deciding who in a family gets paid, how much, and in what way, and how to separate payment from a family's decision to request the withdrawal of care.

retrieval and the payment. The deceased would have waived their rights, so payment and retrieval would not infringe upon them. However, permitting sale only with consent may have little effect on organ supply. As chapter 6 explained, many people do not make their wishes formally known. Moreover, consent from the deceased—as opposed to the absence of their dissent—is hardly anywhere required before retrieval, so why require consent to retrieval and payment specifically? Here we can apply the material from chapter 6. Where people had no views, retrieval with payment to relatives would not infringe upon their rights. Where people did have views, they ought to be followed so far as anyone can tell what they were. Thus if a given person probably would not have objected to retrieval with payment, retrieval with payment would not infringe on her right. If she probably would, it would.

One should be careful in predicting wishes in cases of sale. People may object to their organs being bought even though they would not object to giving them for free. They may oppose the role of money in organ donation, or not want their relatives to have the money, or believe that offering the money to their families would prevent them looking out for their interests while in intensive care. So we could not simply say that in cases when organ donation without the deceased's consent would be justified, so sale must be justified. What would help in trying to determine the deceased's interests would be some empirical evidence about what people think about their organs being sold by their relatives. (It would also be useful to know people's attitudes to selling their relatives' organs so as to predict the effects of sales on supply.)

Whatever we conclude about buying the organs of people who neither consented nor dissented, we can say that, as far as the deceased is concerned, it would not infringe upon their rights if their relatives were paid with their consent.

ARGUMENTS BY ANALOGY

I turn now to organ sales by the living. Whether people should be allowed to sell their organs raises difficult general questions often dealt with at length in philosophical and ethical writings. What rights do people have over their bodies? What agreements are consensual exercises of those rights? Is it unjust to buy organs from the poor, and, if it is, could the injustice be undone by paying more? May a society enforce a moral code against people's rights over their own bodies so as to prevent turning body parts into commodities or to preserve a system with a 'gift relationship'? Perhaps most difficult, how are the various considerations to be combined so as to produce a final conclusion? How, for instance, is someone's autonomy to be weighed against any bad effects on altruism in society?

It is tempting to try to bypass the difficult theoretical questions by using analogous cases of legal permissions and prohibitions. Writers who use such analogies hope their opponent, or disinterested reader at least, will agree with the law in those cases, see that organ sales are similar, and therefore draw the same conclusion about sales. The analogies are important. They can make us think harder about what we take to be the rights and wrongs of free sale and they can help us weigh up the competing considerations to produce some overall conclusion. But they must be treated carefully. To make all of these points, and some others about prohibition, I shall say a bit more about the analogies used in discussion of organ sales.

Supporters of organ sales often draw an analogy with the labour market.[18] They point out that some legal occupations are riskier than having a kidney removed. Commercial fishing is riskier. Working at heights (roofing, steeplejacking, and so forth) is comparably risky.[19] Some people take dreary, uncomfortable, or meaningless jobs. The labour market is segregated by class, race, and sex, so the bad jobs are not simply acquired at random. And yet even severe critics of markets rarely propose banning the jobs outright. By analogy, the argument goes, we should permit people to sell their organs. When we consider whether people know what they are getting into, whether they should be allowed to assume certain levels of risk, and whether they are exploited and, if so, what should be done about it, we can look to see what we already permit and would, on reflection, agree should continue to be permitted. If organ selling is no worse than jobs that are and should be allowed, we have the all-things-considered answer to the question of whether organ sales should be legally permitted. What more is there to say?

The labour market analogy is powerful and instructive. For instance, critics of sales cannot simply say 'the poor will be the sellers and they cannot make voluntary choices' if they also want to allow poor people to sign contracts to be cleaners or checkout operators. A critic must think harder about what is wrong with selling organs; the alleged impossibility of voluntary choice is not enough. Still, this argument by analogy is by no means unanswerable. For instance, critics can point out that, in tolerating some hazardous work, consistency does not require tolerating more (even if it is not so hazardous as what is tolerated).[20]

Writers often look for analogies in other social practices that are legally permitted or forbidden in their societies. For example, American critics of organ sales cite the widespread ban in the US on prostitution while American supporters of permitting sale cite the permission to sell human sperm and eggs.[21] Again, these analogies have an important place in advancing the argument. But they have two instructive limits.

One is created by the problem of multiple rationales. A law could be defensible for many different reasons. Suppose the labour market ought to be regulated despite the interference with freedom of contract. That freedom of contract may permissibly be interfered with in some cases does not show it may be in others. Laws requiring, for instance, a minimum wage or maximum hours legislation could be defended as solving a collective action problem between workers, where they

---

[18] One of the most sophisticated versions is Taylor's. See *Stakes and Kidneys*, ch. 6.

[19] Ibid., pp. 126–7.

[20] The argument has the same structure as the reply to people who believe cannabis should be legalized because more harmful tobacco and alcohol are permitted. Why permit extra harms? (I do not say the argument is persuasive.)

[21] The argument could be reversed in New Zealand, where prostitution is legal but the sale of sperm and eggs is heavily penalized.

gain by being prevented from competing with each other.[22] Suppose now we are considering a law that bans prostitution solely for moralistic reasons, say that sexuality ought not to be the object of a commercial transaction. One mainstream liberal view would say that the state should not use coercion for moralistic reasons, but it would accept that coercion could be legitimate to solve collective action problems. Thus those who hold the liberal view could consistently conclude that working very long hours should be banned without concluding that prostitution should be. Generally, if we are to be persuaded by analogies, we need to know the justifying reasons for a law, not simply what is and is not permissible.

Another limit to the analogy arises from considerations about whether to make something illegal. Even if it is in principle permissible to promote paternalistically people's welfare against their own view, or to try moralistically to secure compliance with a moral code by restricting non-harmful acts, more must be said to justify an actual law. Is it practical to ban or regulate an activity? Would it have worse effects if one tried? How intrusive would be attempts to ban? How expensive would it be, and what good could be done instead? Consider the example of recreational drug-taking, where these considerations are sometimes applied. One may argue for the legalization of recreational drug-taking on the grounds that attempts to prohibit have not worked, they have had harmful effects, through, for instance, creating 'narco-states', and they have involved huge sums of money that could more profitably have been used to treat addiction.[23] It is thus consistent to say that people ought to be legally allowed to take drugs without in any way being committed to a liberal principle that only acts that harm other people may be prohibited. One could conclude that a particular social practice should be permitted simply because the social costs of banning it would be too high rather than because one is, in general, a liberal. We could then argue for permitting organ sales by analogy to a practice permitted for reasons of social cost only if banning sales would have similar costs.

There is nothing for it. Analogies are not enough and we shall have to go into the details of the individual arguments and then try to produce an all-things-considered conclusion. Let me make three more points, which it would be tiresome to keep mentioning, and which we may as well take as read from now on. First, as I said earlier, an ethical assessment of permitting organ sales depends in part on applying difficult concepts, and a really full treatment would be very long. Mine is not a full treatment, but I hope not to have missed out important subtleties. Much of the discussion in earlier chapters is relevant anyway. Second, it must be said that, while numerous articles and several books on transplantation have given impressively detailed defences of the ethical permissibility of sale,[24] those opposed have been much less thorough in setting out their case. In fact, much of the case in favour of

[22] T. M. Wilkinson, 'The Ethics and Economics of the Minimum Wage' *Economics and Philosophy* 20 (2004).

[23] See 'How to Stop the Drug Wars' *The Economist*, 5 March 2009.

[24] To mention the books only, and in addition to the already-cited Taylor, *Stakes and Kidneys* and Cherry, *Kidney for Sale By Owner*, see Stephen Wilkinson, *Bodies for Sale: Ethics and Exploitation in the Human Body Trade* (London: Routledge, 2003) and Michele Goodwin, *Black Markets: The Supply and Demand of Body Parts* (Cambridge: Cambridge University Press, 2006).

sale has involved setting out the details of what the case against ought to have said, before trying to rebut it. Third, perhaps the biggest gap in the anti-sale literature is the absence of any serious attempt to justify punishing would-be organ sellers. If one really believed that sellers would be exploited, coerced, or vulnerable, punishing them seems most unfair. Workers are not generally punished when they are exploited at work; it is their employers who would be committing offences under laws governing health and safety, or wages and conditions. I do not say no argument could be invented to justify punishing the victims, only that it has not been in the kind of detail needed. Punishing the vulnerable sellers is perhaps easier to justify if sale is simply morally wrong than if it is to protect the people who might sell, although again I have seen no serious argument from immorality to justify their criminal punishment.

PERSONAL SOVEREIGNTY AND A RIGHT TO SELL

Do we have a right to sell our organs? Let us first ask what a right to sell would be. A full-blown right to sell an organ can be broken down into several distinct rights. One is the power to waive the duty not to invade one's body. Without this power, the surgery needed to take the organ could not go ahead. Another right is the power to transfer the organ for money so that the seller acquires a right to the buyer's money and the buyer acquires a right to the seller's organ. This power is also protected by two claim-rights. One is that the state not interfere with the sale of the organ by making it illegal and the other is that the state recognize the sale as legally valid.[25] These rights are in principle separable. For instance, someone could have a right against being punished for selling without having the right to keep the money.

The most important reason to think we have a right against sale being made illegal is the value we should attach to personal sovereignty (which was described in chapter 2). People should be able to run their own lives, and deciding what to do with their bodies is an especially important aspect of running their own lives. A few decades ago, with homosexual acts, interracial marriage, and refusing life-saving treatment, the mores of various societies and even the welfare of rightholders were widely thought to have to yield to their decisions over their bodies. The underlying principle of personal sovereignty also makes a powerful case against legally discouraging the sale of organs, whether by making sale illegal and punishing sellers, or by trying to prevent sale by punishing buyers or agents for buyers. Personal sovereignty may make not so strong a case against other methods of discouraging sale, such as confiscating the money, but it still makes a case.

---

[25] See Cécile Fabre, *Whose Body Is It Anyway? Justice and the Integrity of the Person* (Oxford: Clarendon Press, 2006), pp. 126–7. The right to sell is not the right to a sale and, surely, absent some special obligation, no one has a duty to buy someone else's organ. But if no one has a duty to buy, perhaps no one has a duty to perform the operation either. Perhaps a medical guild's instruction to members not to engage in commerce would not infringe on a right to sell even if it would make sale practically impossible. I leave this question aside.

To get a sense of the difficulty of opposing a right to sell, reconsider the right to bodily integrity, which is narrower and less controversial than the right of personal sovereignty. People have the right to refuse their organs being removed even when removal would be greatly to their own good or the good of others. If one accepts the right to bodily integrity, there is no merely saying, against the right to sell the organ, that people cannot have such a right because they would exercise it wrongly or against their interests, or that it is offensive or an error to see people as having rights over their bodies. All those things are true of the accepted right of bodily integrity. Moreover, we should suspect a 'dangling distinction';[26] that is, it is arbitrary to assert a right to consent to the removal of an organ or to donate it but deny a right to sell.

The personal sovereignty account of a right to sell may be called sociologically naïve, overlooking the fact that it is the poor and exploited who would be the sellers of organs, or that allowing sale would perpetuate injustice. Delmonico and Scheper-Hughes write 'even the poorest people of this world "make choices," but they do not make these freely or under social or economic conditions of their own making.'[27] But the account of rights assumes nothing sociological. The poor have the same rights over their bodies as anyone. When agreements to sell are invalid, they do not count as exercises of these rights. But—and this is a conceptual and moral point, not a sociological one—the desperation of great poverty does not on its own make an agreement invalid. Recall the discussion in chapter 8. People whose appendices will shortly burst will usually be desperate for an operation to remove them; their consent to an operation is nonetheless valid. Parents will usually be desperate to save their children; their consent to donate their organs to their children is nonetheless valid. So it is with being poor. When Delmonico and Scheper-Hughes describe how the poor decide by using scare quotes around 'make choices', they are merely arguing by dark hint. They do not say what it would be to decide under social or economic conditions of their own making, or who does this now, or why, if such decisions were not autonomous, the decision of the appendicitis victims would be valid when made under a medical condition not of their own making.

The appeal to personal sovereignty will not persuade all. Possibly personal sovereignty should yield when rightholders would make decisions very much against their interests or other people's, a matter considered in previous chapters and reconsidered shortly in the light of some empirical evidence. I also doubt the principle is consistently followed even in societies that consider themselves liberal. Some readers may be willing to give up personal sovereignty, and it is worth going into the objections to sale specifically to see whether it ought to be given up. That said, it is striking that opponents of sale, when replying to personal sovereignty-type arguments, often do not disagree with the force of personal sovereignty but rather with its applicability to sale. That is, they rarely say 'sales are so bad we should stop people being free to decide what to do with their own bodies' but instead say 'people who sell are unfree'.

---

[26] Shelly Kagan, *The Limits of Morality* (Oxford: Clarendon Press, 1989), p. 14.
[27] Francis L. Delmonico and Nancy Scheper-Hughes, 'Why We Should Not Pay for Human Organs' *Zygon* 38 (2003), p. 694.

I now consider a cluster of arguments against permitting sale that largely start by saying it is the poor who would be the sellers. The arguments say that sale would make sellers worse off in the long run, exploit them, or cause greater injustice than if sale were banned. Most versions of these arguments would not apply to potential sellers who were not desperate, and it is an interesting question whether they would apply to citizens of rich countries with developed welfare states. Since the arguments are unimpressive, I shall leave aside the question of whether non-desperate sellers could be found.

WELL-BEING IN THE LONG RUN

This section focuses on the well-being of people who sell organs, and specifically the well-being of sellers who are poor. It is obviously possible that selling an organ could make people better off, for instance if the money took them permanently out of poverty and they suffered no ill effects. It is obviously possible that selling an organ could make people worse off, for instance if their health were so badly affected they were unable to work. To move beyond bare possibility, we need something like expected utility to take account of the possible effects on sellers' welfare and their probability. To judge expected utility, we would need empirical evidence or theoretical reasoning about, for example, the information sellers typically are or would be given, the extent of any screening for health of any potential sellers, the extent of post-operative care, and the alternative options for people who might sell. In the case of rich countries where sale is not permitted and there is no black market, we would have to speculate about what might happen if sale were permitted. In the case of countries where sale does occur, usually illegally, actual evidence could, in principle, be gathered.

Different countries would no doubt vary greatly, and it would require serious and detailed research to draw well-grounded conclusions about what allowing sales would do to the well-being of the sellers. But it is instructive to consider one study, about kidney sales in Chennai, India.[28] The study is widely cited, and often taken to be unsettling for the pro-sale case. The survey asked 305 adult kidney sellers in Chennai about their incomes and health after sale, and whether they would advise other people, similarly placed, to sell. According to what the sellers said, they were paid substantially less than promised, their average incomes had declined, more were below the poverty line, and their health was worse. 'Of 264 participants who answered this question, 79% would not recommend selling a kidney, while 21% would.'[29] Not surprisingly, these results are often taken to 'explode the proposition that sale is a win-win situation that benefits buyer and sellers'.[30]

---

[28] M. Goyal et al., 'Economic and Health Consequences of Selling a Kidney in India' *Journal of the American Medical Association* 288 (2002).

[29] Ibid., p. 1591.

[30] David J. Rothman, 'Ethical and Social Consequences of Selling a Kidney' *Journal of the American Medical Association* 288 (2002), p. 1641.

Of course, any study has its limitations. In the case of the Chennai study, amongst many questions, it could be asked whether the subjects were genuinely representative of kidney sellers; whether they are correct when they say they are less healthy and poorer; and whether, if they are, they are less healthy and poorer because they sold their kidneys and not for some other reason. For example, in the study, 33 per cent of subjects reported lower back pain—but they were primarily labourers, and the authors do not say how many labourers who did not sell their kidneys have lower back pain. Still, taking the findings at face value, what follows?[31]

The authors say their evidence shows that selling a kidney usually does not pull poor people out of poverty.[32] Rothman, in a commentary, goes so far as to say that '[t]he idea that individuals heavily burdened with debt would be able to use a thousand dollars to purchase capital equipment (farm equipment) or improve their market situation (by renting or buying a shop) and thereby transform their life chances was always fanciful'[33]—although it might be replied that it is not so very fanciful, since the idea of a small capital sum helping people out of poverty is also the idea behind microcredit in poor countries. But if the critics are right, kidney sales cannot be defended on the grounds that they pull people out of poverty. Receiving a median sum equivalent to nearly two years' income for a family at the poverty line may not be enough to get people out of poverty, especially when combined with any effects of ill-health.[34]

However, even if not permanently removed from poverty, sellers need not be worse off for selling. They could be better off for having cleared their debts in the short-run. For this reason, the most striking finding is that so many sellers would advise against selling, particularly if we take the finding as equivalent to expressing regret at their own decision. Even if the poor could have been better off for selling, the finding implies that they were not. This finding is the most unsettling for those who believe permitting sale could help the poor. The finding is, however, striking for another reason too: for people to advise similarly placed people not to do something, they must have felt they had some better alternative. It would make no sense to advise against selling a kidney if the recipient of the advice really had no choice.[35] The advice is a counter-example to the view that the poor act involuntarily because they have no choice, even as it supports the view that, in choosing to sell, they would probably make themselves worse off.

If the poor of Chennai did not have to sell but chose to and worsened their position, their autonomy may appear to conflict with their long-run well-being. But really it looks as if the decision to sell was not voluntary enough to be

---

[31] For a very good discussion of the implications of the Chennai study, see Taylor, *Stakes and Kidneys*, pp. 77–8, 84–9.

[32] Others make the same claim. See e.g. Lawrence Cohen, 'Where it Hurts: Indian Material for an Ethics of Organ Transplantation'. *Daedelus* 128 (1999).

[33] Rothman, 'Ethical and Social Consequences', p. 1641.

[34] Goyal et al., 'Economic and Health Consequences', say the poverty line for Tamil Nadu was US$538 for an average-sized family and the median sum received by sellers was US$1070.

[35] The finding contrasts with Lawrence Cohen's description of some of the sellers he interviewed. They said they would sell a second kidney if they could because they had no alternative. Cohen, 'Where it Hurts', pp.138, 147.

autonomous. The sellers were, if reporting correctly, cheated out of some of the money promised. Their health was worse after the removal of their kidneys in a way and to an extent not to be found generally with living kidney donors, which suggests that they did not get the post-operative care they needed or were not ideally healthy to start.[36] If the sellers were misled, their decision to sell was not fully voluntary and, given where voluntariness standards probably ought to be pitched for selling a kidney, their decision was not voluntary enough. In that case, preventing sale under the conditions they did sell would not be a case of taking sides with their well-being against their autonomous wishes.[37]

The more difficult question is whether sales should be prevented if sellers go in with their eyes open. What if they are not misled, but warned about a lack of post-operative care, their medical unsuitability, and the likelihood of their earnings falling over time? If they really know all this, then perhaps their autonomy would conflict with their long run well-being. But if we focus only on the conflict between autonomy and well-being, and we stipulate that the individual is not coerced (in the sense of being credibly threatened) and is not grossly irrational, I see no reason to give up the conclusion from chapter 8. Either people should be allowed to sacrifice their welfare voluntarily no matter by how much, or they should be allowed to sacrifice it voluntarily to some degree that falls short of catastrophe. Selling organs such as kidneys or liver segments would not be catastrophic to most sellers' expected welfare so on either way of resolving conflicts between autonomy and well-being, people's autonomy should win out and they should be permitted to sell an organ even if they would probably make themselves worse off. But it is hard to see why, as a rule, autonomous choosers would sell if they thought it would make them much worse off in the long run, and the sellers of Chennai appear not to be acting autonomously against their interests because they are not acting autonomously.

EXPLOITATION AND INJUSTICE

The critics of organ sales often argue, as part of their case, that if sales were permitted, the poor would predominantly be the sellers, and this would be unjust. The poor are, it is assumed, themselves already victims of injustice. Letting them sell organs would make them victims of exploitation. It is out of concern for injustice and exploitation that Nancy Scheper-Hughes writes, 'In general, the circulation of organs flows from South to North, from poorer to more affluent

---

[36] There is evidence that sellers have been misled about the effects of selling and not been given the post-operative care promised. Taylor writes, 'accounts are legion of the desperate kidney vendors of Villivakkam and Chennai simply being dumped back on the streets immediately after surgery and left to fend for themselves.' *Stakes and Kidneys*, p. 88.

[37] Taylor says, ibid., p. 87, that the black market trade in Chennai ought to be stopped, but believes a regulated market should be permitted. Care is needed, however. Perhaps trying to or even succeeding in ending the black market traffic would come at too high a cost to potential sellers or others. Perhaps a regulated market would be even worse if, as Lawrence Cohen conjectures, it would allow corrupt government regulators to take their cut. Cohen, 'Where it Hurts', p. 160.

bodies, from black and brown bodies to white ones, and from females to males.'[38] She and Francis Delmonico write: 'The most disturbing issue of organ sales to both Christian and secular ethicists is the formation of an economic underclass of organ donors throughout the world to serve the wealthy.'[39]

When the critics write of exploitation and injustice, some may not be intending to make independent points. Perhaps, when we come to ask why sale is supposed to exploitative or unjust, the critics meant only that the choice to sell is not genuinely autonomous and the retrieval of organs typically makes the seller worse off. If that is what they meant, we need not go into autonomy and well-being again. But there can be more than these familiar ideas behind exploitation and injustice objections to sale. To see the independent points, assume that decisions to sell are voluntary.

Let us take exploitation first. According to David Miller, '[e]xploitation is best regarded as a particularly repugnant form of injustice. It implies not only that the final distribution of resources as between exploiter and exploited is unjust, but that this imbalance arose through the exploiter's use of power of some kind: both the process and the outcome are objectionable.'[40] Miller's is a common enough account of exploitation. We can interpret Scheper-Hughes's comment in its light. She said that organs, as resources, flow from poor to rich, so there is an imbalance in the final distribution. And the reason is due to an imbalance of power, because—even leaving aside coercion and manipulation—the rich have the money to get the poor to give up their organs. We could then conclude that sale would be exploitative and should be prohibited.

More must be said to show whether organ sales would be exploitative and about what would follow if they were. Even assuming Scheper-Hughes's description is correct, the flow of organs one way is countered by a flow of money the other way. Perhaps the flows are equal. If the rich are the buyers of organs, they are also themselves vulnerable, since they need the organs for pressing medical reasons, and the poor have the power to get the rich to give up some of their money.[41] Perhaps the vulnerabilities balance. More generally, not every contractual-type offer to a vulnerable person is exploitative, so some account must be given of when it is. And finally, we need to know what those who cite exploitation are hoping to achieve. They could be making a moral assessment of the character of people who buy or sell organs, or of a world where buying and selling occur. But often enough, the critics

---

[38] Nancy Scheper-Hughes, 'The Ends of the Body: Commodity Fetishism and the Global Traffic in Organs' *SAIS Review* 22 (2002), p. 70.

[39] Delmonico and Scheper-Hughes, 'Why We Should Not Pay for Human Organs', p. 694. This article, and the previously cited one by Scheper-Hughes, invoke nearly all the anti-market arguments considered in this chapter without, unfortunately, taking enough care in setting them out, defending their ethical assumptions, and substantiating their empirical components.

[40] David Miller, *Market, State, and Community* (Oxford: Clarendon Press, 1989), p. 175.

[41] Janet Radcliffe Richards sarcastically writes: 'To hear the organ trade characterized in terms of the greedy rich and the exploited poor, you might think that the rich, tired of gold plating their bathrooms and surfeited with larks' tongues, had now idly turned to collecting kidneys to display with their Faberge eggs and Leonardo drawings. But the rich in question here are *dying*, and desperately trying to save their lives; or, at the very least, to escape the crushing miseries of chronic illness and perpetual dialysis.' See her 'Nefrarious Goings On: Kidney Sales and Moral Arguments' *The Journal of Medicine and Philosophy* 21 (1996), p. 376.

are arguing that sales should be legally prohibited because of the exploitation involved, and they have to show that avoiding exploitation is important enough to warrant the prohibition.

One common view says that exploitation should be avoided because it is unfair. If we take exploitation as unfair, what makes a transaction unfair? A common answer is 'When one of the parties does worse from the transaction than she ought.' This is the sense in which we might think workers are exploited when paid very low wages for working in bad conditions. But 'doing worse than they ought' obviously requires some account of what there ought to be. One account is 'what would be paid in a genuinely competitive market, where parties cannot take advantage of lack of information, barriers to entry or exit, and other market imperfections'.[42] Whatever the account of just reward, an exploitation argument would have to show that sellers would be paid less than they ought. Even if sellers were badly paid, it would have to be shown that the value of what they are selling exceeds what they are paid. Even if the disparity in value can be shown, there would then be the big problem of explaining why exploitation could not simply be avoided by regulating prices. The possibility of exploitation in the labour market is no longer widely taken to be a good reason for prohibiting paid labour, even in unpleasant jobs, but rather a reason for regulating wages and conditions. So why prohibit sale rather than set a minimum price?[43]

A different exploitation argument says that sellers would be taken unfair advantage of simply because it is unfair for people to sell their organs, at any price. The point is not that they get less than the value of what they sell, but that they are in a position where they must sell their organs. The argument is a version of 'wrongful use' exploitation, where what is objected to is the type of use as well as the unfairness in starting positions that causes the offers to be accepted. (The argument cannot simply be that accepting any offer from a poor starting position is exploitative. What if I am poor and you offer to pay me above-market rates for my family silver?) The argument depends on there being something special about organs. One can develop it by appealing to the specialness of the body and hostility to commodification, which I discuss later in the chapter.

INJUSTICE AND IMPROVEMENT

Suppose sellers would typically be poor and suppose it is unjust that they are so poor. Consider an argument for permitting sale anyway. To permit sale is to permit

---

[42] This is Miller's view in *Market, State, and Community*, ch. 7, with the extra requirement that equilibrium prices are the ones that would follow from the correct initial distribution of endowments. See also Alan Wertheimer, *Exploitation* (Princeton: Princeton University Press, 1996), ch. 7.

[43] Suppose minimum price regulation would be ineffective. Even then, an exploitation argument for prohibiting sale has to (1) show that sale would exploit, (2) show that the exploitation is important enough to warrant prohibition, and (3) give some explanation of either why ending the exploitation would not harm the position of the worst off or would be justified if it did. I know of no attempts to show all this in the context of organ sales.

an option that people would, if acting voluntarily, take so as to achieve some end of theirs they otherwise could not achieve. If selling would be voluntary, how could it be more just to stop victims of injustice selling? Either potential sellers start off from a just position, in which case there is no reason of justice to stop them trying voluntarily to improve their positions by selling, or they start off from an unjustly bad position, in which case there is still no reason of justice to stop them trying voluntarily to improve their positions by selling.

The argument has considerable force. Critics of sale sometimes try to blunt it by saying that we should find better ways to resolve problems of poverty than by allowing sales. But the dilemma can then be restated. Either these better ways will be adopted, in which case there is no reason of justice to deny people the option of selling, or they will not, in which case there is still no reason of justice to stop them trying voluntarily to improve their positions by selling.

The restated dilemma has force so long as the option of selling is causally independent of other improvements to the position of the unjustly badly off. But what if permitting sale would prevent the other improvements coming about or would worsen the position of poor people as a class? A government or society may fail to reform an economic system, or fail to give aid to the poor if sales are permitted, perhaps because the poor would no longer be quite so desperate for money if they were able to sell their organs, or perhaps because the rich would prefer to keep people poor so as to get their organs.[44] Or perhaps all members of some class, not only the sellers, would acquire the stigma of organ sellers if enough sell their organs.[45] Obviously, these are mere possibilities without any serious evidence or theoretical reason to believe they would occur. But if we put aside this fundamental weakness in the argument, suppose allowing sales would in some way worsen the position of the poor as a class. What then for individual voluntary choice?

Suppose first that the poor are worse off as a class because each individual in it would end up net worse off if sale were permitted. Suppose this would be because of some collective action problem, rather than because each member makes a mistake about where his or her interests lie. One might then argue for restricting sale on grounds similar to those for minimum wage legislation, which prohibits people having their labour bought below a certain rate. The common argument, mentioned in the section on arguments by analogy, is that legislation prevents a degree of competition among workers, and workers benefit. While people may have rights over their bodies, in the case of organs, or their labour, in the case of the minimum wage, it is a powerful argument (so long as it is true) that all those people would be better off by their own lights if they were prevented from exercising their right in some way. A good case for restricting sale would have been made.

---

[44] As T. Zutlevics suggests in 'Markets and the Needy: Organ Sales or Aid?' *Journal of Applied Philosophy* 18 (2001), p. 299.

[45] Delmonico and Scheper-Hughes, 'Why We Should Not Pay for Human Organs', p. 695, cite some evidence of stigma from Moldova. Note that stigmatized options may be worse for people than high status options but still be better than no options at all.

However, it is entirely implausible that every person who would sell would be net better off if sales were prohibited. At best, some members of the group would gain and others would lose. The argument would then have to be something like: most people would gain from prohibition although some would lose. In that case, the claims of people to determine what happens to their own bodies are overridden for the sake of gains to other people. This requires some justifying, and the justification cannot simply be a utilitarian or majoritarian one. People have rights over their bodies and, not to labour the point made throughout the book, rights stand in the way of crude aggregation. The rights stand in the way of aggregation when the benefits go to fellow members of a class just as much as when they go to the world at large.[46] On the other hand, the right to sell is not absolute, so a substantial benefit to substantial numbers of other badly off people may justify overriding them.

We have been considering the argument for permitting sales that says, whether or not starting positions are unjust, they do not become better and may become worse if the option to sell is denied to the people who occupy them. We have then considered a reply, which says that permitting sale may forestall bigger improvements to the position of the poor as a class or otherwise worsen their position. But to justify overriding the right to sell, there would have to be good evidence that prohibiting sale would cause either each poor person or at least some overriding number of poor people to do better. The evidence does not exist, so, at this stage of evidence and argument, the original dilemma stands. People who are genuinely concerned with the welfare of the badly off have not yet given a reason to stop them selling their organs.

ORGAN SALES AND THE VALUE OF THE GIFT

We have considered some anti-sale arguments about whether poor people who agree to sell their organs would be coerced or act against their interests, or be treated unjustly or exploited. A quite distinct set of arguments opposes permitting the sale of organs because of the damaging effect on social relations of introducing money into the acquisition of organs. According to these arguments, sale should be banned from anyone, not just the poor or easily tempted. Consider a representative opinion, given by John Paul II.

> Every organ transplant has its source in a decision of great ethical value: the decision to offer without reward a part of one's own body for the health and well being of another person. Here precisely lies the nobility of the gesture, a gesture which is a genuine act of love. It is not just a matter of giving away something that belongs to us but of giving something of ourselves, for by virtue of its substantial union with a spiritual soul, the human body cannot be considered as a mere complex of tissues, organs and functions . . . rather it is a constitutive part of the person who manifests and expresses himself through it. Accordingly, any

---

[46] Perhaps class solidarity would cause people to waive their rights to sell, but that would be the exercise of a right, not its infringement.

procedure which tends to commercialize human organs or to consider them as items of exchange or trade must be considered morally unacceptable, because to use the body as an 'object' is to violate the dignity of the human person.[47]

John Paul II's view, as stated in this passage, speaks for several different kinds of critic of the market, not only Roman Catholics or even Christians more generally. Many oppose the extension of market norms into the disposition of human bodies and their parts for reasons similar to or the same as John Paul II's. For example, political critics of the market, whether religious or not, often speak warmly of the voluntary gift of blood by contrast with its sale.[48] They say that the selfless act of giving with no expectation of reward is particularly valuable and should not be driven out by private sale.

John Paul II, in the quoted passage, makes two different, but related, points. He states that paying a person for his organs compromises his dignity and he says that organs should instead be given out of genuine love. These points differ from each other; one is about the bad side of money and the other about the good side of donation. In principle, they are separate, but, as I shall explain, they are best taken together as a compound argument if they are supposed to support the current widespread criminal prohibition of organ sale and purchase. Altruism, on its own, cannot be used to make a case for banning sales.

The previous chapter considered the value of altruism and gift, and the extent to which it genuinely characterizes the existing systems of donation. I want to make some further points specifically in the context of sale. How are we to explain the special value of altruism in organ donation? It cannot be simply because organs are important and what is important should be acquired and distributed outside a market. Food is more important than organs for transplant and yet '[i]t is not from the benevolence of the butcher, the brewer, or the baker that we expect our dinner, but from their regard to their own interest.'[49] The point may be about the *extension* of market norms, that is, about taking the market to where we do not already have it. It could be said that, in capitalist societies dominated by monetary exchange, we should cherish those parts of it—whatever they are—that are not so dominated. Permitting sale would undermine the existing valuable practice of donation.

As against the argument, one could make some familiar points. Why think we have a valuable practice of donation, since not enough organs are donated by the families of dead people and very few organs from live donors fit the model of altruistic stranger donation to a blood bank? Since sale and donation could coexist,

---

[47] John Paul II, statement to the 2000 International Congress of the Transplantation Society, quoted in Robert Arnold et al. (the Ethics Committee of the American Society of Transplant Surgeons), 'Financial Incentives for Cadaver Organ Donation: An Ethical Reappraisal' *Transplantation Forum* 73 (2002), pp. 1362–3. Although John Paul said every transplant has its value from the decision to offer one's own body, he is wrong if he meant that all organs for transplant are in fact taken only from those who have decided to donate. More commonly, retrieval follows the family's decision. Note too that John Paul's stricture against exchange appears to conflict with the existing practices of paired exchange.

[48] The critics usually cite Titmuss, *The Gift Relationship*.

[49] Adam Smith, *The Wealth of Nations* (Harmondsworth: Penguin English Library, 1982), Bk. 1, Ch. 2, Par. 2.

why think sale would drive out donation? Why think, even if sale would drive out donation, that altruism would not find other, equivalent, outlets?[50] These are all telling questions, and they give the critics of sale a reason to think more clearly about the facts they need to show and the value they need to defend.

The most difficult problem for the critic of sales is to explain why criminal prohibition is justified. One reason for any criminal prohibition is to prevent harm. But if all the participants act voluntarily, who would be harmed? On what grounds could third parties complain that their interests have been wrongly set back? People could still donate their organs if they want to. One could try to make some capital out of the point that one's option to donate has been changed when in the presence of sale, but why would it have been changed for the worse,[51] and why would it be anything like the wrongful setback of an interest? Some people may feel offended, but any offence they feel is not from the unavoidable public display of an organ transaction occurring, but from the bare knowledge that the transaction has taken place. No legal rule against offence should try to prevent just any feeling of upset, or we should have no freedom and we should be hostage to the strangest views.

So the argument would have to be that the altruism of organ donation is of such value that it may be preserved through the criminal law, even though no one would be harmed if it were not. The argument would then be an illiberal one. At this point, a really full discussion would assess the liberal view that the criminal law must be reserved for preventing harm or, perhaps, certain forms of offence. But to cut a long story short, how plausible is it to ban commercial transactions for the sake of preserving altruism, even assuming the illiberal case could be made out? Suppose a society has a tradition of seeking advice from family and friends without, of course, paying money for it. Suppose people in the society start to move around more and can no longer get all the advice they seek. Suppose they pay for the advice. We may regret the rise of professional psychiatrists and counsellors; we may think a society that has turned advice and comfort into a commercial transaction has lost something of value. But who would seriously suggest that professional counselling or psychiatry should have been made illegal so as to prevent the extension of a market norm?

The obvious reply is that selling body parts is not like selling advice. Indeed, it is not—but not because of the value of altruism taken alone. The idea is surely that organs are special not because, or not just because, they are important but because they come from people's bodies; and that what comes from people's bodies is not suitable for sale. The appeal to the positive value of altruism needs to be taken together with the argument about the evil of selling body parts. To conclude this section, if altruism is taken on its own, it gives no reason for criminal prohibition.

---

[50] Wilkinson, *Bodies for Sale*, pp. 109–16.
[51] Martin Wilkinson and Andrew Moore, 'Inducements Revisited' *Bioethics* 13 (1999), pp. 125–6. See also Taylor on 'the domino effect', *Stakes and Kidneys*, pp.155f. Titmuss claims we have a right to give which would be infringed upon if a market were permitted, but he does not explain either the right or its alleged infringement clearly enough to comment on. He also has a slippery slope argument about the bad effects of markets in healthcare that would arise if sale of blood were permitted, but that is not clear enough either. See *The Gift Relationship*, ch. 14.

As for the other ways of discouraging sale, such as not enforcing contracts, any reason to discourage would depend on the value of altruism, which would have to be set against the value of sale. Even then, altruism may or may not give a reason (of unspecified strength) depending on whether it can be shown that altruistic practices exist, that they would be threatened unless sales were discouraged, and that altruism would not simply be displaced into other valuable activities.

COMMODIFICATION

Not only would permitting sales drive out the good of altruism, according to the critics, it would permit and encourage a market price for parts of persons. But persons and their parts ought not to have a price upon them and they should not be traded in a market. To permit sales is to commodify people; to make people or their parts into commodities is wrong; and what is wrong about it may be prevented by the criminal law. So, at any rate, goes a familiar chain of argument.

What is wrong with turning body parts into commodities? The question is not redundant. 'Commodification' on one interpretation simply describes a process without being pejorative. People who want a market in organs obviously realize that organs would become commodities of a sort and just calling the process 'commodification' does not give a reason against it. If we ask what critics have said to be wrong about commodification, often what they object to is the alleged exploitation, coercion, or temptation of the vulnerable living, or, in the case of paying families for organs from their dead relatives, the prospect of flouting posthumous wishes. 'Commodification' is then a label for a process they object to rather than the summary of a distinct objection.[52] However, 'commodification' is sometimes the label for a distinct objection, which I now consider.

In the Kantian language often used, there are persons and there are things. Persons do not, or should not, have a price because they have dignity. People should not be treated as mere means but always as ends-in-themselves. If people were to sell their organs, they would be selling parts of themselves, that is, parts of an entity with dignity but not price. They, and the buyers of their organs, would consequently be treating them as mere means and not ends. The underlying idea, without the Kantian language, is that persons have something morally special about them which in some way means they should be outside the market. This something special is often described in terms of what Ronald Dworkin called 'the vague but powerful idea of human dignity'.[53] Note that the ideas in this paragraph had better be powerful, since the conclusion is supposed to be the criminal prohibition of purchase and it is supposed to be a final conclusion, that is, even after taking into

---

[52] 'Commodification' is not a distinct objection but only a heading in Donald Joralemon and Phil Cox, 'Body Values: The Case against Compensating for Transplant Organs' *Hastings Center Report* 33 (2003), pp. 29f.

[53] Ronald Dworkin, *Taking Rights Seriously* (Cambridge, MA: Harvard University Press, 1978), p. 198. For some examples, of very many, of the Kantian ideas, dignity, or both being used in action in arguments against organ sales, see the quotation from John Paul II above; Cynthia B. Cohen, 'Public

account people's rights, need for organs, the expense of using the law, the harm caused by enforcement, and so forth. Whether or not powerful, the ideas are certainly vague. What do they mean? And how could such a demanding conclusion follow?

Let us try to work out what the opponents of sale had in mind. They believe that the dignity of persons is somehow compromised if those very persons choose to sell their organs. The organs themselves are not persons, so it cannot be claimed that to sell an organ is to sell a person. But the organs, before sale, are inside persons. To remove the organ is to do something to the person, not only a body part. If you touch my arm, you touch me-the-person.[54] Moreover, unlike touching my arm, taking my organ is to take something important to my functioning as a person.

Suppose we agree that taking my organ is doing something to my person. Why is this incompatible with dignity? One cannot say dignity means persons cannot or may not be separated from their body parts. The critics of organ sales usually support living donation, so they do not object to the removal of organs as such. It is payment they object to. But then they need to say what difference payment makes. To illustrate some typical tangled reasoning, here is what Cynthia Cohen writes:

> The donation of a kidney can be taken to uphold human dignity just because this would allow the donor to share something of him- or herself as a gift to another member of the realm of ends and yet would not destroy human functioning. Donation is a gesture of altruism and of solidarity with other human beings. It is the *sale* of a kidney, however, to which Kant would object because, *at the time of donation* [retrieval? sale?], the kidney is essential to the person. It is not a mere appendage. To put a price on a human being in this way would be to deny embodied human dignity.[55]

I can see only two ways in which this passage could be reconstructed. The first says taking a body part that is essential to a person denies dignity, and kidneys are not essential when donated but somehow are when sold. On this interpretation, we would have a kind of reason against sale, but one resting on an obviously false or mysterious distinction. Alternatively, kidneys are both essential to a person whether bought or sold and thus a kidney possesses the dignity of the person; and sale, but not donation, puts a price on a person and denies dignity. On the second interpretation, no reason has been given to think putting a price on a person who consents denies dignity. Moreover, kidneys are not essential to a person if by that one means the person ceases to exist without it—and what else could 'essential' mean? Certainly, my kidney does not count as essential merely because, if someone touches it, they touch me-the-embodied-person. If you touch my hair or the wax in my ear, you touch me-the-embodied-person, and neither of those is essential to my

Policy and the Sale of Human Organs' *Kennedy Institute of Ethics Journal* 12 (2002); Delmonico and Scheper-Hughes, 'Why We Should Not Pay For Human Organs'.

[54] Cohen, 'Public Policy and the Sale of Human Organs', p. 57.

[55] Ibid., p. 58. Cohen clearly agrees with the position she believes Kant would have taken. Cohen is not the only writer who starts with a premise about persons and bodies, endorses donation but opposes sale, and ties herself into all sorts of knots trying to explain away the appearance of inconsistency. See Taylor's account of critics' contortions in *Stakes and Kidneys*, pp. 153–5.

person. So why think putting a price on a kidney is putting a price on a person? Mysteries abound.

The dignity of persons can be taken in another way, which does not support the prohibition of sale. People, unlike things, should be able to direct themselves. People are capable of being autonomous, of having their own ends in life, and deciding how to pursue them. People should be treated as autonomous and, unlike mere things, not be the subject of direction by others for their own ends. People have rights and they are not mere cogs in a social machine. People do indeed differ from typical commodities, such as cars and computers—it is much more of an insult to people as possessors of dignity to tell them what they can do with their own bodies than it is to tell them what to do with their mere possessions. The conclusion would be that sale from the autonomous should not be banned.

To say the least, this ringing declaration of the importance of personal autonomy is not what the opponents of permitting sale had in mind. If we are to express the idea of human dignity, what is wrong with this expression? Why is the anti-sale version the right one? Have the opponents been misled by the historical enslavement of people against their wishes and failed to see the difference made by consent?[56]

Clearly, people can be subject to indignities, in a more normal sense of the term, within a consensual framework. People can be ignored, humiliated, treated as fools, or treated as expendable; it will often be wrong to treat people in these ways, and it may sometimes be wrong of the victims to consent. One can think of fictional cases, as when Dr Fischer of Geneva routinely humiliates his 'toads', guests who put up with it for the sake of the expensive objects he gives them despite being rich already;[57] and one can also bear in mind the all-too-common cases in work, particularly low-paid unskilled work. But not all badly paid workers suffer indignities; low-paid work need not be humiliating; and even those who would like to use the law to raise pay do not think the jobs themselves should become illegal. People who consent to sell their organs should not be subjected to indignities. They should not be treated as merely expendable, ignored, or humiliated. But nothing in the nature of sale requires such behaviour.

Let us turn to the question of criminal prohibition. The argument starts from premises about dignity and moves to an all-things-considered conclusion of criminal prohibition. Consider Cynthia Cohen again:

> Public resistance to the sale of body parts, no matter how voluntary or well-informed it may be, is grounded in the conviction that such a practice would diminish our human dignity and common humanity. It derives from the belief that if people were to turn themselves into commodities, not only their humanity but that of everyone would be degraded.[58]

---

[56] Wilkinson, *Bodies for Sale*, ch. 3 has a fuller and more patient analysis than mine of commodification and objectification.
[57] Graham Greene, *Dr Fischer of Geneva or the Bomb Party* (New York: Simon and Schuster, 1980).
[58] Cohen, 'Public Policy and the Sale of Human Organs', p. 59.

She later says 'Turning human organs into commodities . . . is contrary to values at the core of our life together and should therefore be prohibited.'[59] These passages illustrate two common ways by which the demanding conclusion of criminal prohibition is supposed to be reached: first, dignity is a sufficiently important element of morality that it may be legally enforced and, second, opposition to sale is such a deep part of a social code that a society is entitled to enforce it. The first requires that the moral argument is actually correct, whatever people in a society think, and the second requires that people in a society actually think sale wrong, whether or not they are right to do so.

There is not much more to be said about the argument that considerations of dignity conflict with consensual sale and are important enough to justify criminal prohibition. As far as respect for dignity is concerned, treating people as criminals for making decisions about what they do with their own bodies with other consenting adults is no more justified in the case of organ sales than it was when homosexual acts were illegal.

A similar point could be made about the argument that society may enforce its code. The dignity of autonomy could stand in the way of that too. But to take it on its own terms, the argument that society may enforce its code by prohibiting sale presupposes that society has a code that condemns sale as wrongful commodification (as opposed to exploiting the poor or some such). This empirical presupposition needs evidence to show that people tend to oppose sale and they oppose it deeply enough for their opposition to count as a fundamental part of their mores.[60] Suppose—probably contrary to fact—that such evidence exists. What would justify society in enforcing its code when, as Cohen is willing to assume, sale would be voluntary and well-informed? One common argument says that a majority may shape its moral environment, but there are familiar objections. Why must shaping an environment be winner-takes-all rather than something each of us can shape a bit within the rights we have?[61] Another argument, including perhaps Cohen's, envisages all of us in some way being affected for the worse if people are permitted to sell. But in what way, and how? Some people already sell organs, illegally in most cases, and close to legally in Iran. Were we degraded by this? Did we feel degraded by this? If we are already degraded, will we become more so if sales are permitted, or have we already been as degraded as we are going to be? Possibly to say that anyone may sell an organ is to say that all of us may sell our organs, that the organs of each of us are sellable. So if selling organs were permissible, the status of each of us would change. But so what? To say organs may not be sold is to say of each of us that we

---

[59] Ibid., p. 61.

[60] The claim needs more evidence than the seven writers Cohen cites at ibid., pp. 59–60 as representative of the United States, especially when two of those quoted do not cite only considerations about commodification. By contrast Kaserman and Barnett write '[i]n general, surveys have found that most individuals are not disturbed or morally offended at the prospect of paying organ donors', *US Organ Procurement System*, p. 91.

[61] Ronald Dworkin, *Sovereign Virtue* (Cambridge, MA: Harvard University Press, 2000), pp. 213–16; Joel Feinberg, *Harmless Wrongdoing* (New York: Oxford University Press, 1990), pp. 50–5.

should not be free to decide what happens to our bodies, and that is a matter of status too.

Commodification is not a sound basis for prohibiting sale. The arguments from dignity against sale are either mysterious or false. If anything, considerations of dignity oppose punishing sellers as criminals. It is hard to see how it can be argued that society may prohibit sale as a violation of its moral code. The evidence that sale would violate its code has not been produced, and in any case, there are all the familiar powerful arguments against a society enforcing its code independent of its truth.

PUTTING IT ALL TOGETHER

So far, we have considered the supply of organs, personal sovereignty, well-being, exploitation and injustice, altruism, and anti-commodification. I said the effects on supply were uncertain, but sale would be worth trying. I claimed that part of personal sovereignty includes being able to decide what happens to one's body, which includes deciding whether to sell one's organ. While not every sale would express personal sovereignty, being desperate for money does not, in and of itself, make a sale invalid. Sales could be against the sellers' interests but, unless catastrophically so, their autonomy should take priority over their welfare. I argued that considerations of exploitation, injustice, repugnance, altruism, and commodification provided no or weak reasons against permitting sales.

It might be thought, from the arguments so far, that the case for permitting sale is decisive. However, an assessment of sales involves some variables. If sales are permitted, the supply of organs may go up, down, or stay the same. Regulations designed to filter out non-voluntary sellers—those secretly being coerced or grossly irrational—or sellers who would suffer badly may be more or less successful. (On a liberal view, people whose health would be greatly harmed by selling should be warned but perhaps not prevented; on a modified liberal view, they should be prevented.) A society may find sales highly repugnant, somewhat distasteful, or unobjectionable. It may become much less altruistic, if donation is driven out, or no less altruistic if, for instance, it had no practice of donation anyway, or its practice was merely supplemented by sale. If the variables turned out a certain way, the case for permitting sale would be decisive. If they turned out a different way, they could be enough to tip the balance against permitting sale. Consider two possibilities.

First, suppose that if sales were permitted (1) supply increases a good deal, (2) regulation effectively filters out the non-voluntary would-be sellers, (3) the society does not find sale repugnant at all, and (4) the extent of altruism in the society is unaffected. If the variables turn out this way, all that is left to say against permitting sale is that it wrongly commodifies body parts, an objection that rests on an inadequately explained and controversial account of the meaning and weight of human dignity. The case for sales would be decisive.

Second, suppose that if sales were permitted (1) supply would fall a good deal, (2) regulations would be ineffective filters, so many sellers would be agreeing non-voluntarily, (3) the society finds sale utterly repugnant, and (4) it becomes much less altruistic.

If 1–4 occur, the strongest case could be made for preventing sales. Even then, people have a right voluntarily to accept offers of money for their organs, and blocking sales would stop some exercising that right. This still seems to me a powerful consideration, and perhaps enough to rule out the widespread existing practice of punishing sellers. But there are other ways to block sales besides threatening would-be sellers. One could threaten buyers or their agents instead. If the most unfavourable circumstances did occur, it may well be right to block sales in some—not all—ways.

The two possibilities are extremes and there are intermediate possibilities. Perhaps supply would increase but society would find selling repugnant. Perhaps supply would decline but all sellers would be deciding voluntarily. Without better evidence about the size of the effects, it is not worth attempting to set out in detail how trade offs should be made, but I want to make a few final comments.

After discussing the various considerations separately, the important ones are the effects on supply and the autonomy and welfare of potential sellers. By comparison, enforcing a social code, preserving altruism, and the supposed wrongs of commodification have no or little weight. Thus if supply were to go up and sellers to be acting both voluntarily and not catastrophically against their likely interests, I regard the case for permitting sale as decisive. The difficulties in reaching a final conclusion arise where supply would fall or many sellers would be acting non-voluntarily, or both.

Suppose regulation was not very effective, and many sellers would be acting non-voluntarily. A trade off must then be made within the category of respecting personal sovereignty. If the state blocks sales, it would directly infringe on the personal sovereignty of some would-be sellers, but if it permitted them, it would allow third parties to infringe on the personal sovereignty of some sellers. Where the trade off should be made would depend on such further considerations as how many were in each category and how much they would lose by having their personal sovereignty infringed upon.

A trade off may also have to be made with the effect on supply. Strict regulation may prevent non-voluntary sale but lead to fewer organs than would either relaxed regulation or donation alone. One would then be trading off personal sovereignty both against itself and against the supply of organs. As things become more complex, it is worth bearing in mind the following points. A right to sell, as derived from personal sovereignty, is not absolute, so the interests of potential recipients may outweigh it. This may be a point in favour of sale, tolerating some loss of personal sovereignty for the sake of more organs, or against, preventing the exercise of some personal sovereignty to forestall a loss of organs. A right to sell seems the worse infringed upon by direct punishment than indirect methods of blocking sale, so even if the needs of recipients warrant blocking sale, direct punishment may still be unjustifiable and should at least be the last resort. Finally, the evidence may make it unnecessary to specify trade offs in detail. If supply would increase and regulation would be effective, which is reasonably likely in some countries, personal sovereignty need not be traded off against the needs of recipients. In such a case, sales should not be discouraged.

Bibliography

Abadie, Alberto and Gay, Sebastien, 'The Impact of Presumed Consent Legislation on Cadaveric Organ Donation: A Cross Country Study' *Journal of Health Economics* 25 (2006), 599–620.

Alderson, P., Sutcliffe, K., and Curtis, K., 'Children's Competence to Consent to Medical Treatment' *Hastings Center Report* 36 (2006), 25–34.

American Society of Transplant Surgeons, 'Statement on Directed Donation and Solicitation of Organs', 23 October 2006, available at <www.asts.org> (last accessed 5 November 2009).

Archard, David, Untitled review article, *Journal of Applied Philosophy* 24 (2007), 209–21.

——'Informed Consent: Autonomy and Self-ownership' *Journal of Applied Philosophy* 25 (2008), 19–34.

Ariely, Dan, Bracha, Anat, and Meier, Stephan, 'Doing Good or Doing Well? Image Motivation and Monetary Incentives in Behaving Prosocially' *American Economic Review* 99 (2009), 544–55.

Arnason, Wayne, 'Directed Donation: The Relevance of Race' *Hastings Center Report* 21 (1991), 13–19.

Arneson, Richard, 'Autonomy and Preference Formation', in Jules Coleman and Allen Buchanan (eds.), *In Harm's Way* (Cambridge: Cambridge University Press, 1994), 42–75.

Arnold, R., Bartlett S., Bernat, J., Colonna, J., Dafoe, D., Dubler, N., Gruber, S., Kahn, J., Luskin, R., Nathan, H., Orloff, S., Prottas, J., Shapiro, R., Ricordi, C., Youngner, S., and Delmonico, F. (the Ethics Committee of the American Society of Transplant Surgeons), 'Financial Incentives for Cadaver Organ Donation: An Ethical Reappraisal' *Transplantation* 73 (2002), 1361–7.

ASERNIP–S (Australian Safety and Efficacy Register of New Interventional Procedures—Surgical), 'Live Donor Liver Transplantation—Adult Outcomes: A Systematic Review' (2004).

Audi, Robert, 'The Morality and Utility of Organ Transplantation' *Utilitas* 8 (1996), 141–58.

Australian National Health and Medical Research Council, *Donating Organs After Death: Ethical Issues* (Commonwealth of Australia, 1997).

Australian and New Zealand Intensive Care Society, *The ANZICS Statement on Death and Organ Donation* (3rd edition) (Melbourne: ANZICS, 2008).

Bagheri, Alireza, 'Criticism of "Brain Death" Policy in Japan', *Kennedy Institute of Ethics Journal* 13 (2003), 359–72.

——'Compensated Kidney Donation: An Ethical Review of the Iranian Model' *Kennedy Institute of Ethics Journal* 16 (2006), 269–82.

Baron, Jonathan, *Against Bioethics* (Cambridge, MA: MIT Press, 2006).

Barry, Brian, *Justice as Impartiality* (Oxford: Clarendon Press, 1995).

BBC News, 'Organ Donor System Overhaul Call', 13 Jan. 2008.

Bell, M. D. D., 'The UK Human Tissue Act and Consent: Surrendering a Fundamental Principle to Transplantation Needs?' *Journal of Medical Ethics* 32 (2006), 283–6.

Birmingham Mail, 'Kidney Sale Man Found Dead', 25 September 2007.

Blackburn, Simon, *Ruling Passions* (Oxford: Clarendon Press, 1998).

Boddington, Paula, 'Organ Donation After Death: Should I Decide, or Should My Family?' *Journal of Applied Philosophy* 15 (1998), 69–81.

Brazier, Margaret, 'Retained Organs: Ethics and Humanity' *Legal Studies* 22 (2002), 550–69.

——*Medicine, Patients and the Law* (3rd edition) (London: Penguin Books, 2003).

——'Organ Retention and Return: Problems of Consent' *Journal of Medical Ethics* 29 (2003), 30–3.

Brennan, Samantha, 'How is the Strength of a Right Determined?' *American Philosophical Quarterly* 32 (1995), 383–92.

——'Thresholds for Rights' *The Southern Journal of Philosophy* 33 (1995), 143–68.

Broome, John, *Weighing Goods* (Oxford: Basil Blackwell, 1991).

——*Ethics Out of Economics* (Cambridge: Cambridge University Press, 1999).

Buchanan, Allen and Brock, Dan, *Deciding for Others* (Cambridge: Cambridge University Press, 1990).

Bühler, L., Friedman, T., Iacomini, J., and Cooper, D. K. C., 'Xenotransplantation: State of the Art Update—1999' *Frontiers in Bioscience* 4 (1999), 416–32.

Callahan, Joan, 'On Harming the Dead' *Ethics* 97 (1987), 341–52.

Caplan, A. and Coelho, D. (eds.), *The Ethics of Organ Transplants* (Amherst, NY: Prometheus Books, 1998).

Chamberlain, Jenny, 'To Give or Not to Give?' *North and South* (March, 2004).

Chan, Ho Mun, 'Sharing Death and Dying: Advance Directives, Autonomy and the Family' *Bioethics* 18 (2004), 87–103.

Cherry, Mark, *Kidney for Sale by Owner* (Washington, DC: Georgetown University Press, 2005).

Christmas, Ashley, Burris, Gary, Bogart, Tyson, and Sing, Ronald, 'Organ Donation: Family Members NOT Honoring Patient Wishes' *The Journal of Trauma* 65 (2008), 1095–7.

Clayton, M. and Williams, A. (eds.), *The Ideal of Equality* (Basingstoke: Macmillan, 2000).

Cohen, Cynthia B., 'Public Policy and the Sale of Human Organs' *Kennedy Institute of Ethics Journal* 12 (2002), 47–64.

Cohen, G. A., *History, Labour, and Freedom* (Oxford: Clarendon Press, 1988).

——*Self-Ownership, Freedom, and Equality* (Cambridge: Cambridge University Press, 1995).

Cohen, Lawrence, 'Where it Hurts: Indian Material for an Ethics of Organ Transplantation' *Daedelus* 128 (1999), 135–65.

Cohen, M., Nagel, T., and Scanlon, T. (eds.), *Medicine and Moral Philosophy* (Princeton, NJ: Princeton University Press, 1981).

Coleman, Jules and Buchanan, Allen (eds.), *In Harm's Way* (Cambridge: Cambridge University Press, 1994).

Cronin, Antonia and Douglas, James, 'Directed and Conditional Deceased Donor Organ Donations: Laws and Misconceptions' *Medical Law Review* 18 (2010), 275–301.

Crouch, Robert and Elliot, Carl, 'Moral Agency and the Family: The Case of Living Related Organ Transplantation' *Cambridge Quarterly of Healthcare Ethics* 8 (1999), 275–87.

Csillag, C., 'Brazil Abolishes "Presumed Consent" in Organ Donation' *The Lancet* 352 (1998), 1367.

Daniels, Norman, *Just Health* (Cambridge: Cambridge University Press, 2008).

Delmonico, Francis L. and Scheper-Hughes, Nancy, 'Why We Should Not Pay for Human Organs' *Zygon* 38 (2003), 689–98.

Department of Health, *An Investigation into Conditional Organ Donation* (London: Department of Health, 2000).

Devlin, Patrick, *The Enforcement of Morals* (London: Oxford University Press, 1965).

Dowding, Keith, Hughes, James, and Margetts, Helen (eds.), *Challenges to Democracy: The PSA Yearbook 2000* (Basingstoke: Palgrave Macmillan, 2001).

Dworkin, Ronald, *Taking Rights Seriously* (Cambridge, MA: Harvard University Press, 1978).

——*Life's Dominion* (London: HarperCollins, 1993).

——*Sovereign Virtue* (Cambridge, MA: Harvard University Press, 2000).

Elliott, Carl, 'Doing Harm: Living Organ Donors, Clinical Research and *The Tenth Man*' *Journal of Medical Ethics* 21 (1995), 91–6.

Ellis, Anthony, 'Thomson on Distress' *Ethics* 106 (1995), 112–19.

Elster, Jon, 'The Market and the Forum: Three Varieties of Political Theory', in Jon Elster and Aanund Hylland (eds.), *Foundations of Social Choice Theory* (Cambridge: Cambridge University Press, 1986), 103–32.

——Hylland, Aanund (eds.), *Foundations of Social Choice Theory* (Cambridge: Cambridge University Press, 1986).

Epstein, Richard, 'Justice across the Generations', in P. Laslett and J. Fishkin (eds.), *Justice Between Age Groups and Generations* (New Haven: Yale University Press, 1992), 84–106.

——*Mortal Peril* (Cambridge, MA: Perseus Publishing, 1999).

Erin, C. and Harris, J., 'Presumed Consent or Contracting Out' *Journal of Medical Ethics* 25 (1999), 365–6.

Fabre, Cécile, *Whose Body Is It Anyway? Justice and the Integrity of the Person* (Oxford: Clarendon Press, 2006).

——'Posthumous Rights', in C. Grant, B. Holburn, A. Hatzistavrou, and M. Kramer (eds.), *The Legacy of H. L. A. Hart: Legal, Political, and Moral Philosophy* (Oxford: Oxford University Press, 2008), 225–38.

——'Reply to Wilkinson' *Res Publica* 14 (2008), 137–40.

Feinberg, Joel, *Social Philosophy* (New Jersey: Englewood Cliffs, 1973).

——*Harm to Others* (New York: Oxford University Press, 1984).

——*Harm to Self* (New York: Oxford University Press, 1986).

——*Harmless Wrongdoing* (New York: Oxford University Press, 1990).

——*Freedom and Fulfilment* (Princeton, NJ: Princeton University Press, 1992).

Feldman, Fred, 'Some Puzzles About the Evil of Death', in J. Fischer (ed.), *The Metaphysics of Death* (Stanford: Stanford University Press, 1993), 305–26.

——'The Termination Thesis' *Midwest Studies in Philosophy XXIV* (2000), 98–115.

Fellner, Carl and Marshall, John, 'Kidney Donors: The Myth of Informed Consent' *American Journal of Psychiatry* 126 (1970), 1245–51.

Fischer, J. (ed.), *The Metaphysics of Death* (Stanford: Stanford University Press, 1993).

Fleck, Leonard, 'Children and Organ Donation: Some Cautionary Remarks' *Cambridge Quarterly of Healthcare Ethics* 13 (2004), 161–6.

Frankfurt, Harry, *The Importance of What We Care About* (Cambridge: Cambridge University Press, 1988).

Gaston, Robert, Ayres, Ian, Dooley, Laura, and Diethelm, Arnold, 'Racial Equity in Renal Transplantation: The Disparate Impact of HLA-based Allocation', in A. Caplan and D. Coelho (eds.), *The Ethics of Organ Transplants* (Amherst, NY: Prometheus Books, 1998), 308–20.

Gauthier, David, *Morals By Agreement* (Oxford: Clarendon Press, 1986).

Gill, Michael, 'Presumed Consent, Autonomy, and Organ Donation' *Journal of Medicine and Philosophy* 29 (2004), 37–59.

Glannon, Walter, 'Do the Sick Have a Right to Cadaveric Organs?' *Journal of Medical Ethics* 29 (2003), 153–6.

Goodwin, Michele, *Black Markets: The Supply and Demand of Organs* (Cambridge: Cambridge University Press, 2006).

Gostin, Lawrence (ed.), *Public Health Law and Ethics: A Reader* (Berkeley and Los Angeles: University of California Press, 2002).

Goyal, M., Mehta, R., Schneiderman, L., and Sehgal, A., 'Economic and Health Consequences of Selling a Kidney in India' *Journal of the American Medical Association* 288 (2002), 1589–93.

Grant, C., Holburn, B., Hatzistavrou, A., and Kramer, M. (eds.). *The Legacy of H. L. A. Hart: Legal, Political, and Moral Philosophy* (Oxford: Oxford University Press, 2008).

Greene, Graham, *Dr Fischer of Geneva or the Bomb Party* (New York: Simon and Schuster, 1980).

Greenhalgh, Trisha, *How to Read a Paper* (3rd edn.) (Oxford: Blackwell Publishing, 2006).

Griffin, James, *Well-Being* (Oxford: Clarendon Press, 1986).

Grover, Dorothy, 'Posthumous Harm' *The Philosophical Quarterly* 39 (1989), 334–53.

Grubb, Andrew, '"I, Me, Mine": Bodies, Parts and Property' *Medical Law International* 3 (1998), 299–317.

Hare, R. M., *Moral Thinking* (Oxford: Clarendon Press, 1981).

Harris, J. W., 'Who Owns My Body?' *Oxford Journal of Legal Studies* 16 (1996), 55–84.

Harris, John, 'The Survival Lottery' *Philosophy* 50 (1975), 81–8.

—— *The Value of Life* (London: Routledge & Kegan Paul, 1985).

—— *Clones, Genes, and Immortality* (Oxford: Oxford University Press, 1998).

—— 'Law and Regulation of Retained Organs: The Ethical Issues' *Legal Studies* 22 (2002), 527–49.

—— 'Organ Procurement: Dead Interests, Living Needs' *Journal of Medical Ethics* 29 (2003), 130–4.

Hart, H. L. A., *Essays on Bentham* (Oxford: Clarendon Press, 1982).

den Hartogh, Govert, *Farewell to Non-commitment: Decision Systems for Organ Donation from an Ethical Viewpoint* (The Hague: Centre for Ethics and Health, 2008).

—— 'When Are Living Donations Voluntary Enough?' in W. Weimar et al. (eds.), *Organ Transplantation: Ethical, Legal and Psychosocial Aspects* (Lengerich: Pabst Science Publishers, 2008), 221–31.

Hilhorst, M. T., '"Living Apart Together": Moral Frictions between Two Coexisting Organ Transplantation Schemes' *Journal of Medical Ethics* 34 (2008), 484–8.

Hitchen, Lisa, 'No Evidence that Presumed Consent Increases Organ Donation' *British Medical Journal* 337 (2008), 1614.

Holmes, Stephen, *The Anatomy of Antiliberalism* (Cambridge, MA: Harvard University Press, 1993).

Horvat, Lucy, Shariff, Salimah, and Garg, Amit, 'Global Trends in the Rates of Living Kidney Donation' *Kidney International* 75 (2009), 1088–98.

House of Lords European Union Committee, *Increasing the Supply of Donor Organs Within the European Union* (2008).

Howard, David H., 'Producing Organ Donors' *Journal of Economic Perspectives* 21 (2007), 25–36.

Ibrahim, H., Foley, R., Tan, L., Rogers, T., Bailey, R., Guo, H., Gross, C., and Matas, A., 'Long-Term Consequences of Kidney Donation' *The New England Journal of Medicine* 360 (2009), 459–69.

Independent Review Group on the Retention of Organs at Post-Mortem, *Final Report* 2001, recommendation 4 available at <http://www.sehd.scot.nhs.uk/scotorgrev/Final%20Report/ropm.pdf> (last accessed 8 August 2009).

Jacob, Marie-Andrée, 'Another Look at the Presumed-Versus-Informed Consent Dichotomy in Postmortem Organ Procurement' *Bioethics* 20 (2006), 293–300.

Jansen, Lynn, 'Child Organ Donation, Family Autonomy, and Intimate Attachments' *Cambridge Quarterly of Healthcare Ethics* 13 (2004), 133–42.

Jenkins, Roy, *Gladstone* (New York: Random House, 1995).

Johnson, E. and Goldstein, D., 'Do Defaults Save Lives?' *Science* 302 (2003), 1338–9.

Joralemon, Donald and Cox, Phil, 'Body Values: The Case against Compensating for Transplant Organs' *Hastings Center Report* 33 (2003), 27–33.

Jowsey, Sheila and Schneekloth, Terry, 'Psychosocial Factors in Living Organ Donation: Clinical and Ethical Challenges' *Transplantation Reviews* 22 (2008), 192–5.

Kagan, Shelly, *The Limits of Morality* (Oxford: Clarendon Press, 1989).

——'The Limits of Well-Being' *Social Philosophy and Policy* 9 (1992), 169–89.

——'Me and My Life' *Proceedings of the Aristotelian Society* 94 (1994), 309–24.

——*Normative Ethics* (Boulder: Westview Press, 1998).

Kamm, F. M., *Morality, Mortality*, vol. 1 (New York: Oxford University Press, 1993).

——*Morality, Mortality, vol. 2* (New York: Oxford University Press, 1996).

Kaserman, David, L. and Barnett, A. H., *The U.S. Organ Procurement System: A Prescription for Reform* (Washington, DC: AEI Press, 2002).

Katz, Jay, *The Silent World of Doctor and Patient* (Baltimore and London: Johns Hopkins University Press, 2002).

Kluge, E.-H., 'Designated Donation: Private Choice in Social Context' *Hastings Center Report* 19 (1989), 10–16.

——'Improving Organ Retrieval Rates: Various Proposals and their Ethical Validity' *Health Care Analysis* 8 (2000), 279–95.

Kramer, Matthew H., Simmonds, N. E., and Steiner, Hillel, *A Debate over Rights* (Oxford: Clarendon Press, 1998).

Lamont, Julian, 'A Solution to the Puzzle of When Death Harms its Victims', *Australasian Journal of Philosophy* 76 (1998), 198–212.

Langone, A. J. and Helderman, J. H., 'Disparity Between Solid-Organ Supply and Demand' *New England Journal of Medicine* 349 (2003), 704–6.

Laslett, P. and Fishkin, J., *Justice Between Age Groups and Generations* (New Haven: Yale University Press, 1992).

Leng, Tan Hui, 'More Seek Organ Donation Opt-Out Forms after Hospital Scuffle', TodayOnline (28 February 2007).

MacFarquhar, Larissa, 'The Kindest Cut' *The New Yorker*, 27 July 2009.

Machnicki G., Seriai, L., and Schnitzler, M., 'Economics of Transplantation: A Review of the Literature' *Transplantation Reviews* 20 (2006), 61–75.

Manson, Neil and O'Neill, Onora, *Rethinking Informed Consent in Bioethics* (Cambridge: Cambridge University Press, 2007).

Marx, Karl, 'On the Jewish Question', reprinted in Jeremy Waldron (ed.), *Nonsense Upon Stilts* (London: Methuen and Co., 1987).

Matas, A., Bartlett, S., Leichtman, A., and Delmonico, F., 'Morbidity and Mortality after Living Kidney Donation, 1999–2001: Survey of United States Transplant Centers' *American Journal of Transplantation* 3 (2003), 830–4.

May, T., Aulisio, M., and DeVita, M., 'Patients, Families, and Organ Donation: Who Should Decide?' *The Milbank Quarterly* 78 (2000), 323–36.

McCunn, Maureen, Mauritz, Walter, Dutton, Richard, Alexander, Charles, Handley, Christopher, and Scalea, Thomas, 'Impact of Culture and Policy on Organ Donation: A Comparison between Two Urban Trauma Centers in Developed Nations' *The Journal of Trauma: Injury, Infection, and Critical Care* 54 (2003), 995–9.

McGuiness, S., and Brazier, M., 'Respecting the Living Means Respecting the Dead Too' *Oxford Journal of Legal Studies* 28 (2008), 297–316.

McMahan, Jeff, *The Ethics of Killing* (New York: Oxford University Press, 2002).

Mill, J. S., *On Liberty* (Harmondsworth: Penguin English Library, 1982).

Miller, David, *Market, State, and Community* (Oxford: Clarendon Press, 1989).

Mocan, N. and Tekin, E., 'The Determinants of the Willingness to Donate an Organ Among Young Adults: Evidence from the United States and the European Union' *Social Science and Medicine* 65 (2007), 2527–38.

Morris, John A. Jr, Wilcox, Todd R., and Frist, William H., 'Pediatric Organ Donation: The Paradox of Organ Shortage Despite the Remarkable Willingness of Families to Donate' *Pediatrics* 89 (1992), 411–15.

Munson, Ronald, *Raising the Dead* (New York: Oxford University Press, 2002).

Muyskens, James, 'An Alternative Policy for Obtaining Cadaver Organs', in M. Cohen, T. Nagel, and T. Scanlon (eds.), *Medicine and Moral Philosophy* (Princeton, NJ: Princeton University Press, 1981), 187–98.

Nadel, Mark and Nadel, Carolina, 'Using Reciprocity to Motivate Organ Donations' *Yale Journal of Health Policy, Law and Ethics* 5 (2005), 293–325.

Nagel, Thomas, *The View From Nowhere* (New York: Oxford University Press, 1986).

——*Equality and Partiality* (Oxford: Clarendon Press, 1991).

——'Death' in J. Fischer (ed.), *The Metaphysics of Death* (Stanford: Stanford University Press, 1993), 59–69.

Narveson, Jan, 'On Dworkinian Equality' *Social Philosophy and Policy* 1 (1983), 1–23.

New Zealand Ministry of Health, *Review of the Regulation of Human Tissue and Tissue-Based Therapies: Discussion Document* (Wellington: Ministry of Health, 2004).

Nozick, Robert, *Anarchy, State, and Utopia* (Oxford: Basil Blackwell, 1974).

——*The Examined Life* (New York: Simon and Schuster, 1989).

Oberdiek, John, 'Specifying Rights Out of Necessity' *Oxford Journal of Legal Studies* 28 (2008), 127–46.

Olson, Mancur, *The Logic of Collective Action* (Cambridge, MA: Harvard University Press, 1965).

O'Neill, Onora, *Autonomy and Trust in Bioethics* (Cambridge: Cambridge University Press, 2002).optn.transplant.hrsa.gov (last accessed August 2010).

Organ Donation Taskforce, *The Potential Impact of an Opt Out System for Organ Donation in the UK* (London: Department of Health, 2008).

Page, Edgar, 'Parental Rights' *Journal of Applied Philosophy* 1 (1984), 187–203.

Paine, Thomas, *Rights of Man* (Harmondsworth: Penguin, 1969).

Parfit, Derek, *Reasons and Persons* (Oxford: Clarendon Press, 1984).

——'Equality or Priority?' in M. Clayton and A. Williams (eds.), *The Ideal of Equality* (Basingstoke: Macmillan, 2000), 81–125.

Partridge, Ernest, 'Posthumous Interests and Posthumous Respect' *Ethics* 91 (1981), 243–64.

Pitcher, George, 'The Misfortunes of the Dead', in John Martin Fischer (ed.), *The Metaphysics of Death* (Stanford: Stanford University Press, 1993), 159–68.

Potter, Stephen, *The Complete Upmanship* (London: Rupert Hart-Davis Ltd., 1970).

President's Council on Bioethics staff paper by Eric Cohen, 'Organ Transplantation: Defining the Ethical and Policy Issues', available at <www.bioethics.gov> (last accessed 20 August 2009).

Price, David, *Legal and Ethical Aspects of Organ Transplantation* (Cambridge: Cambridge University Press, 2000).

——'From Cosmos and Damian to van Velzen: The Human Tissue Saga Continues' *Medical Law Review* 11 (2003), 1–47.

——*Human Tissue in Transplantation and Research: A Model Legal and Ethical Donation Framework* (Cambridge: Cambridge University Press, 2009).

Qing, Koh Gui, 'Scuffle for Organs Sparks Donor Debate in Singapore' Reuters, 28 February 2007.

Quinn, Warren, *Morality and Action* (Cambridge: Cambridge University Press, 1993).

Rakowski, Eric, *Equal Justice* (Oxford: Clarendon Press, 1991).

Rawls, John, *A Theory of Justice* (rev. edn.) (Oxford: Oxford University Press 1999).

Raz, Joseph, *The Morality of Freedom* (Oxford: Clarendon Press, 1986).

Reynolds, Gretchen, 'Will Any Organ Do?' *The New York Times Magazine* 10 July 2005.

Richards, Janet Radcliffe, 'Nefrarious Goings On: Kidney Sales and Moral Arguments' *The Journal of Medicine and Philosophy* 21 (1996), 375–416.

Rieber, S. D., 'Causation as Property Acquisition' *Philosophical Studies* 109 (2002), 53–74.

Roach, Mary, *Stiff* (New York: W. W. Norton, 2003).

Robertson, C., 'Desperate Patients Solicit Volunteers' *The Journal of Law, Medicine, and Ethics* 33 (2005), 170–4.

Ross, L. F., *Children, Families, and Health Care Decision Making* (Oxford: Clarendon Press, 1998).

Ross, L., Thistlethwaite J., Jr., and the Committee on Bioethics, 'Minors as Living Solid-Organ Donors' *Pediatrics* 122 (2008), 454–61.

Rothman, David J., 'Ethical and Social Consequences of Selling a Kidney' *Journal of the American Medical Association* 288 (2002), 1640–1.

Rothman, S. M. and Rothman, D. J., 'The Hidden Cost of Organ Sale' *American Journal of Transplantation* 6 (2006), 1524–8.

Ruben, David-Hillel, 'A Puzzle About Posthumous Predication' *The Philosophical Review* 97 (1988), 211–36.

Scanlon, T. M., 'Rights, Goals, and Fairness', in *The Difficulty of Tolerance* (Cambridge: Cambridge University Press, 2003), 26–41.

Scheper-Hughes, Nancy, 'The Ends of the Body: Commodity Fetishism and the Global Traffic in Organs' *SAIS Review* 22 (2002), 61–80.

Schoeman, Ferdinand, 'Rights of Children, Rights of Parents, and the Moral Basis of the Family' *Ethics* 91 (1980), 6–19.

Sen, A., *Collective Choice and Social Welfare* (San Francisco: Holden-Day Inc., 1970).

Shalowitz, D., Garrett-Mayer, E., and Wendler, D., 'The Accuracy of Surrogate Decision Makers: A Systematic Review' *Archives of Internal Medicine* 166 (2006), 493–7.

Sheehy E., Conrad, S., Brigham, L., Luskin, R., Weber, P., Eakin, M., Schkade, L., and Hunsicker, L., 'Estimating the Number of Potential Organ Donors in the United States' *New England Journal of Medicine* 349 (2003), 667–73.

Shiffrin, S., 'Paternalism, Unconscionability Doctrine, and Accommodation' *Philosophy and Public Affairs* 29 (2000), 205–50.

Siegal, M. and Peterson, C. (eds.), *Children's Understanding of Biology and Health* (Cambridge: Cambridge University Press, 1999).

Siminoff, L. and Chillag, K., 'The Fallacy of the "Gift of Life"' *Hastings Center Report* 29 (1999), 34–41.

——Lawrence, Renee, 'Knowing Patients' Preferences about Organ Donation: Does it Make a Difference?' *The Journal of Trauma* 53 (2002), 754–60.

——Mercer, Mary Beth, 'Public Policy, Public Opinion, and Consent for Organ Donation' *Cambridge Quarterly of Healthcare Ethics* 10 (2001), 377–86.

Singer, Peter, *Rethinking Life and Death* (Melbourne: The Text Publishing Company, 1994).

Slaughter, V., Jaakkola, R., and Carey, S., 'Constructing a Coherent Theory: Children's Biological Understanding of Life and Death', in M. Siegal and C. Peterson (eds.), *Children's Understanding of Biology and Health* (Cambridge: Cambridge University Press, 1999), 71–98.

Smith, Adam, *The Wealth of Nations* (Harmondsworth: Penguin English Library, 1982).

Sperling, Daniel, *Posthumous Interests* (Cambridge: Cambridge University Press, 2008).

Spike, Jeffrey, 'Cultural Diversity and Patients with Reduced Capacity: The Use of Ethics Consultation to Advocate for Mentally Handicapped Persons in Living Organ Donation' *Theoretical Medicine* 22 (2001), 519–26.

Spital, Aaron, 'Mandated Choice for Organ Donation: Time to Give it a Try', in A. Caplan and D. Coelho (eds.), *The Ethics of Organ Transplants* (Amherst, NY: Prometheus Books, 1998), 147–53.

——'Conscription of Cadaveric Organs for Transplantation: Neglected Again' *Kennedy Institute of Ethics Journal* 13 (2003), 169–74.

——'Should People who Donate a Kidney to a Stranger be Permitted to Choose their Recipients? Views of the United States Public' *Transplantation* 76 (2003), 1252–6.

——Taylor, James S., 'In Defense of Routine Recovery of Cadaveric Organs: A Response to Walter Glannon' *Cambridge Quarterly of Healthcare Ethics* 17 (2008), 330–6.

Steinberg, David, 'An "Opting In" Paradigm for Kidney Transplantation' *American Journal of Bioethics* 4 (2004), 4–14.

Steiner, Hillel, *An Essay on Rights* (Oxford: Basil Blackwell, 1994).

Streat, Stephen, 'Moral Assumptions and the Process of Organ Donation in the Intensive Care Unit' *Critical Care* 8 (2004), 382–8.

——'When Do We Stop?' *Critical Care and Resuscitation* 7 (2005), 227–32.

Sumner, L. W., *The Moral Foundation of Rights* (Oxford: Clarendon Press, 1987).

Sunstein, Cass, *Worst-case Scenarios* (Cambridge, MA: Harvard University Press, 2007).

Taylor, James S., 'The Myth of Posthumous Harm' *American Philosophical Quarterly* 42 (2005), 311–22.

——*Stakes and Kidneys* (Aldershot: Ashgate, 2005).

——'Personal Autonomy, Posthumous Harm, and Presumed Consent Policies for Organ Procurement' *Public Affairs Quarterly* 20 (2006), 381–404.

Temkin, Larry, *Inequality* (Oxford: Clarendon Press, 1993).

Textor, Stephen and Taler, Sandra, 'Expanding Criteria for Living Kidney Donors: What are the Limits?' *Transplantation Reviews* 22 (2008), 187–91.

Thaler, Richard and Sunstein, Cass, *Nudge: Improving Decisions about Health, Wealth, and Happiness* (New Haven: Yale University Press, 2008).

The Economist, 'Logical Endings: Evidence-based Ethics', 17 March 2007.

——'How to Stop the Drug Wars', 5 March 2009.

——'Where There's a Will There's a Row', 17 October 2009.

The Royal Liverpool Children's Inquiry Report (London: The Stationery Office, 2001).

The Times, 'Dying Woman's Last Wish to Donate Kidney to her Mother Denied by Rules', 12 April 2008.

Thomson, Judith Jarvis, 'Feinberg on Harm, Offense, and the Criminal Law' *Philosophy and Public Affairs* 15 (1986), 381–95.

——*Rights, Restitution, and Risk* (Cambridge, MA: Harvard University Press, 1986).

——*The Realm of Rights* (Cambridge, MA: Harvard University Press, 1990).

Tilney, Nicholas, *Transplant: From Myth to Reality* (New Haven: Yale University Press, 2003).

Titmuss, Richard M., *The Gift Relationship* (Harmondsworth: Pelican Books, 1970).

Turia, Tariana, 'Speech: The Circle of Life—the Human Tissues Bill', 14 November 2006. <www.maoriparty.com> (last accessed October 2007).

UK Transplant *Potential Donor Audit: Summary Report for the 24 Month Period 1 April 2007–31 March 2009*, available at www.uktransplant.org.uk (last accessed August 2010).

<www.uktransplant.org.uk> (last accessed August 2010).

<www.unos.org> (last accessed August 2010).

Veatch, Robert, *Transplantation Ethics* (Washington DC: Georgetown University Press, 2000).

——Pitt, Jonathan, 'The Myth of Presumed Consent', in Robert Veatch, *Transplantation Ethics* (Washington, DC: Georgetown University Press, 2000).

Volk, Michael and Ubel, Peter, 'The Impracticality of Overriding Family Rejection of Donation' *Transplantation* 86 (2008), 1631.

Waldron, Jeremy (ed.), *Theories of Rights* (Oxford: Clarendon Press, 1984).

——(ed.), *Nonsense Upon Stilts* (London: Methuen and Co., 1987).

——*The Right to Private Property* (Oxford: Clarendon Press, 1988).

——'A Right to Do Wrong', in *Liberal Rights* (Cambridge: Cambridge University Press, 1993), 63–87.

——'When Justice Replaces Affection: The Need for Rights' in *Liberal Rights* (Cambridge: Cambridge University Press, 1993), 370–91.

Weimar, W., Bos, M., and Busschbach, J. (eds.), *Organ Transplantation: Ethical, Legal and Psychosocial Aspects* (Lengerich: Pabst Science Publishers, 2008).

Wellman, Carl, *A Theory of Rights* (Totowa, NJ: Rowman and Allanheld, 1985).

Wertheimer, Alan, *Coercion* (Princeton: Princeton University Press, 1987).

——*Exploitation* (Princeton NJ: Princeton University Press, 1996).

——*Consent to Sexual Relations* (Cambridge: Cambridge University Press, 2003).

Wilkinson, Martin and Moore, Andrew, 'Inducements Revisited' *Bioethics* 13 (1999), 114–30.

Wilkinson, Stephen, *Bodies for Sale: Ethics and Exploitation in the Human Body Trade* (London: Routledge, 2003).

Wilkinson, T. M., 'Parental Consent and the Use of Dead Children's Bodies' *Kennedy Institute of Ethics Journal* 11 (2001), 337–58.

——'Research, Informed Consent, and the Limits of Disclosure' *Bioethics* 15 (2001), 341–63.

——'Last Rights: The Ethics of Research on the Dead' *Journal of Applied Philosophy* 19 (2002), 31–41.

——'What's Not Wrong With Conditional Organ Donation?' *Journal of Medical Ethics* 29 (2003), 163–4.

——'The Ethics and Economics of the Minimum Wage' *Economics and Philosophy* 20 (2004), 351–74.

——'Individualism and the Ethics of Research on Humans' *HEC Forum* 16 (2004), 6–26.

——'Racist Organ Donors and Saving Lives' *Bioethics* 21 (2007), 63–74.

Wilkinson, T. M., 'Consent and the Use of the Bodies of the Dead' *Journal of Medicine and Philosophy* (forthcoming).

Williams, Bernard, *Moral Luck* (Cambridge: Cambridge University Press, 1981).

Wodehouse, P. G., *Life with Jeeves* (Harmondsworth: Penguin, 1981).

Wolfe, R. A., Merion, R., Roys, E., and Port, F., 'Trends in Organ Donation and Transplantation in the United States, 1998–2007' *American Journal of Transplantation* 9 (Part 2) (2009).

Wolff, Jonathan, 'Levelling Down', in Keith Dowding, James Hughes, and Helen Margetts (eds.), *Challenges to Democracy: The PSA Yearbook 2000* (Basingstoke: Palgrave Macmillan, 2001), 18–32.

——*Why Read Marx Today?* (New York: Oxford University Press, 2002).

Youngner, Stuart, Arnold, Robert, and Schapiro, Renie (eds.), *The Definition of Death* (Baltimore: Johns Hopkins University Press, 1999).

Zargooshi, J., 'Iran's Commercial Renal Transplantation Program: Results and Complications', European Platform Conference, Rotterdam, April 2007.

Zutlevics, T., 'Markets and the Needy: Organ Sales or Aid?' *Journal of Applied Philosophy* 18 (2001), 297–301.

2007 OPTN\SRTR Annual Report: Transplant Data 1997–2006 'Pediatric Transplantation: Common Themes', <optn.transplant.hrsa.gov> (last accessed August 2010).

Index

Printed and bound by CPI Group (UK) Ltd, Croydon, CR0 4YY